DIMENSIONS OF MORAL EDUCATION

Robert E. Carter's introduction to the philosophy of moral education is rooted in the Socratic method of teaching and learning. To begin to know, you must first recognize what you don't know – or see. Carter shows the value of that myopia (his striking metaphor for partial knowing) over either blindness (hopeless ignorance) or 20/20 vision (intellectual arrogance). All education which is philosophically enriched is seen as an activity, rather than as a body of knowledge or a collection of answers. The author seeks to chart a path between authoritarianism and radical scepticism.

Applying the same 'critical method' to moral education, Carter first examines the fashionable Values Clarification approach, then critically analyses Lawrence Kohlberg's stages of moral judgment. Building on his conclusions he focuses on the importance of the person in existentialist thought. The notions of choice, responsibility, and commitment are examined, and it is argued that existential absurdity may prevent intellectual and moral senility (at any age), but possibly only at the cost of moral paralysis: the inability to find any reason for doing or caring about anything.

Carter addresses this problem by discussing the various meanings of 'value' and by examining empathetic learning and valuing. He analyses three kinds of evaluative perspectives and concludes that 'intrinsic valuation' is identifying yourself with whatever you are actively involved with. As the painter may be said to become the object painted, so the educator must come to know the student, or the subject-matter, as though from the inside. The teacher also needs to be concerned with the harmonious integration of the whole person. This can be achieved through the excitement which can come only from authentic involvement in a genuine search for self-understanding in an environment of moral seriousness and purpose. Education is inseparable from the processes of critical reflection and from being fully involved in what you are doing and caring deeply about.

ROBERT E. CARTER is Professor of Philosophy at Trent University.

ROBERT E. CARTER

Dimensions of
Moral Education

UNIVERSITY OF TORONTO PRESS
Toronto Buffalo London

© University of Toronto Press 1984
Toronto Buffalo London
Printed in Canada
Reprinted 1987

ISBN 0-8020-6540-6 (paper)

Canadian Cataloguing in Publication Data

Carter, Robert Edgar, 1937–
    Dimensions of moral education
    Includes index.
    ISBN 0-8020-5640-7 (bound). – ISBN 0-8020-6540-6 (pbk.)
    1. Moral education – Philosophy. I. Title.
    LC268.C37 1984   370.11′4′01   C83-098960-9

To all those in my life who have,

in the many ways of living,

helped to make this book possible

Contents

Foreword

Robert Carter's excellent introduction to the philosophy of moral education begins with a readable, sound statement of how philosophy can help the educator to confront the moral dimensions of teaching. His enlightening presentation of the Socratic method shows what moral philosophy has to offer educators.

Chapter 2 presents my theory of moral development and moral education in a clear but constructive critical approach. It is useful to educators who may want to use the theory without accepting all of its claims. His distinction between the more disputable claims and those which are less controversial is one which I would largely accept, and I recommend this chapter from that point of view. It presents a balance between the extremes of relativism and universalism.

The next chapter, while keeping the balanced view held throughout the book, explores the insights of the existentialists. The one on value theory is comprehensive and original, and his concluding chapter on the integrated person thoughtfully and systematically guides us to a more humane conception of education.

I recommend this book to anyone seeking a clear and illuminating presentation of the questions addressed by the philosophy of moral education.

LAWRENCE KOHLBERG
Professor of Education and Social Psychology
Harvard University

Acknowledgments

Many have contributed to the writing of this book in very specific ways. None of them are to be blamed for whatever deficiencies there still are. Professor Fraser Bleasdale of the Psychology Department of Trent University gave many hours of his time to introduce me to the wonders of word-processing, and remained enthusiastically supportive throughout. His critical comments have helped to sharpen my focus. Roy Wright has provided invaluable assistance with style, having read the entire manuscript with care and understanding. He has picked apart sentences whose elements appeared to be intolerant of one another, and put them together again in the form of harmonious community. Mrs Margaret Parker of University of Toronto Press has made countless invaluable suggestions (and corrections) to make the book better than it might have been. Roy Wright and Miss Heather Spiller of Trent University have helped in the preparation of the index with the same dedication.

Several people have been involved in the typing of the manuscript, at various stages; Ms Heather Collins, my son, Scott Carter of Lakefield College School, Dickson Davidson of Bishop's College School, Miss Rita Young, and Mrs Grace Dyer. To all of these people I extend my thanks.

Others, too, have read the manuscript at various stages, and have made helpful comments: Professors Lionel Rubinoff and Trudy Govier of Trent University, Miss Amanda Parr, now a graduate student at the University of Waterloo, David R. Raynor of the University of Ottawa, and my daughter, Meredith Carter, whose charge of 'It's boring' kept me reaching for something better.

Professor Lawrence Kohlberg of Harvard University has not only written the foreword, but has been more than generous in making materials available to me, and in genuinely encouraging dissent.

Financial assistance for the research which led to this volume has come from several quarters; the Trent University Research and Travel Grants Committees have provided funds for consultation with Professor Kohlberg in Leicester, England, and Cambridge, Mass; Professor R.S. Peters in Leicester and London; and Professors R.M. Hare and John Wilson at Oxford University. The same committees also made possible my first research journey to Japan. A Social Sciences and Humanities Research Council Research Fellowship made it possible for me to experience Japan a second time, in 1978 for a more extended period. A Canada Council Doctoral Fellowship in 1968 enabled me to work extensively with Professor R.S. Hartman, in Cuernavaca, Mexico, for a period of several months. Trent University has also assisted in the cost of typing and preparing the manuscript for publication. Last, but certainly not least, my thanks to the Canadian Federation for the Humanities, whose subvention of manuscripts which it deems academically worthy has done so much to keep academic publishing strong in Canada. Thus, I acknowledge that this book has been published with the help of a grant from the Canadian Federation for the Humanities, using funds provided by the Social Sciences and Humanities Research Council of Canada. Support has also come from the Publications Fund of the University of Toronto Press.

I have drawn on material I have previously published, in a few places, although most of what follows appears in print for the first time. Grateful acknowledgment is made for permission to draw on those articles and chapters: 'Existentialism: Subjectivity and Responsible Choice' in *Ethical Options* ed Clark Kucheman (Boston: Beacon Press 1978) 31–47 and 141–3; 'Comparative Value Theory' in the *Journal of Value Inquiry* 13, no 1 (spring 1979) 33–56; 'What Is Lawrence Kohlberg Doing?' in the *Journal of Moral Education* 9, no 2 (January 1980) 88–102.

Grateful acknowledgment is also made for permission to make use of excerpts from copyrighted material, as follows: from 'A lesson in oversimplification' *Maclean's* 94, no 24 (15 June 1981) by Barbara Amiel; and, on pages 203–6, the appendix, 'The Six Stages of Moral Development,' from *Essays on Moral Development*, volume 1: *The Philosophy of Moral Development* by Lawrence Kohlberg, copyright © by Lawrence Kohlberg, reprinted by permission of Harper & Row, Publishers, Inc.

DIMENSIONS OF MORAL EDUCATION

Introduction

THE VIRTUES OF INTELLECTUAL MYOPIA*

It is difficult for teachers of a philosophical bent to explain to others what it is that they strive to achieve. Whatever their discipline or subject, a philosophical approach to it is likely to be question-oriented rather than answer-oriented, exploratory rather than conclusive, developmental rather than fixed or authoritative. Such a teacher (like Socrates) often gives the impression of having nothing to teach. The primary skills of such an approach centre around the ability to point out the weaknesses in the various positions, doctrines, beliefs, or ideologies studied.

To borrow an analogy from optometry, critically philosophical teachers are myopic. They don't claim to see any issue clearly enough to pronounce an answer absolutely, or as self-evident. On the other hand, they see well enough to know that the claims of certainty made by others are far too indistinct, blurred, and insecurely based to be left unchallenged. Rather

---

* Another name for myopia is near-sightedness, and this results from the imperfect curve of the eye, causing parallel rays to come to focus in front of the retina rather than on or at it. One's vision is, in such cases, better for near objects than for far or, put another way, defective with respect to objects at any distance. The Greek root *myein* means 'to narrow (the eye) or squint' and so myopic intellect is one narrowed to new ideas and able to focus only on that which is at hand, recognizing only the familiar and habitual. Inasmuch as I advocate intellectual myopia in the pages that follow, it is imperative that I reject such closedness, and encourage the openness that results from the liberating recognition that, as humans, we don't know with apodictic certainty. In this latter sense, awareness of one's myopia is the beginning of, and a necessary condition for, a dedicated search for something better.

than wallow in the disappointment of not having 20/20 vision, they view it as a great miracle that we are not all totally blind. Myopia is a great human achievement, and it allows for indefinite gradation of clarity and accuracy of vision all the way from blindness to myopia. Such a modest conclusion is bothersome only if you have your sight set on perfect vision, or certainty. If you must settle for less, then the excitement and pride come from seeing less poorly, less confusedly, and therefore less prejudicially. Education's greatest achievement is myopia, and philosophy is myopia's chief trustee. The problem with this alleged result is that it is no easy matter to impress the public with the fact that, after years of study and preparation, you are now professionally myopic. It is not an easy condition to 'sell' or explain. Difficult as it is to understand the virtues of myopia, it is singularly easy to misunderstand it altogether. Just as Socrates, in the *Apology*, appeared to be an underminer of the beliefs, ideals, and character of his pupils, so the skilled myoptician (teacher) may be thought of in purely negative terms, as someone who can see the weaknesses in other positions but is unable to put anything better in their place.[1] While it does not follow that the purpose of criticising foundations is to make the superstructure built on them topple (for you might desperately wish to make a firmer foundation for just such a superstructure), it is the likely first reaction of someone watching a professional skilfully and relentlessly digging away at the foundations of others.

It is a tenet of this book that most diggers at foundations are also superstructure-oriented, but it requires considerable explanation and patience to make a case to this effect. Socrates, the longstanding 'hero' of critical inquiry, was given but a few hours to make the case that what appeared to be his corruption of youth was really improving them. Plato successfully showed in the dialogues which dramatize the life and death of Socrates that a sympathetic understanding of the work of the myopic Socrates is possible (but even then not certain) only after many discussions, debates, confrontations, and corrections stemming from precisely those beliefs and 'facts' which were heretofore thought to be adequate. A central message of the dialogues is that you have to be brought to the point where you see for yourself that your own answers are not good enough, thereby initiating a search, alone or collectively, for more adequate and defensible ones. Without this negative insight, this negative education, positive education is impossible and irrelevant. To know that you do not know, particularly where you previously thought that you did know, is a necessary pre-condition for educational growth. Unless you come to see that your answers are confused and inadequate, you are unlikely to be motivated to search for something better. To become motivated to seek a better answer is not, however, to be committed to discover the answer. A 'better' answer may be many shades away from a 'best' answer in any final sense, and in any case even the possibility of there being a 'best' answer is a very controversial matter. Surely it is sufficient to insist that you are in need of a better answer because the inadequacies of your present answer have become all too clear, with the help of the skilled questions raised by the provocative myoptician.

MYOPIA AND MORALITY

Most people are willing to admit that myopic imperfection may be the best that you can hope for in the realms of gardening, manufacturing automobiles, and writing novels. On the other hand, morality, though notoriously riddled with conflicting views and bombarded by the claims of subjectivity, relativism, and scepticism, is regularly thought to be necessarily absolute, certain, and even sacrosanct. The only alternatives available are said to be 20/20 vision or total blindness. Given that choice, the world publicly opts for the former and gives every evidence of believing and living by the latter. Enter the moral myoptician! He claims to be able to distinguish between blindness and myopia, as well as between indefinitely varied degrees and kinds of myopia. Unless he can distinguish between better and worse sight, he is no better off than the morally blind.

One of the aims of what follows is to suggest that many of the current disagreements about the teaching of values and morality in the schools result from supposing that the only alternative to the current wave of moral blindness and rampant insensitivity is the moral rigour of absolutism. Social commentators seem agreed that we are in the age of the 'me' generation, but it is less than obvious that the way from rampant egoism to altruism is moral absolutism. If morality is concerned with the well-being of the other person, and with actions which treat and recognize the other person as being as worthy of respect and justice as oneself, or anyone else, then it follows that what ought to occupy our attention is how to foster in others the capacity to empathize by placing themselves in another's place, and to apply generally such principles as justice, fairness, and equality of treatment. The opposite of selfishness is not absolutism but universalism or 'not-just-me-ism.' Moral principles are binding on everyone alike and must pay no heed to the desires, aims, and goals of an individual out of relation to others and the greater social context. A moral point of view is one which faithfully surveys the interests of all those likely to be affected by an action, who have agreed to decide on what is to be done on the basis of general principles which apply to everyone equally. It does not follow from the fact that moral principles apply to everyone equally that moral principles are not open to question, may not be altered, expanded, or reduced in application, or integrated into a more systematic and encompassing moral theory. To be moral appears to mean to act on principle, and principles do apply to everyone equally. Such universal application does not rule out alteration, exceptions built into the rule so as to apply with fairness to anyone meeting the requirements, or changes designed to accommodate new and changing circumstances. Just as progress and knowledge in science is not dependent on discoveries and theories being guaranteed for ever not to change, so moral growth and moral principles do not require such ultimate fixity. The decision to be moral, however, does require such fixity and assurance. To be moral it is not enough to go along with general principles most of the time and then abandon them either when the going gets rough or when it appears not to be in your self-interest. The fixity of morality is the decision to do what is required by your principles, your imaginative capacity to place yourself in another's shoes, and your overall philosophy of life without fail, and even if doing so appears to run counter to your own self-interest. In both science and morality you must be unmovable in your determination to follow the evidence and the requirements of your principles. But just this determination and resoluteness often requires that you abandon certain assumptions and interpretations in favour of modifications and additions which appear to be more supported by what is now the evidence and your altered or new principles. In science, your concern is to find the truer, not to defend the present understanding of science; in morality, your concern is to determine and enact what is better, or right, or your duty, not to defend the present status of the art *per se*. If the present status of the art corresponds to what, upon examination, appears to be the better moral viewpoint, so much the better and easier. Let us, though, come to see this for ourselves. The aim of education, in all fields of inquiry, ought to be to encourage and assist us in coming to see the 'truths' and 'principles' of a subject for ourselves. Anything short of that, at least in the long run of education, is to assume either that not everyone can be made to see what is alleged to be the case or that it is too difficult to bring them to see for themselves. Either way, the idealism of education and educators is greatly tarnished.

CREATIVE AMBIGUITY

At the centre of the philosophic method lies creative ambiguity. To be sure, only the sceptics in philosophy's history have also made it the end of their activity, but virtually all have taken ambiguity as at least the starting point of philosophic activity. Socrates is famous for his announcement that the only thing that he knew with certainty was that he didn't know anything else with the same certainty. Philosophy begins in ignorance, with confusion and ambiguity, and whether it turns phoenix-like into creative ambiguity is a factor of the success with which a given response to the darkness generates light.

My use of the term 'response' needs explanation. Philosophy is often characterized by its claims to wisdom, or truth, or the finding of solutions. In fact, this tendency is dominant in most fields of educational theory and practice, where it is common to place emphasis on the answers rather than on the methodology, or on a position or theory which itself is viewed as a myopic squinting at that which has become visible. One who is myopic does not eradicate blurred vision or any of the other forms of ambiguous seeing. He does avoid blindness and the curse of total indistinguishability. As a result, it is precisely because he does not see well enough to eliminate all darkness, imprecision, ambiguity, and indistinctness that he elects to emphasize the problematic in what he holds and teaches. For even the most 'factual' answer is grounded on a variety of theoretical assumptions and postulates and may well rest on an entire system of thought. On this very point, Plato had Socrates remark that the worry about mathematics, and the reason why it was less adequate than dialectic, is that its first beginnings are not proved but only assumed.[2] It is a commonplace that an argument can lead to a conclusion that is, at best, no better than its premises. Among the exact sciences, the beginnings are usually axioms, predefined primitives and postulates. We say of these that they are either so clear and distinct or necessary, or both, that unless we presupposed and posited them we could not otherwise erect a system of exact knowledge. It is just at this point, however, that it is easiest to go wrong. In order to preserve the foundation, and indeed to bolster it, we are tempted to hold that anyone who does not affirm the self-evident starting points as being descriptive of things as they really are is intellectually deficient, or a renegade who would benefit from discipline in the worst way. Or you might choose to emphasize the fact that not to accept any starting points is to be unable to get started at all. You would then have opted for blindness on the grounds that myopia does not offer all that you hoped for. The two extremes of 20/20 vision or total blindness have reappeared as the only options open to us.

The history of educational theory and practice about which I am concerned in this book (that is, as I shall attempt to reconstruct it) is the history of intellectual myopias. Sometimes it is difficult to distinguish between the corrective lenses of one system when compared with another, while at other times the differences are staggering. Often, too, you must wear the lenses for a considerable period of time before the benefits of the correction can be enjoyed and experienced. Even so, it remains the case that even with corrective lenses there is much that cannot be seen, and that what can be seen is plagued by old habits, expectations, prejudices, or simply by the inability to take the time to see with care what has been visible all along. What is most important with corrective lenses is what the wearer uses them for, just as what is important about a violin is what the player does with it. A skilled musician can make remarkable music even on a toy, and a dolt can scratch and howl on a Stradivarius. The great moments in human cultural history have generally resulted either from an unexpectedly skilled use of the instruments at hand or from a novel and untried application. Thus, creativity includes both the expansion of capacity in the sense of skill or excellence at something and a unique application or way of looking. When Picasso saw the world cubistically, he saw it in a new way, and when the pianist Glenn Gould put aside all previous interpretations of a Beethoven sonata, both his own and those of others, in order to experience it afresh and to interpret it in yet another novel and unique way, he was searching for perspectives which would achieve something not heretofore revealed.[3] You can read poetry in countless ways and drain a single verse of more meaning than the poet ever intended or even dreamt. It is undoubtedly a mistake to think that a critic of poetry, or of any literature, is supposed to remain faithful to only those interpretations which are accepted by the author or by a single school of interpretation. What is important is seeing what has not usually been seen, or seeing it in a new way, or seeing its significance as something other than the expected.

The main point of this discussion of 'response' has been to suggest that the problems, the darkness, and the ambiguity out of which the response comes are as important as the actual response itself. For example, to say that Plato held a view usually called the 'theory of forms' is by itself only marginally informative. To understand that he maintained such a theory because, as he saw it, it would otherwise be impossible to show that knowledge of any kind was achievable is informative. More important still is his own recognition that the theory of forms itself was fraught with difficulties, ambiguities, and possible inconsistencies, and that there remained a vast darkness which the theory was unable to illuminate.[4] This is philosophic humility in action and represents a central part of the methodological stance of myopia. It is also true that Plato was at times considerably less humble than this. Be that as it may, to know what Plato said is one thing, and to know why he came to say it is another. More important still is the awareness that he held a position tentatively and with grave doubts about its accuracy and capacity of explanation. This is to come closer to that search for wisdom which Plato tried to instantiate in a concrete form in the dialogues. The centre of philosophy and of education is as much in the seeking as it is in the resultant wisdom in the form of answers. It should also be apparent that it is my view that so-called wisdom is not to be taken as final or sacrosanct but as a perspective, a set of lenses to see through, and possibly to reject as inadequate for your own tasks. It is such active and continuing response to your initial stance, or to someone else's response to it, that keeps alive that original creativity which fostered it in the first place. An idea can only remain alive if it elicits a response. If it is passively received, it is already a dead issue.[5]

PASSIVE ACCEPTANCE (OR REJECTION)

While creative ambiguity has been described as the continuation of the philosophical search for better and more adequate answers, the attitude which it expresses has been identified by the psychologist Rollo May: 'Creative people ... are distinguished by the fact that they can live with anxiety, even though a high price may be paid in terms of insecurity, sensitivity, and defenselessness for the gift of the "divine madness," to borrow the term used by the classical Greeks. They do not run away from non-being, but by encountering and wrestling with it, force it to produce being.'[6] It would not be too much to say that the art of philosophical inquiry is the development of a tolerance for ambiguity and frustration. It is more commonly the case, however, that we are protected from such ambiguity and anxiety by those who consider it their job to pass on to us that information which will 'tell it like it is,' thus enabling us to put the matter in question aside, once and for all. It is comforting to be told what the answers are, what things are really like, what you ought to do, and how a proper life plan is to be constructed. You can passively go through the motions of choosing, selecting, adopting, and living in accordance with pre-packaged alternatives in such a way as to appear to be working things out for yourself. Not only is it easy to come to identify with the accepted and acceptable standards, it takes strength of character actually to recognize that the design and the production are your own. Just as an automobile may serve as an extension and symbol of your own personality even though you may have done nothing more than purchase it, so a series of courses, pre-defined life goals and expected character traits may provide sufficient apparent variation for the expression of personal freedom and growth. It is this deceptiveness of passive acceptance, of reacting superficially, out of habit and along expected paths, that makes the development of what Paulo Freire calls 'critical consciousness' so difficult and so important in contemporary society.[7] It is so easy for what one habitually is and does to become the standard for what is worth doing and what ought to be done.

It is interesting to observe that the deceptiveness of passive acceptance masquerading as active inquiry was no less a concern in classical Greece. The circumstances were different, as was the nature of the passive educational system against which Socrates and Plato reacted, but the translation to our own circumstances is remarkably applicable. Plato's attack on educational content and methodology was a call for a thorough-going reform. However, it is either so subtle that it can be mistaken altogether or so dangerous as to be avoided at all costs. It is best analogized in the well known 'myth of the cave' from the *Republic*.[8] Prisoners are chained in place at the bottom of a cave so that they can only look at shadows on the wall of the cave before them. This wall, deep within the cave, is a wall of illusion, of flickering images arising from habit, unreflective acceptance, and ordinary expectations. The prisoners need but turn their heads to reject the images reflected on the cave wall and see what is in the cave and the world behind them, but their habits restrict their possibilities. Even though the chains are psychological chains of their own making, they cannot bring themselves to do it. They resist giving up the comfort and familiarity of the cave for the possible dangers and uncertainty lurking behind them. All they need do in order to be transformed is turn their heads and look in another direction. It is rather like the childhood sketches and drawings of the hidden faces and animal shapes in the gnarled trees and branches of the forest, where at first it is virtually impossible to see anything but trees in the picture, until you change your visual perspective and see the faces and animals hidden amongst the lines for yourself, and then this change of mental perspective makes it virtually impossible to see only the trees again. Your perspective on the drawing has allowed you to see much more than you originally saw, and the drawing will never be exactly the same again. For the prisoner in the cave who has broken the chains of habit and customary perspective, the world has radically changed as well, and yet it is but the result of a turn of the head, a subtle openness to the possibility of a new perspective. The dangers resulting from this subtle change are not nearly so subtle. They include the anxiety of leaving your old and familiar world behind, of being out of step with your peers and the authoritative point of view on things, and seeming to undermine the virtues and stability which society has worked so hard to establish.

In the pages that follow, I will look at education and its relationship to values and also to morality and ethics. It will be my contention throughout that to entertain well-thought-out perspectives on values and ethics which differ from your own is to enrich your understanding and encourage growth, and is a necessary aspect of general education. The first chapter expands on the methodology and justification for the critical or philosophical approach in education and leads to more specific exemplification of this methodology in practice through discussion of moral education (chapter 2), the importance of choice and the taking of responsibility for what one is and does (chapter 3), the examination of values (chapter 4), and the sensitization of the person to values and the integration of the person as a harmony of intellect, feeling, and will (chapter 5).

The main argument of the book, particularly as it applies to educational practice, can be gleaned by reading the first, third and fifth chapters, and half of chapter 2 (pages 43–61 and 81–105). While the entire manuscript is an extended discussion of a distinctive approach to education, and in particular to moral education, the more technical material can be left until the main argument is in hand.

1

The method as message

It is in the *Symposium* that Plato defines the 'lover of wisdom' or philosopher as neither as wise as a god nor as devoid of wisdom as an ignoramus. The philosopher is inspired by the demi-god *Eros* – a *daimon* – who acts as an intermediary between gods and men, and who stands as 'a mean between ignorance and knowledge.'[1] The philosophic person, too, might be thought of as an intermediary being, as *daimon*-like. The priestess Diotima, through whom Plato says these startling words, additionally warns that the evil of ignorance is 'that he who is neither good nor wise is nevertheless satisfied with himself; he has no desire for that of which he feels no want.'[2] It follows from this that the task of the philosophical educator is to kindle the desire for knowledge and moral goodness within students, making them aware of their ignorance, of the inadequacy of the beliefs and assumptions they hold, and of the incredible complexities to be puzzled over in any serious, thorough inquiry into any subject. The philosopher is a gadfly, persistent in his attempts to get under the saddle of comfort and complacency, thereby creating sufficient discomfort to call attention to a moral or intellectual itch.[3] The philosophical educator and the willing student are both perched precariously between knowledge as certainty, and total ignorance. The image aptly characterizes the activity and character of Socrates. While there continues to be much discussion about whether Plato's own philosophy increasingly departed from that of his teacher, Socrates, there is little doubt that Socrates was a master at demonstrating that neither he nor his disputants knew with certainty. That he knew that he did not know seems to be the only unassailable statement of which Socrates was capable. As *daimon*-like, and as *daimon*-inspired (his inner voice), he was not wise enough to determine the absolute truth of things, but neither was he so stupid as to accept any answer as worthy or believable. As critic, he claimed to be able to recognize an answer which fell short of the very standards that he, as a demanding aspirant after truth and goodness, had but tentatively set forth and defended. Philosophic education is, on this account, the development of the capacity for critical reflection upon the answers, traditions, and habits of your own age undertaken in an attempt to ascertain which of them is more or less adequate and acceptable. There is no better place to encounter this dimension of Socrates than in Plato's dialogue *Meno*.

THE *MENO*

The dialogue takes place between Meno, a young and well-educated aristocrat from Thessaly, and the great Socrates. Meno is not only familiar with the sophists, and with the sophist Gorgias in particular, but has learned the sophistic approach to argument and debate as well. Perhaps the most often quoted sophistic boast is that of being able to make the better argument appear to be the worse and the worse the better. As with the least admirable aspects of our own contemporary debating societies, the object of a debate may be taken to be to win the argument at all costs, regardless of the evidence. The skill of the debater becomes all-important, and the truth of the arguments themselves becomes irrelevant. It is little wonder that sophistry became the model of relativistic education, for if it is the quality of the debater that determines which of the arguments is the winner, then it is the debating skill of the teacher that determines what is worthy of being taught and learned. On this model, and taken to its extreme, teaching becomes a great ego trip, a forum for manipulation and indoctrination. One 'cooks' the evidence to produce the desired result. Of course, simply to manipulate others as you arbitrarily wish can lead to outrage and disgrace. The sophist, however, is ready for this unwanted challenge, defending himself by claiming to be preparing his students for real success in everyday society. 'Success' for the sophist means reputation, position, power, and wealth. The successful public figure is not a zealous seeker after truth or the saint, but the one who gets elected to public office time and time again, who speaks impressively on whatever issue he is obliged to address, and who wields sufficient power amongst his colleagues and in society to be of considerable influence. Even today it is a commonplace that a politician, or a businessman, or even a lawyer need not be honest, only successful, impressive, and influential. The lawyer must win his case to be effective, but he does not have to 'prove' that the case he won was worthy of being won. It is not uncommon in our time to hear of praise being heaped upon a lawyer for winning a 'bad' case, that is, for getting someone off the hook on a technicality, or for winning a decision purely as a result of his own brilliance and skill as a debater. He has made the better case appear the worse and the worse the better. On this relativistic note, success and reputation in education may become the passing of examinations and the mere regurgitation of information. It may be the adopting of the 'safe' opinion, the backing of the *status quo* not because you believe in it but because it is safer and a necessary ingredient in 'success.' To lose your reputation or your job through the backing of an unpopular cause is the route to failure. Thus it can be seen that the advantage of relativism is that it allows you to cast aside as unimportant concern about principles, weighing of the evidence, the degree of justification of a position, or its moral worth, all in favour of considering only what sort of behaviour and personal advocacy will result in success, applause, and power in the everyday world. It is not hard to take the path of least resistance and 'give them what they want.' Such a decision may well eliminate conflict with authorities and (for an educator) conflict with the school board and parents as well. Ironically, the major argument against such a stance may strike you as considerably less robust than those for it. To adopt the majority conformist position simply because it pays to do so is to suspend your critical capacities and to ignore the requirements of morality. Questions about the morality or truth of what you are teaching or doing are replaced by a pragmatic concern about your own well-being, reputation, and social position. The Socratic types, by contrast, are nearly always in trouble.

RELATIVISM AS SCEPTICISM

The sophistic position is a relativism of opportunity which, in philosophical terms, may well reduce to scepticism. If any position held is as worthwhile as any other position simply because it brings success to someone or to some group, then any imaginable position or theory is, or could be, as worthwhile as any other. The consequence of such a position is that distinctions between the more and less valuable, the good and the evil, the beautiful and the ugly, all collapse to a one-dimensional concern about whether holding one view rather than another will bring success and reputation. All considerations here are extrinsic to the arguents *per se* and independent of the weight and adequacy of the evidence in support of them. Emphasis has been shifted to the circumstantial context of popular opinion and the consequences resulting from a decision to act so as to enhance popular reaction to yourself.

This is Meno's intellectual heritage. The implied and unspoken background which Plato weaves into the dialogue is even more dramatic and concerns the life and death of Socrates. While Socrates appears alive and well in the dialogue, in fact Plato is writing this piece some time after Socrates' death in an effort to make the general public come to grips with what Socrates had actually taught, and with the tragedy of Socrates' having been put to death for being, among other things, a sophist. The irony is effective. Socrates, the enemy of sophistry, is put to death for being a sophist. The message is that it is so easy to confuse the philosophical approach to inquiry and learning with the sophistical. For Plato this means that, even in methodology, the worse may be taken to be the better and the better the worse. The justification of the method of philosophy as opposed to sophistry is an oft-repeated one in the dialogues and is a focus of the *Meno*.

PHILOSOPHY AS UNLEARNING

The opening sentence of the *Meno* announces that the issue to be examined is whether virtue can be taught, can be achieved with practice, or is a natural aptitude. Taking a position which appears sophistical, Socrates claims not to be able to deal with the question since he does not know the meaning of the key term in it – 'virtue.' Since he does not know what virtue is, he cannot decide whether it is teachable. Meno is astonished by this and repeats from memory some of the teachings of the sophist Gorgias who held that 'virtue ... consists in managing the city's affairs capably' and also requires that he 'help his friends and injure his foes while taking care to come to no harm himself.'[4] The criterion of success is apparent, and several definitional variations are offered, each shown by Socrates to be inept, until Meno, dizzied from the sting of refutation and subtle distinction, remarks:

Socrates, even before I met you they told me that in plain truth you are a perplexed man yourself and reduce others to perplexity. At this moment I feel you are exercising magic and witchcraft upon me and positively laying me under your spell until I am just a mass of helplessness. If I may be flippant, I think that not only in outward appearance but in other respects as well you are exactly like the flat sting-ray that one meets in the sea. Whenever anyone comes into contact with it, it numbs him, and that is the sort of thing that you seem to be doing to me now. My mind and my lips are literally numb, and I have nothing to reply to you. Yet I have spoken about virtue hundreds of times, held forth often on the subject in front of large audiences, and very well too, or so I thought. Now I can't even say what it is. In my opinion you are well advised not to leave Athens and live abroad. If you behaved like this as a foreigner in another country, you would most likely be arrested as a wizard.[5]

The crime which Athens did come to charge Socrates with was much worse than wizardry. The charge was that of corrupting youth and challenging the beliefs of the State.[6] The penalty was death. But why should you be put to death for assisting in revealing the inadequacies of others? The sophistic background provides some of the answers. An immoral person might feign discomfort with the arguments of another and convince him that they were inadequate by means of a glib tongue. He might do this to gain power over the individual, or to gain support in high places were the colleague an important official, or to incite others to action for his own purposes. A skilful debater can exercise tremendous influence, and that influence is only as moral as his character. No wonder Plato wrote so many dialogues to make evident just what sort of person Socrates was. The way to defuse the charges against Socrates was (1) to show that he was not evil but a dedicated and good man, and (2) to demonstrate that the aim of his critical method was not selfish gain or the propagation of some dogma or ideology but the clarification and justification of answers to questions of great human importance through the use of reason itself. His ends were not self-interest and personal gain but intellectual honesty and critical vigilance in uncovering logical inadequacies; in short, greater understanding. Athens put to death the wrong man, partly because of a misconception and partly because Socrates was persistent in disrupting the *status quo*. One who doesn't play the game is always a considerable threat to those who do, for he undermines the sense of security of the players and the authority of the team captains, and can easily paralyse them. Socrates attacked claims of expertise in areas such as morality, teaching, and political leadership, where it was not easy to find evidence supporting such claims. In so doing he was attacking established reputations and undermining the inflated authority of those who claimed knowledge but could not produce under scrutiny. He was a corrupter of youth if that means that he transformed his students by causing them to investigate all claims to authority – philosophical, societal, or personal – before placing their trust in that authority. His students were never the same again.

The possible implications of the image of Socrates as sting-ray are both numerous and exciting. To sting oneself as well as others, teachers as well as students, is to make the *question*, rather than the answer, the problem, rather than the solution, the subject matter of education. What makes a good teacher, in this model, is the quality of his questioning, the extent to which he loses sight of solutions which, if accepted, might well cause one not to look further, or to think again.

Paradoxically, the less one knows in this sense, the better teacher one can be. All of this seems counter-intuitive. Surely the purpose of education is to make knowledge available, yet on the Socratic model, not only is there an open question as to whether there is any such thing as knowledge, there is also the added and questionable assumption that the goal of teaching is to criticize so-called knowledge in order to create a profound ignorance, a not-knowing. We are much more than ignorant, even though teaching the humility of ignorance is the starting point of Socratic education. As *daimones* we can approach the divine in being able to recognize untruth, and can find answers that are less deficient than others. We are capable of degrees of myopia.

DAIMONIC RECOLLECTION

In the *Thaetetus* Socrates compares himself to a midwife. As a midwife assists a mother in giving birth to the child needing to be born, so the teacher/philosopher assists a student in giving birth to those ideas and insights which are there, within the student's mind, awaiting expression. Of course, it is important to be clear about what is there already and what is not. Many of the impatient attacks on Plato's *Meno* result from people assuming that what Plato is saying is that all our ideas are already within our minds, at birth, and in something like their fully developed form. Taken to the extreme, such a claim would hardly be believable. To assume that today's stock-market reports were already in the minds of the young stockbrokers-to-be does stretch credulity. But insight is another matter. Insight is simply the capacity to recognize that an answer to a question is wrong, or at least insufficient, ambiguous, vague, unclear, or confused. At its best, it is the capacity to recognize a correct answer, or at least one that is better than available alternatives in the directions of sufficiency and clarity, and away from ambiguity, vagueness, and confusion. Putting my thesis into Plato's mouth, the miracle is not that we have inborn ideas of the goings and comings of the stock-market but that we can use reason itself to establish standards of consistent reasoning and systematic argument, to detect similarities amongst past occurrences and the like, and to weight the evidence so as to be able to 'order' events like those of the stock-market. How is insight possible? What makes us able to distinguish the better evidence from the worse? How does knowledge begin and gain a foothold amidst the 'blooming, buzzing confusion' of perception, consciousness, and life?[7]

MEMORIZATION OR INSIGHT

What has been said thus far places Socrates and Plato in the tradition of non-absolutist thinkers. Yet the standard history of philosophy often places Plato at the vanguard of absolutist, dogmatic, and totalitarian theorizing.[8] He has also been regularly associated with the architects of democracy.[9] There is considerable evidence on both sides, and, as with most philosophical questions, the stand taken is heavily the result of the approach, sensitivities, background, hopes, and fears of the interpreter, yielding an emphasis which is distinctive if not actually unique. There is no need to rehearse the evidence for and against Plato's totalitarianism, although it is worth singling out Sir Karl Popper as a contemporary critic of Plato who considers him to be a dangerous totalitarian. He contrasts Plato's rigid stance to his own open-ended, democratic, and ever-revisable approach.[10] Popper is to be singled out here simply because I will enlist him in making clearer some of the grounds for a theory of myopic knowledge. Obviously something odd is at work here, for it is my claim that Popper and Plato are really colleagues at the same task and with similar aspirations, whereas Popper views Plato as aptly representative of what he is most opposed to.

A simple explanation of this dissonance is that I have thus far been at pains to write more of Socrates, who was less systematic, and less about Plato, who was more rigid in his stance. Socrates was more the critic, the questioner in search of a philosophy, while Plato found and systematized it. Much of this is true, and yet the answer is more complex, as Norman Gulley notes.[11] It was Plato who, in looking back at his teacher and friend, saw that Socrates' search went on to the very end of his life. It was Plato who emphasized that fact in his dialogues about Socrates. It is well known that Socrates comes to figure less and less prominently in the dialogues of the middle and later period, and he ceases to appear at all in much of the later writings of Plato. This may be Plato's own device for calling to the reader's attention that he is leaving the explicit teaching of his master behind and going on to develop his own position. His 'theory of forms' served as the foundation for his own philosophy, and the forms bring to rest the search for truth as they are the eternal, absolute, unchanging ground of all knowledge and insight. If there were no fixed truth, then we would have no standard by means of which to decide whether one insight was closer to the mark than another. On the other hand, if we already had a glimpse of the truth, we would not need to search. We will explore this paradox shortly, as it appears in the *Meno*. What matters here is whether Plato held to this theory as being the fixed and final word about knowledge and its possibility. It is no small point that the entire history of philosophy in the West has been labelled but a series of critical and appreciative footnotes to Plato and to his main thesis of the forms. It is apparent enough to those who have come after him that his work was open to critical reaction, rejection, refinement, and renovation. While there have been relatively few who have accepted Plato's view more or less as it is, there are fewer still who have not been significantly affected by their encounter with his philosophic insight, challenge, and pains-taking analysis. What is even more remarkable is that Plato was one of his own most severe critics, as a study of the more mature dialogues will reveal. We shall return to this in a moment. For the present, it is the *Meno* that may place in perspective how the forms might be taken on as an interpretation of Plato that lays emphasis on search rather than fixed truth.

KNOWLEDGE AS RECOLLECTION

Imagine for a moment that you have to teach Plato's philosophy to a beginners' class in the following way. Make certain that you first teach Plato's basic doctrines, and having provided a list of his main ideas and concepts, you might then proceed as follows. The necessity for believing in reincarnation is outlined in the *Meno* and elsewhere. Because we have all lived many times before, we are filled to the brim with knowledge which we need only recollect. In the *Phaedrus* Plato amplifies this and describes a previous encounter, in another realm before birth into this one, with the forms themselves. Our 'chariot-like' souls soar upwards, some to the clouds, some above, and to a greater or lesser extent gain glimpses of the shimmering forms, before sinking back below the clouds again. Prior to birth into this world our souls drink from the river of Unmindfulness or Forgetfulness, erasing the memories of these visions from ordinary waking consciousness, but not eliminating them altogether. The skilled philosophical midwife, if he or she happens along, will assist in bringing them to the surface of consciousness by asking penetrating questions, forcing us to dig deeper until we are able to rediscover answers to those questions. The example of the ignorant or unschooled slave boy of the *Meno* serves us well here. Never having studied geometry before, the boy is asked to double the area of a square drawn before him in the sand. His first instinct is to assume that he need only double the length of the sides of the square. If the square were two feet by two feet (2×2 or 4 square feet in area), then doubling the length of the sides would make the square four feet by four feet, and the resultant area would have quadrupled, not doubled (4×4 or 16 square feet). This first answer is clearly wrong. But how is the slave boy able to recognize that this is clearly not the right answer? The Platonic 'facts' of the case seem to indicate that the boy was able to recognize the answer as incorrect because, in a previous life in another realm, his soul fluttered above the clouds long enough to glimpse the forms of 'Doubleness,' 'Area,' 'Square,' etc ... Such an approach to Plato would be disastrous. Students in such a class would put philosophy aside as useless and farfetched. The answers alone are lifeless doctrines, discrete pebbles removed from the shores where they were found intelligibly placed in an appropriate context. Out of the context of the queries and perplexities which occasioned them, they are without a frame of reference which will tell us which questions they were deemed adequate or hopeful answers to. Unless we are led to see why Plato felt compelled to put forward a doctrine as a more adequate solution to a problem than the other alternatives of which he knew, then we will be confused by his figurative language, metaphors, analogies, myths, and well known folktales, which supplement his more literal philosophical descriptions of the cosmos. By themselves separate doctrines, or even a string of doctrines, do not carry with them their own defence or compelling force apart from occasioning perplexity. This is why the problem itself is often viewed by philosophers as more important to master in depth and detail than any of the 'great' answers given as possible solutions. To come to understand a philosopher's doctrines as responses to problems is to interpret him and to incorporate what you learn from him into a web of interpretation which includes far more than you find in the literal answers and isolated examples taken from his writings. You have to recreate the problematic context itself.

Now let's alter our approach, making Plato's answers secondary to our main purpose, namely, to understand how you grasp problems such as those which perplexed Socrates and Plato enough to cause them to strive for answers to them. The central problem is whether and how knowledge of any kind is possible. You must think with Plato in order to determine whether you can give grounds for resisting the sophists and their criterion of success. Returning to Meno's dilemma, we must focus once again on this profound statement of the problem:

MENO: But how will you look for something when you don't in the least know what it is? How on earth are you going to set up something you don't know as the object of your search? To put it another way, even if you come right up against it, how will you know that what you have found is the thing you didn't know?[12]

Unless you already know what is being sought, by somehow innately possessing the knowledge or the latent knowledge which makes recognition possible, there will be no way of determining whether what is found, even if it is immediately before you, is what you have set out to find. The same point is driven home in a thoroughly delightful passage from A.A. Milne's *Winnie-the-Pooh*, in which Pooh and Piglet wander around the 'hundred acre wood' again and again:

'Hallo!' said Piglet, 'what are you doing?'
'Hunting,' said Pooh.
'Hunting what?'
'Tracking something,' said Winnie-the-Pooh very mysteriously.
'Tracking what?' said Piglet, coming closer.
'That's just what I ask myself, I ask myself, What?'
'What do you think you'll answer?'
'I shall have to wait until I catch up with it,' said Winnie-the-Pooh.
'Now, look there,' He pointed to the ground in front of him. 'What do you see there?'
'Tracks,' said Piglet. 'Paw-marks.' He gave a little squeak of excitement. 'Oh, Pooh! Do you think it's a - a - a Woozle?'
'It may be,' said Pooh. 'Sometimes it is, and sometimes it isn't. You never can tell with paw-marks.'[13]

Since neither Piglet nor Pooh have ever seen a Woozle, it is unlikely that they would ever succeed in tracking one, and if they did they would be unable to know whether or not it was a Woozle. Pooh's final remark that 'you can never tell with paw-marks' is even more devastating, for it implies that what are one day Woozle tracks, the next day are not. This is relativism verging on chaos! Nothing stands still or remains the same. The world of experience is in a continual state of flux. It was the hopelessness of such a vision which caused the ancient Cratylus, elder contemporary of Socrates, to sit in the middle of downtown Athens, refusing to speak or to do much else besides wiggle his fingers in quiet desperation in order to make a philosophical point.[14] To say anything at all requires that things remain constant, that words continue to mean what they mean and that they apply to things consistently. The scepticism of Cratylus results from viewing the world and everything in it as being in continual and hopeless flux, and so all knowledge walks away as well. Logically even his finger-statement is inconsistent, for it, too, will come to mean what he didn't intend it to mean. Short of utter scepticism, Pooh had found the only answer possible in an inquiry without a standard: 'I shall today, just now, mean by Woozle an animal that makes tracks like those in front of us. For now, a Woozle, if discovered, will be a large, brown, hoppity animal.' It is more than apparent that, if pressed, this conventional relativism will give way to the scepticism of the foundationless. Unless you have a starting point, that is, unless you already have some indication of what what you are searching for is required to be, then any answer is as good or bad as any other, which means that none of them are based on anything more than temporary whim.

R.B. Perry draws a similar result when he pin-points the central dilemma of education: 'To define in advance an end result and then to seek by all possible means to achieve it, is held to be too narrowing, too repressive, too authoritarian. But if, on the other hand, there is no end in view, educational activity is confused and incoherent. Its various parts and successive phases do not add up to anything. Without a definition of the end there is no test by which means can be selected, and no standard by which practice can be criticized and improved.[15] Once again it appears that the ground between 20/20 vision and blindness closes, leaving no alternative between the two. The educational choice is between indoctrination, which places emphasis on the established answers, and scepticism, which places emphasis on the unanswerability of the questions. In the slave boy example from the *Meno*, the educational implications are paralysing. If he already knows the answer, actually or latently, he does not need to 'learn' it. If he does not know the answer, then he cannot learn it, for he is incapable of ever recognizing a correct answer. Either way, education is impossible. The slave boy has no means whereby he can come to accept or reject various answers which attempt to double the area of a square. Yet he does see that his answer is incorrect! He is not immediately able to reach the correct answer, but the ability to recognize an incorrect answer at least suggests that he is not totally blind but badly myopic. And in seeing how not to double the area of a square, he is a little less myopic than he says. His myopia, however, was present before Socrates' teaching began. His capacity to see was not Socrates' doing. It is this capacity to 'see' on which a teacher must count, if there is to be any learning at all. A child must come to class already able to see that something is or is not so. A child does not come to class to be told that something is or is not so. For then he need not see it at all but, like Piglet, will accept any answer as the right one. He need only listen and memorize. He will memorize the theorems of geometry and the principles of law and morality, and begin a detailed list of the examples and situations to which they apply. He will not be able to apply such theorems and principles deftly to other similar situations, for he has not come to 'see' the force of such generality, he may forget the formula and thus lose the entire benefit, and so on. But bring him to see the answer for himself, and he has the insight and probably the method for applying the answer to other instances; he may even qualify and refine it, and the issue of forgetting disappears altogether. Not having memorized the formula, but having worked it out for himself, he knows the method of solving problems, in geometry and, we shall assume for the moment, in morality as well. He is an independent thinker, capable of solving problems on his own, no longer in need of lists of specifics to which his memorization of rules and regulations apply. It is this seeing for oneself that is central to the Socratic/Platonic method of education. Specific doctrines, even that of the forms, are but attempts to think something out. The answer is used only in an attempt to re-create the problem which occasioned it. Then, having looked at the alternative answers to the same problem, you criticize and then evaluate each of them, eventually reaching the conclusion that a particular answer is preferable, although not without its own difficulties. The answer achieved, however, is one that has taken much struggle and has been carved out of confusion by and for yourself.

You may emphasize Plato's answers to questions, detailing his doctrines as static notions about which you can have opinions or as insights to problems which so involve you in them that you cannot help but stand on your own two feet in deciding whether the answers are good enough. A Platonic answer, I am contending, involves the reader by necessity as well as by design, and makes of him a co-disputant and fellow seeker. We will return to the example of the slave boy shortly, for we have not yet spoken of the correct answer to the geometrical problem, or of how correct answers are possible in general. First, however, it will be helpful to expand on the importance of involvement which makes of you a co-disputant and fellow seeker in problem solving.

ARE YOU THERE?

In his *Preface to Plato* Eric Havelock remarks that the live 'performances' of ancient Greek poetry in Socrates' time were 'truly a form of hypnosis' and concludes that this 'surely is the reason why Plato so often describes the non-philosophical state of mind as a kind of sleep-walking.'[16] In Plato's time live narrative or dramatic performance of poetry was not just literature, but a cultural encyclopaedia maintained by the 'Greek culture bearers.'[17] Until the fifth century BC Greek culture was almost exclusively an oral culture, and the mechanism of transmitting the traditions of society from generation to generation included neither schools nor manuscripts, but public recitation. Havelock maintains that the techniques of the oral culture of Greece were overwhelmingly anti-philosophical. On all sides the young were bombarded with repetitions of the cultural tradition, performed as part of the family rituals or in public.[18] Always they were to identify with what was being portrayed, for a performance is a dramatic recreation of certain material or traditions so convincingly done as to cause you to identify with the characters portrayed. It was this that Plato was fighting against, for when you identify with a performance in this way you become passively uncritical of the ideas being presented. You become temporarily identified with the characters and their deeds and are unable to stand apart from the 'objects' being presented so as to analyse and evaluate them.[19] Of course, such identification was an important aspect of the act of memorization, for years after seeing or hearing a performance one could easily recall the vivid experience and quote it from memory. In addition to uncritical identification, rhythm and rhyme as well acted as hypnotic suggesters. Even the actor or rhapsode might have been unaware of 'the cultural meaning of what he was preserving.' You can be sure that he was aware of whatever techniques he had to assist him in making his words stick in the minds of his audience. Education and performance are here identified. Writes Havelock: 'You were not asked to grasp their principles through rational analysis. You were not invited to so much as think of them. Instead you submitted to the paideutic spell. You allowed yourself to become "musical" in the functional sense of the Greek term [ie, possessed or enchanted by the Muse].'[20] You can almost imagine Socrates or Plato adding to this that education becomes a sort of sleep-walking when it resorts to memorization, authority, or tradition and standardizes the results of the educational process in terms of 'information gained.' A truly philosophic education, Socrates might have observed, has little to do with the information gained and a great deal to do with the development of the capacity to see for yourself whether something is or is not to be accepted as given, and precisely why. Then, and only then, can a student take off on his own. By contrast, a sleep-walker is one who dimly sees what is around him, except what is directly before him, and possibly not even that. 'Am I going in the right direction?' – what sleep-walker would be able to ask such a question? A curriculum, like a play or the path of a sleep-walker, is to be taken as given, to be identified with. It was Socrates and Plato who, according to Havelock, startled the sleep-walkers of ancient Greece by asking, 'What do you mean? Say that again.'[21] This is the beginning of the so-called Socratic *elenchus*, or cleansing, that is the necessary preparation for learning:

But to say, 'what do you mean? Say that again' abruptly disturbed the pleasurable complacency felt in the poetic formula or the image. It meant using different words and these equivalent words would fail to be poetic; they would be prosaic ... In short, the dialectic, a weapon we suspect to have been employed in this form by a whole group of intellectuals in the last half of the fifth century, was a weapon for arousing the consciousness from its dream language and stimulating it to think abstractly. As it did this, the conception of 'me thinking about Achilles' rather than 'me identifying with Achilles' was born.[22]

The passive spell is broken, unthinking listening and memorization are cast aside, and the individualistic stand is born which requests the evidence for the claim. You are no longer a passive identifier with either participant in a dialogue, following whatever is said or thought, but an active participant in the dialogue; you reason and speak for yourself. It has become necessary to establish the support for any assertion or claim if it is to bear conviction. If the support is missing, it is necessary to consider the case again and to dialogue further. This is the spirit in which the dialogues of Plato are to be taken. Whether or not you agree with Plato and accept his conclusions, you are forced to walk with him in the lengthy and twisting ins and outs of the argument, in order to be brought to the point where you can see for yourself whether to reject or accept, to modify or revise. Often, when reading the dialogues, you find that a seeming solution is soon dashed to bits by Socrates himself, or that it is first articulated and then re-examined by another and found to be weak. It is as though Plato is teaching by placing arguments before you which appear to be sound, but some of which will prove, upon examination, to have been unworthy. Did you see that for yourself? Are you awake? Are you still there, still paying attention? In the context of teaching and education, it is as though you were asked, 'Did you see the mistake? Did you work it out for yourself before I pointed it out to you?' If not, then you must work harder until you, too, can begin to see for yourself what a good philosophical argument is. In the mean time, the most important thing is to remain alert, vigilantly critical, and searching for errors, for shortcomings, or for conclusions reached with insufficient evidence and support.

But how are good philosophical arguments recognizable?

ANSWERS

Returning to the *Meno*, we find that after seeing that his first answer was incorrect, the slave boy next tries increasing the sides of the original square by half, in his attempt to arrive at a figure double in area. What is required is a square whose area is exactly twice that of the original figure ($2 \times 2 = 4$), or an area of eight square feet. This second solution, however, is still off base, for it yields a figure with an area of nine square feet ($3 \times 3 = 9$). Significantly, the slave boy can again see this answer to be incorrect. Socrates now proceeds to lead the boy to the correct answer. Hardly a commentator on this passage has not emphasized that the boy is indeed being led to the right answer by Socrates, but most take this to be a clear instance of 'cheating' on Plato's part. In order to establish that knowledge is recollection, he leads the slave boy to see the very answer which he wants him to see, and then says that it was the boy himself who got there on his own. It is not acceptable to lead someone carefully to a preferred answer and then praise him for his own autonomous efforts in getting there on his own. Surely, though, this is to miss the point of the passage. Plato, through Socrates, openly and candidly leads the slave boy to the correct answer. It is hardly a hidden passage, and that is precisely why almost everyone has noticed it. What has been less often noticed is that the slave boy was solely in possession not of the path to insight but of his own insight itself. You can lead a student to insight, but you can't make him see. He, and he alone, has that power. By drawing a square on the diagonal of the original square, you produce a square exactly twice the size in area. We now have the solution to the mathematical puzzle. The slave boy is able to see that this is so, and I can see it, and so can anyone else. The point of the *Meno* is not that the boy recollected the details of this geometric solution (actually, the Pythagorean theorem) from a previous existence, but that he could come to learn because he was capable of seeing for himself the truth of the third answer. How he was able to do so is considerably less clear and remains one of the central problems of philosophy. Plato simply points out that we do claim to have knowledge, and that such a claim is, by necessity, based on the capacity to recognize something as an instance of knowledge, as a correct answer, or as a member of a class, when we stumble upon it. Unless something like recollection was so, we could never get the process of cognition started. Cognition is recognition, that is, re-cognition. Otherwise, alleged knowledge would be but stipulation, or frivolous naming, of the sort the sophists retreated to in order to win arguments. No wonder Cratylus sat and wiggled his fingers in consistent defiance of the arbitrary games called tradition, education, and political and social virtue!

Plato's answer to the question 'How is knowledge possible?' may be taken as something like the following. Cognition implies re-cognition, in some sense. To see that something is such and such requires that you already have the capacity to identify such and suches. This capacity must be inborn, or simply there already, before recognition can occur. One possible answer as to how this is possible is to imagine a time when the soul of each person gained this knowledge in a previous life. Is such an answer sufficient or acceptable? Plato himself warns his readers that this answer is one that he has 'heard from certain wise men and women who spoke of things divine.'[23] The original source of this tale is the priests and priestesses whom he has so often ridiculed in the past for being unable to tell why what they teach is worthy of being taught. Then he himself adds that some of the things which he goes on to say about the theory of recollection he is 'not altogether confident' about.[24] Plato may be taken to be saying that he is using an unproven myth and that he cannot vouch for its truth, or at least that it would take many more dialogues to be able to determine whether it could be done. He does not argue for its acceptance here or even break it down into its component arguments; in fine, he does not weigh the evidence in support of this theory but defends it purely pragmatically, showing its superiority to Meno's theory of unknowability: 'We ought not then to be led astray by the contentious argument you quoted. It would make us lazy, and is music in the ears of weaklings. The other doctrine produces energetic seekers after knowledge; and being convinced of its truth, I am ready, with your help, to inquire into the nature of virtue.'[25] Meno's doctrine is that knowledge is impossible, for we have no means of recognizing it. What Plato appears to be claiming is that unless something like recollection is so, that is, unless we have within us a capacity for distinguishing a better from a worse argument, then knowledge is impossible. It must never be forgotten that Plato left dialogue after dialogue inconclusive as to the result achieved, almost as though his chief point was that he provided theories and hypotheses as possible solutions to significant questions, but only to encourage others to engage with him in the inevitable revisions and further struggle required. Answers lead to new problems or questions more often than they yield quiet and sufficient solutions. A student confronting Plato in this spirit is forced to decide for himself whether he can establish some other basis for knowledge and insight, or whether he will stand with Plato on ground which the philosopher himself saw as shaky. In any case, the student is now a participant in the dialogue, in the philosophical search for truth through critical inquiry into the sufficiency of answers provided. He comes to see a problem for himself, to understand Plato's own tentative solution, to recognize its shortcomings in the light of his own experience and understanding, and perhaps to have a hunch or two about the direction of the answer which will serve to ground his own philosophic position in the future. The real issue is not whether he accepts Plato's solution but whether he has learned to be vigilant enough to persevere in his quest for a solution which is sufficiently well-grounded to convince him and to motivate him further in his search for understanding.

The standard of knowledge which Plato comes to establish is that of the unchanging, absolute, and eternal forms, recollected by us in this life through considerable struggle. Yet Plato writes dialogues which are consistently inconclusive, calling again and again on the disputants, and by implication the reader, to come back another time to try to better the present results. In his so-called later dialogues, Plato is critical of his own position, and in particular of the theory of forms itself.[26] That he changed his mind and his position is evident from his own writings. That he ever made up his mind in a philosophically definitive way is debatable. At all events, to resolve issues of this kind is a task for Plato scholarship. What matters here is that the method of questions and answers begun by Socrates and Plato serves well as the model of open-ended inquiry and may be viewed as an adequate description of what Western philosophers have been about for the past 2500 years in their varied responses to Plato's position.

ENEMIES IN LEAGUE WITH EACH OTHER

Karl Popper's attack on Plato's dogmatism was briefly discussed above. In the light of my interpretation of Plato's method as itself being open-ended, it becomes apparent that Plato and Popper may be seen as allies in search of non-dogmatic understanding. Popper, in his book *Objective Knowledge*, stresses the tentativeness of all knowledge claims, and in particular of those so often thought to be immune to doubt, namely, the findings of science:

We have reached a point from which we can see science as a magnificent adventure of the human spirit. It is the invention of ever new theories, and the indefatigable examination of their power to throw light on experience. The principles of scientific progress are very simple. They demand that we give up the ancient idea that we may attain certainty (or even a high degree of 'probability' in the sense of the probability calculus) with the propositions and theories of science (an idea which derives from the association of science with magic and of the scientist with the magician): the aim of the scientist is not to discover absolute certainty, but to discover better and better theories [or to invent more and more powerful aids to vision: searchlights, spectacles, etc] capable of being put to more and more severe tests [and thereby leading us to, and illuminating for us, ever new experiences]. But this means that these theories must be falsifiable: it is through their falsification that science progresses.[27]

Falsifiability is an initial tenet which forces us to compare our theories with the world of everyday reality, and then, if our 'facts' are found wanting, we can try a new and more satisfactory hypothesis.[28] The urge to try a new hypothesis is the result of recognizing that a previous hypothesis has been shown to be inadequate. A new hypothesis is an opportunity for more adequate 'feedback' from the world of nature which we are trying to understand and explain. A major interpreter of Popper, Bryan Magee, writes of Popper's method that it is undogmatic in essence, for 'it holds that we never actually know – that our approach to any and every situation or problem needs to be always such as to accommodate not merely unforeseeable contributions but the permanent possibility of a radical transformation of the whole conceptual scheme with which, and even within which, we are operating.'[29] Scientists do not aim at certainty and try to solve all the major problems of thought; they are more like artists who, 'by use of creative imagination subjected to critical control,' seek to find answers which are more acceptable than previous ones.[30]

There is little in this brief account of Popper's open-ended theory of knowledge that does not accord with Plato's methodology as I have described it. What is missing is some mention of how knowledge is possible in the first place. In his *Unended Quest* Popper reflects back upon his own grappling with this foundational issue and comes to admit that cognition is not possible without some sort of re-cognition: 'All this led me to the view that conjecture or hypothesis must come before observation or perception: we have inborn expectations; we have latent inborn knowledge, in the form of latent expectations, to be activated by stimuli to which we react as a rule while engaged in active exploration. All learning is a modification (it may be a refutation) of some prior knowledge and thus, in the last analysis, of some inborn knowledge.'[31] Popper's admission does not carry with it the baggage of reincarnation, recollection, and the theory of forms, but it clearly is a sympathetic footnote to the Platonic challenge that something innate is required for knowledge to begin, and that that something must in some way serve as a standard for determining whether a statement is correct or incorrect, defensible or indefensible, justified or whimsical. Plato's problem orientation and his central concern of knowing whether and how knowledge is possible are no less dominant in Popper's and our own day, and the struggle for insight into the matter is no less apparent.

THE BUCKET THEORY

If the primary concern of education is to bring learners to 'see for themselves,' and if the methodology best serving it is that of dialogical interaction which enlists learners in appraising the problem situation, then educational practice ought to be more a process of drawing out than of putting something into the minds of students. To help someone see is to enrich and sharpen already existing powers. As they mature, learners ought to be increasingly encouraged to enter into an analysis of the major solutions offered to significant issues, with the goal being their own knowledgeable evaluation of each of them. To concentrate on problems is to de-emphasize any particular answer or set of answers, and to increase markedly the level of perplexity amongst those involved in the inquiry. In this sense, education is the development and intensification of ambiguity, but it is also the development of a tolerance for ambiguity. Perplexity is a necessary first step in learning, for it is perplexity alone that reveals to you, the learner, that you do not know. Ambiguity reveals that previous assumptions, habits, and beliefs are not, as they stand, adequate to handle the issues before you. Furthermore, perplexity, frustration, and the recognition of the inadequacies of your views may yield a high motivational thrust in aid of working out something better. It should be directed to that end, and with the thrust of passion awakened (re-awakened) by the paradoxical knowledge of your own ignorance. Socrates saw clearly that the desire to know must precede learning; otherwise, you assume that you are not in need of anything further – that what you believe and think you know is true and sufficient, and that additional search is not called for. To be brought to your intellectual knees, on the other hand, is to be made aware of a lack. As one who is akin to a *daimon*, you do not possess the wisdom of the gods. The first act of becoming aware of your status as *daimon* is seeing that you do not know, after all. The method of revealing the not-known is dialogue. The function of dialogue is to upset habitual ways of looking at people and ideas, to break the hold of prejudice, to attack blind assumption, and even to challenge the truisms and clichés of your culture. Such aphorisms as 'Never put off until tomorrow what you can do today' find their way into nearly every home and most schools at one time or another. Sayings are traditionally assumed to be concentrated glimpses of a distilled wisdom which has stood the test of time and changing circumstances. In this same folk wisdom we also learn that 'Haste makes waste,' although the apparent conflict between the two aphorisms is obvious when they are considered back to back. The aphorisms alone without interpretation and analysis cannot help us decide whether to hurry up or slow down. We must consider whether haste is the only alternative to procrastination, or whether there is a golden mean between the two ... and so on. Unreflective 'knowledge' is often inconsistent and considerably less than universally applicable in spite of being formulated for general application. Without a method of application and of resolving conflicts between contradictory claims, there is no way of determining whether a common truth is applicable to a given situation or not.

Learners who see that they do not know may well search for knowledge with remarkably increased zealousness. To ask them to memorize an answer for which they have no corresponding problem is to cause them to work to possess something which for them has no relevance and little significance. Alfred North Whitehead calls such learning the mastery of 'inert ideas,' although his concern was with ideas which were long since dead, whereas we have added to his list those ideas 'killed' in the teaching of them.[32] Any idea and any solution to a problem can become inert in a context which does not bring it to life. Education which operates by filling heads with answers for which corresponding problems and related difficulties have not been emphasized may be termed 'bucket theory' education. Popper writes of the bucket theory in science: 'According to this view, then, our mind resembles a container – a kind of bucket – in which perceptions and knowledge accumulate.'[33] Francis Bacon contrasts 'the men of experiment' who, like ants, only collect and heap up discrete particles or nuggets of information, with 'the reasoners,' who, like spiders, make intricate cobwebs out of their own substance. He advocates that we emulate the middle course of the bee, which 'gathers its material from the flowers of the garden and of the field,' while digesting it and transforming 'it by a power of its own.'[34] In contrast, R.M. Hare explains his version of the bucket theory where the student is merely a passive recepticle for bits of information (which is sometimes called 'impartiality'): 'It is to be hoped that [recent research showing the mind to be an active agent in creating knowledge] will finally and effectively remove from the repertoire of philosophical theories that one which Professor Popper has called "the bucket theory of the mind" – the theory that facts drip into the mind like water into a bucket where they accumulate and are called "knowledge."'[35] A mind crammed full of inert ideas is one devoid of binding material to systematize them. Without such congealing material, the great danger is that the information will, if you tip your head to one side, run out of the ear. You have to make the material you own, and the reliable way of doing this is to possess the problems which occasioned the initial response, and to share in the difficulties and complexities which serve to keep the issue very much alive. Working harder at memorizing material only makes the matter worse, leaving less time and less incentive for working over ideas already in one's possession in an attempt to evaluate them, relate them, and go beyond them. The encouraging of flexibility and independence of mind is the aim of education, not the amassing of information *per se*. To have both is better still.

EDUCATING FOR UNIQUENESS

In *Teaching as a Subversive Activity*, Neil Postman and Charles Weingartner emulate the Socratic method and aim to encourage the student to think and to see for himself. The goal of education, they argue, is to create learners who have become expert 'crap detectors,' that is, who refuse to accept uncriticially the outpourings of wisdom from any source.[36] Such students do not simply sit and listen, but question and attempt to assimilate what is being presented into their own developing perspectives. They do not accept what authorities say but test the claims and arguments offered in the light of the evidence, or lack of it, provided. It is the teachers, however, who ought to be the best at 'crap detecting,' in order that they might pass on the skill to those who encounter them. The problem is that it is all too easy to rely on your earlier worked-out answers, or your own earlier education, or simply the established view, rather than to subject yourself to the uncertainty, frustration, and need to build which arise from the method of beginning yet again. It is an important characteristic of capable educators that they continue to endeavour to learn. But can it be sustained as a salient characteristic over an entire career, and beyond?

One of the more interesting sources of support for the possibility and desirability of non-terminating learning and continued intellectual openness and flexibility is to be found in the work of the physiologist J.Z. Young. In *Doubt and Certainty in Science* Young argues that by and large the rules by which the brain works are not inherent but have been learned. This is not to say that the capacity to see for yourself is also learned, but only that your rules and point of perspective are learned, that is, developed (not poured in), over a period of time. He is not concerned with the Platonic question about how seeing, or the gaining of rules in the first place, is possible. Be that as it may, the rules for processing information gained from within and without and turning it into a coherent system of recognition and understanding are slowly and progressively developed by each and every one of us. The rules themselves are not 'poured in' but emerge, and can be encouraged or drawn out for examination. Precisely because they are learned, they may also be altered or even eliminated. We may be 'taught' to process materials according to new rules, that is, we may be led to see things in new ways. By analogy, the difficulties encountered by those adjusting to sight, having been blind from birth, may be compared to the difficulties affecting the mind which encounters new perspectives or encounters someone who 'blows his mind' because of a radically different way of looking at things. The process of learning to see physically involves a great deal of unlearning before new avenues of association can be formed and utilized. Objects do not 'look' the way they feel, sound, taste, and smell. Those who are learning to see must be led again and again to the same objects which they have come to know in these other sense-ways, in an attempt to reinforce the correlation of the visual patterns with them. Linking the sight of an orange with its texture and shape when felt, for example, regularly seems incredibly difficult and generally pointless to the newly sighted. What the sighted person does from childhood with ease, the heretofore unsighted views as an unnecessary relational complication which must be slowly and painfully grasped. You may be reminded here of the long and arduous journey out of the cave of ignorance described in Plato's *Republic*, where the ascending, that is, developing, prisoner has to wait patiently for his eyes to adjust to the more intense light at each level of ascent. At all events, returning to the analogy of physical seeing, the blind person has for years successfully distinguished oranges from chairs and it is only now that this simple action has become problematic as a result of the addition of the capacity to see and the recently acquired need to correlate this ability with the other sense abilities. What has to be shown is that the ability to see actually enhances your capacity to deal with objects in the everyday world and will yield considerable enjoyment as well.

Leaving the analogy behind, if the teacher is thought of as one who must provide a 'new point of view' by means of which the learner may either gain new information which may force him to change his 'rules' or see old information in a new light, then he may be thought of as a source of new input, information, or perspective. Just as the eye must be taught to see by learning to pick out from the confusion of brilliantly coloured, bright and dark, moving and still visual sensations which impinge upon it every waking moment, so the brain must make sense of the 'blooming, buzzing confusion' which impinges on it every waking moment (and perhaps every sleeping moment as well, if we are to take into account the activity of the mind itself, even during sleep and when unconscious). The brain is not just a simple recording system, as a camera with film is thought to be. Rather, the camera must be understood as a device used to select from a much vaster field certain prominent characteristics relevant to its user. It is a limited instrument with enormous applicability, but always within a specific framework of purposes and capacity. Its products have two dimensions rather than three, may be either coloured or black and white, may not catch the too dark or the too light, the too near or the too distant, never capture odours, and usually are most valuable when altering the size of the original visual field. The brain, if indeed it has to learn to see the world as it does, differs from the camera in that there is no standard by means of which its products may be compared to a seen and possibly restructured reality. The brain may be as relative and selective as a camera, with its selected lens, film used, and photographer, but there is no way of detecting with certainty what the seer's brain has done to an already known landscape. To the contrary, the brain may well have produced both the already known landscape and the photographic recreation as one experience. As the creator of reality by means of its own rules, learned in the very process of growing up in your culture, the brain may question its point of view only by undoing or restructuring itself, that is, by growing up all over again, at least in some respects. To relearn something once learned, using different principles, is extraordinarily difficult and obviously unsettling. For example, it must have been extremely difficult for people living at the time of Galileo to accept and actually imagine the sun appearing to rise because of the earth rotating on its axis. Or, to take a different example from the arts, it is much more difficult to teach someone to learn to play a musical instrument well who has previously been poorly and incorrectly taught than it is to start at the beginning with the learner. In either case, the instructor must painstakingly assist in the erosion of old habits and ways of conceiving before being in a position to instruct in the 'correct' and more fruitful techniques and approaches. Similarly, to learn to see, when you have already learned to cope with the world by means of the other senses or through habitual and encrusted 'tried and true' ways, is extremely difficult, and seemingly pointless in addition. Thus, to advocate a method of teaching which requires that we continually re-examine any theory or belief or fact may well be viewed as pointless, or dangerous, or both.

Suppleness of mind, the ability to rethink an issue or an answer or to see someone or something as though for the first time, is not a common quality. How is it possible to encourage or to maintain suppleness of mind when the very process of maturation and formal education requires that we rule out avenues of conception, interest, and inquiry in becoming who we are, in learning what we 'need' to know, and in becoming citizens of our own culture's way of life? J.Z. Young provides a remarkable answer. He notes that existing and habitual organization does reduce the number of alternative or fresh organizational patterns open to the brain: 'The cortex of the new-born baby has perhaps few innate traits; it is in the main a blank sheet of possibilities. But the very fact that it becomes organized minute by minute, day by day, throughout the years, reduces progressively the number of possible alternative ways of action.'[37] Learning is commonly thought of as a process of cramming into the minds of the young as much as possible, since it is so much more difficult to add to or alter such information when the mind of the young person sets, like the plaster in a thin rubber mould. 'Get them while they are young and they will be set for a lifetime' is a much more common educational principle than one might at first suppose (or wish). However, there is no more reason to suppose that this inflexibility of mind and closing off of alternative patterns of learning-organization is an unavoidable inheritance than to suppose that brittle and quick-setting plaster is the only substance which can be poured into a mould. In fact, there is strong reason to suppose that the plaster may be the substance provided by our existing educational systems, and not by our brains or minds. In this connection, Robert Hogan and David Schroeder, in a hard-hitting critique of contemporary university training in psychology, write of 'the failure of graduate education in America to encourage students to reflect critically upon the really quite controversial material being taught': 'Education properly conducted would include making students aware of their values and theoretical presuppositions. But in America we do graduate training, not education: graduate school is more like barber college than like Plato's *Symposium*. Students are taught how to do research (in the approved manner): the focus is almost exclusively on professional training rather than on a careful examination of theoretical premises. Biases persist in part because they are unexamined.'[38] We could adopt a different approach to teaching and abandon the bucket theory activity of 'training,' adopting in its place the 'problem framing' approach of Plato and the 'trial and error solving' of Popper. In any case there is hope, Young tells us, for new circumstances may themselves come to our aid by reversing or altering brain patterns which seem inflexibly and unalterably present and operative: 'We may forget, or learn new ways of speaking about the world. Some people manage to go on learning new ways much longer than others. Probably a part of their secret is that they constantly seek new circumstances. The temptation to go on relying only upon the rules already used year in and year out is very strong. A really useful and interesting brain is always starting off on new ways. But it is a common experience that this gets more difficult as we grow older.'[39] A willingness to encounter new perspectives and to engage in continuing critical reflection may achieve the suppleness of mind that Young, as well as most teachers and adults, might desire. In any case, successful educational method not only transmits information but keeps open the channels of learning and relearning in the mind and attitudes of the student and the teacher. The greatest deterrent to this sort of capacity for fresh insight is the assumption that your ways are the true ways, or that it is an attack on the 'holy' itself to inquire and to re-inquire about the status of any fact, belief, idea, ideal, or theory. Such irrevocable commitment is the plaster not only of rigidity but of senility as well. Senility, of course, can occur at any age and, as many teachers will admit, regularly afflicts the young as often as the elderly.

Without a perspective there is no ground of selection by means of which

anything may be picked out from the indefinitely rich source of information which surrounds us. Like good photographers, we should feel
obliged to change our lenses, film, and even camera frequently in order to
enlarge our overall creative aptitude for insight into variety. The first step
in being willing to exchange our hard and fixed point of view for another
experimental perspective is the recognition that no point of view or
perspective is, or ought to be, beyond doubt or final. Philosophical truth
is at best approximate, a hypothesis with considerable evidence in its
support, but a hypothesis nevertheless. Fixed points are wrested from the
otherwise uncharted, but ultimate truth is not only too much to claim, it is
unnecessary for those who recognize what our actual myopic needs are.
Our intellectual thirst, of course, will unceasingly direct us towards
perfect sight in the sense that we will always strive for more understanding than we have.

To claim final and absolute truth or to accept matters as given without a
critical glance are the surest ways of committing intellectual suicide. You
acquire a mental stance and attitude as hard set as plaster of Paris. The fine
line between commitment, without which there can be no facts, and
absolute commitment to a position about which there can be no change or
fruitful debate is very narrow indeed. Perhaps this explains why good
people and good educational aims so often go awry. Commitment is
necessary to avoid paralysis of action. Irrevocable commitment, on the
other hand, is to be avoided, if only because we do not know nearly
enough about this surprising cosmos of which we are a part. The great
and learned answers of the centuries, from East and West, are still as hotly
and profitably debated as when first entertained. The question of the
need for robust commitment to the values which you hold will be taken up
in succeeding chapters. Let it be noted here, though, that a major theme of
this book will be that commitment to a belief, way of life or moral code,
country or another person does not necessitate either blind and uncritical
acceptance or irrevocable commitment. Commitment does necessitate
firmness and resolve, but the difference between pledging yourself to
uphold the best that you have found in your years and pledging yourself
to a supposed absolute truth seems to me to be unimportant if you are
capable of reflection issuing in action in accordance with the best that you
have come to see and hold dear. If the process which leads you to see for
yourself that a certain way of life or moral code is the best that you have
encountered and can imagine and is itself infused with the passion
resulting from your original and authentic frustration and perplexity,
then it will be every bit as enlivened and vigorous as any absolutism might

be. There is one additional caution to be observed, however. To hold open-endedness of inquiry as a doctrine or dogma is to rob it of its distinctive character and integrity, and may further serve to shut off honest search for clarity and understanding. Genuine critical inquiry must turn against dogmatic assumptiveness wherever it occurs, for assumptiveness is but fatigue or fear in the face of the ambiguities of new challenges. Critical thinking is to be nourished until there is good reason to suppose that it will nourish and sustain itself in the character and expression of a person. On this hope, as John Anderson writes, rests the health of both education and democracy: 'Neither democracy nor education can exist without controversy, they cannot exist without initiative, without spontaneous movements of the "rank-and-file," and the greatest danger to both is the spurious agreement involved in submission to the "expert," the official judge of "fitness" and "unfitness." '[40]

One last point of clarification is in order before leaving the contributions of J.Z. Young behind us. It is true that he argues for a model of the brain as more or less blank at birth, a *tabula rasa*, while Plato argues that at least some knowledge must be inborn in order for knowledge to arise. The contradiction is evident, but it results from the fact that the two are talking about different moments in the life of learning. Plato raises questions about how knowledge is possible at all. Young takes for granted that it is possible and shows that sound brain physiology indicates that seemingly inflexible ways of seeing and thinking are really acquired, can be unlearned, and can be kept from hardening in those still flexible. A modern Plato would accept the flexibility thesis as helpful evidence that learning can continue to take place even amongst those rigidly cemented in place in the cave, and would enlist the help of Young in trying to do more than speculate about how any rules come to be recognized, distinguished, and established in the first place. Young, like Plato, argues that we must release our protective grip on customary and traditional answers to questions. The uncritical acceptance of tradition is not learning, but memorization. In attempting to undermine or break this protective and instinctive grip on the answers of tradition through critical inquiry, you may find it awkward at the least to explain that the teacher's goal in breaking the learners' grip on things is to help them towards an even stronger grip, one more rewarding, effective, and applicable.

INDOCTRINATION AND EDUCATION

In sharp contrast to the dialogical method of education thus far proposed is education by means of the appeal to authority. Not only do some political ideologies, religions, and a variety of voluntary associations teach by requiring the acceptance of creeds, codes, and principles, but even in our schools there is an overwhelming temptation to educate via the appeal to authority. I.A. Snook, in *Indoctrination and Education*, makes the point well in the following passage: 'I would argue that schools are concerned not so much with "truth" (over which men differ philosophically and factually) but with what is "established" by those who are regarded as competent in the area in question. This does not mean that the man in the street has no part to play at all. He plays his role by the acceptance of certain experts as experts.'[41] Not only are we taught in school to accept and respect authority qua authority, but this training is viewed by us as being important preparation for the obedience to authority that is to count for so much throughout one's adult life in society. From the perspective of education as critical inquiry leading to seeing for oneself, this is a great pity. Evidence and reasoned argument should carry their own authority, and authority for its own sake should have little influence. The uncritical acceptance of authority can become a passive, hypnotic state of awareness where one is watching the players, checking the program for the statistics, and not once entering into the activities of life and education as an active participant, but only viewing them as a spectator. This pattern of education and adult response to events in life is akin to the characteristic state of TV watching – silent, passive, glazed stares not requiring independent reaction.

The recognition of the myopic state that we find ourselves in and the emphasis on evidence and quality of argument rather than acceptance of facts and authority are but minor alterations in our outlook on the world and educational stance. Yet the result is an overwhelming revolution. Just as the Copernican revolution resulted from a slight change in expectation and perspective whereby what was first seen as the sun going round the earth came to be seen as the earth going round the sun, so the revolution in thought contemplated here requires only that you approach ideas and theories not as fixed and final fact but as firmly held hypotheses, as clearest possible attempts of the myopic to wrest sight from the complexity and confusedness of the field of knowledge. It is a revolution requiring that teachers enlist students in the reconsideration of answers, leave aside the claims based on authority, his own and that of the expert, and focus instead on the wonder of insight and the dedication to evidence and reasoned justification. The aim of education thus becomes not to provide answers but to provide a context of excitement and critical capacity through which children can come to see for themselves what is at stake and weigh the evidence in accordance with standards of consistency, social significance, and whatever else pertains to the discipline and problem area in question. For the philosophical educator, the answers are always secondary to the questioning process and to the evidence for those answers. Again quoting Snook:

I have argued that the indoctrinator intends that the pupil believe P [ie, proposition 'P'] 'regardless of the evidence.' In full-blown cases of intention, this captures very well the difference between the indoctrinator and the educator. For the educator, the beliefs are always secondary to the evidence; he wants his students to end up with whatever beliefs the evidence demands. He is concerned with methods of assessing data, standards of accuracy, and validity of reasoning. The answers are subsidiary to the methods of gaining answers. The indoctrinator, however, is typically most concerned with the imparting of the beliefs.[42]

To try to convince someone of something other than as a result of a review of the evidence in support of it is to indoctrinate. To rely on authority is to rely on the influence of the answer or the answerer, but not on the force of the evidence itself. If you have been taught to view the answers as all important, then you do not wish your children to be educated, for that would be to invite corruption. Rather, you ask that the answers be given and that the young be prepared to get on with the living of life in the same way that you have done. Passive acceptance breeds passive acceptance. Authority is highly contagious.

COMMUNIQUÉS

Paulo Freire, the Brazilian educator whose writings have provided renewed vigour and excitement to democratic educational theory and practice, convincingly contrasts the dialogical and the anti-dialogical educational methods. Dialogue requires that there be a relation of empathy amongst the participants such that those involved are 'engaged in a joint search,' and are related by an attitude of love, humility, trust, and critical search.[43] These attitudes constitute the atmosphere of dialogue. Anti-dialogue, by contrast, sets teacher over student and follows the pattern or habit of the issuing of communiqués, of statements of authority for the 'oppressed' to take in as given and to store away for successful entrance into the culture. The attitude and hence the anti-dialogical atmosphere are, according to Freire, 'loveless, arrogant, hopeless, mistrustful, acritical.'[44] Given this provocative list of atmospheric characteristics, it is instructive to ask which atmosphere you live and work in and what sort of environment serves as the learning place for your children. The dialogical relation is horizontal, or rather stretches outward to embrace the other as an active and contributing participant. The relationship need not be conceived as one between actual intellectual equals but as one between democratically free and potentially insightful partners engaged in an adventure of searching inquiry. It is, of course, quite true that one of the 'partners' may not only have more of an idea where the search will lead than the other, but may even be responsible for the path taken, as, for example, the designer of the curriculum to be followed. It remains no less true, however, that he too must reconsider the problem matrix and the offered solutions as myopic views of a scene capable of being understood in many ways and in deeper ways.[45] The dialogical relation is horizontal interchange, not vertical pronouncements. Freire's involvement in dialogical curricula design was occasioned by his interaction with illiterate peasants in his own country whose predictable attitudes towards education and authority caused them to listen submissively to their 'superiors,' to take in whatever issued from the bureau of information and to suppose that all learning was the result of attending to communiqués. Brazil and its institutions were skilled at producing quiet, passive, accepting subjects. Such a mental stance thrives on the assumption that there is nothing wrong with authoritarianism, for it is a given, a fact of life. Aside from the fear of punishment should you stray from what the communiqués require, there is the positive incentive that some day one may be the issuer of communiqués to a new generation of listeners. In this case, the system perpetuates itself, with success being defined not as a change in the system, but as being on top and doing unto others what others have done to you. The teacher who was taught at, whose bucket was filled with fact after inert fact, rejoices in the long run at being able to *teach at* others with an even greater store of facts to be mastered.

Paradoxically, to be opposed to Socrates or Freire is to join them. For if you come to reject their answers and their analysis of the situation, you have nevertheless been engaged by their questions. This very engagement in the act of critical reaction and reflection places you squarely in their methodological camp. Answers are secondary to the evidence and to the insight gained through the weighing of that evidence. Authoritarianism is emphasis on answers rather than on the methodology of insight and intellectual independence. Freire puts this wonderfully well in a powerful passage in *Education for Critical Consciousness*:

One subverts democracy (even though one does this in the name of democracy) by making it irrational; by making it rigid in order 'to defend it against totalitarian rigidity;' by making it hateful, when it can only develop in a context of love and respect for persons; by closing it, when it only lives in openness; by nourishing it with fear when it must be courageous; by making it an instrument of the powerful in the oppression of the weak; by militarizing it against the people; by alienating a nation in the name of democracy.

One defends democracy by leading it to the state Mannheim calls 'militant democracy' – a democracy which does not fear the people, which suppresses privilege, which can plan without becoming rigid, which defends itself without hate, which is nourished by a critical spirit rather than irrationality.[46]

If equality is not defended in practice, but just in theory, in the schools and in the homes of a nation, it is not likely to stand with firmness in the world. That which aids in developing the capacity for independent judgment is likely to be an aid to a democratic society, for liberty exists 'in the struggle of diverse interests or in the character of certain of the struggling forces and not in the system as a whole, so that the policy of reducing diversity is actually inimical to liberty.'[47] That which destroys or discourages independence of judgment is probably an aid in fostering a more rigid societal form and individuals who have long since either become intellectually senile or count on the senility of others to keep the system going in the most orderly way possible. Freire's account of 'militant democracy' could profitably become the constitution of any public or private school, as well as of any nation, and could serve as an insightful guide to the development and implementation of actual curricula and classroom atmospherics.

2

Ethics and moral education

The complexities identified thus far have been intended as representative of those lurking behind and within almost all human inquiry, in every discipline and in every stand which we take as individuals or as societies. The basis and essential nature of education is the development of the capacity to stand on your own intellectual abilities, to think for yourself, and to come to 'see' for yourself – in short, to take an inquiring stance with respect to any subject-matter whatsoever. To be critical in this way is not to be a negative or destructive thinker but only to work out for yourself the reasons for any position, to weigh the evidence, to clarify ambiguity and imprecision, and then to come to hold firmly the best conclusion which you can reach and now defend. The critical stance, represented by dialogue, is contrasted with the passive acceptance of answers (either because it is considered wrong or even bad actively to question them or because one has fallen asleep or become numbed by communiqués from above which 'they,' the authorities or experts, have issued). Consider the frequency with which people speak of the 'they' of authority: 'They tell us that it is okay' or 'They have found that ...' This habitual formula is one to be avoided in reflective language by anyone of critical independence, for it is regularly a smokescreen for authority resting outside yourself or for intellectual senility. It is the television mentality which, after several hours of vacant observation, numbs us into believing that if it is said on the tube, then it must be so. Indeed, the remarkable phenomenon of 'Advertised on TV' labelling marks the problem. Whether a catchy ad is paid for on TV or sings its way onto the radio, or makes it only to the handbill stage has absolutely nothing to do with its truthfulness, accuracy, or worth. So what difference does it make whether it was 'advertised on TV?' None, unless you have adopted the communiqué mentality, thereby passively accepting such pronouncements as some-how 'official' and therefore authenticated. Communiqués can be effective only when people have become passively receptive, just as slavery requires that people become subdued and docile. The circumstances for totalitarianism must be right, and these consist of far more than just strong and ruthless power at the top. Passive acceptance is at least as much a requirement for authority to gain its strength as is the strength at the top. This is precisely why educators must recognize that what is at stake is not simply a professional choice about which theory of education we find most appealing. Unless we remain purveyors of the critical development of individuals as centres of worth and independent appraisal, we are adopting a view of education as training in 'passivity' or acceptance because of the 'correctness' of what is being taught, of 'pouring into the bucket' what is worth having there. The critical educator assumes that what is worth having there will come to be there, chosen by the student, indeed worked out by the student himself from a problem situation, that is, being in a situation which creates a problem and fixes its importance. If he succeeds, he has won not only a passionate defender of the 'best' but a capable and compelling dialectician as well.

Ethics can be taught in the 'bucket' fashion – indeed, it usually is. We can tell the young what to think, believe, and do. They will predictably not listen. I have been surprised to find that most high school students with whom I have had discussions about 'moral education' classes consider them to be moralizing sessions, variations on the theme of religious indoctrination. Most of them take such classes lightly (or not seriously) or resentfully (seeing them as unwarranted), or both. Morality becomes the only classroom subject area where one feels it inappropriate to raise doubts of any kind. This is a modern tragedy. And while I will argue below that it is equally a tragedy to disembowel ethics by teaching that any firmly held personal decision is as good as any other, it remains a fact that the relativist at least tries to force the student to come to grips with his own views and to become clear about them. Nevertheless, it is difficult to choose between the numbness and thoughtlessness of passive acceptance required by dogmatism and the hopelessness and vacuous-ness of the self-examination required by relativism. Indeed, the mis-guidedness of the latter position may go a long way towards pinpointing why some wag has characterized American society as consisting of 250 million egos pulling in different directions simultaneously. The chaos of the 'me' generation, a partial result of making each and every personal stance as good as any other, is every bit as destructive as the vacant passivity which breeds the sort of uniformity which is persistently a breeding ground for various species of totalitarianism. It is hard to choose between the despair and naïvety of intellectual and moral blindness and the arrogance and ideology of alleged 20/20 vision.

ETHICS

Just as the study of methodology and the possibility of knowledge is complex, unresolved, and in need of patient and careful inquiry, so ethics, too, is brimming over with heated disagreement and restless debate. Philosophically viewed, ethics is not the passing on of the 'truths' of the ages but an active inquiry into the concepts and foundations of the various and competing claims made by the leading theorists and schools, classical and contemporary. As William Frankena puts it, 'Moral philosophy arises when, like Socrates, we pass beyond the stage in which we are directed by traditional rules and even beyond the stage in which these rules are so internalized that we can be said to be inner-directed, to the stage in which we think for ourselves in critical and general terms (as the Greeks were beginning to do in Socrates' day) and achieve a kind of autonomy as moral agents.'[1] Reflecting directly upon the prevailing attitudes in contemporary education in the field of ethics, Frankena observes, 'The two besetting sins in our prevailing habits of ethical thinking are our ready acquiescence in unclarity and our complacence in ignorance – the very sins that Socrates died combatting over two thousand years ago.'[2] From my own perspective, the cardinal sin is to teach as though these problems, these debates, these alternative moral stances did not exist. Absolutes are hard to achieve, except, perhaps, for the one just stated, the wrongness of teaching passive acquiescence and complacency. And yet it is commonly assumed that unless you teach in an authoritative way, you simply open the floodgates of hopelessness or encourage immorality and selfishness; but this common assumption just does not stand up. Why must you declare that what is taught is authoritative, and that any straying from dogma is indicative of a defect in the questioner's character? Why not confess to being less than omniscient? The definitive ethical answers are not in; the problems, puzzles, and unclarities of ethics are so enormous as to make it a major contemporary focus in philosophy, where the search goes on and on, and is unlikely to come to rest in a lifetime of reflection, for that is the nature of philosophic issues and their preferred answers. Why not engage students in the attempt to erect an edifice of clarification and defence that will stand criticism? Why not show them where the 'best' evidence of the day seems to reside, even if it leaves unresolved which of several views is the likely winner? One major contemporary debate centres around the notion of 'justice' and whether it can be fully explained and accounted for on utilitarian grounds, or whether a formalist or deontological position is preferable – and whether the two are in some way compatible. The distinction arises from the general question 'What is the criterion of moral value?' – that is, what is the standard by means of which it can be correctly decided whether an action is morally right or wrong? The utilitarian is a consequentialist in ethics, maintaining that the goodness or badness of the results or consequences of an action is the sole determinant of the moral worth of the action. By contrast, the deontologist or formalist argues that it is the nature of the act in question, and not just its results, that serves as the criterion of a moral act. Thus, the very nature of an instance of promise-keeping, whatever else might result from its being performed, is sufficient to make it morally incumbent on us to keep that promise. Perhaps it is now apparent that the formalist can accuse the utilitarian of paying insufficient attention to the binding force of classes or kinds of actions of a certain type, while the utilitarian accuses the formalist of encouraging actions of a certain sort, in spite of the likelihood of inferior or even bad consequences resulting. Either way, you are left doing justice to some but not all of our ordinary as well as our more sophisticated moral sensitivities and expectations. I will raise this issue again when I examine the philosophy of moral education developed by Lawrence Kohlberg, but for now it is enough to emphasize that a class in moral philosophy should be designed not to stop debates but to start them. If the utilitarians and the deontologists cannot settle the issue between them, why should I become upset if I can't? My task, as teacher, is to cause my students to see the problems from which the dispute has arisen, to examine carefully the concepts and the positions in question, and to invite them to try a tentative resolution of the problem, either by siding with one or the other of the positions or by striking out on their own and providing a hint of a solution which is neither of the two studied.

MORAL EDUCATION – THE DEBATE

Should the teaching of ethics be part of the school curriculum? This is the hottest educational issue of the day. At the beginning, it is well to become clear about the impossibility of any school remaining totally aloof from moral guidance, moral example, and moral atmosphere. The point is succinctly made in a book entitled *Moral Education ... It Comes with the Territory*, edited by David Purpel and Kevin Ryan:

The schools cannot avoid being involved in the moral life of the students. It is inconceivable for schools to take the child for six or seven hours a day, for 180 days a year, from the time he is six to the time he is eighteen, and not affect the way he thinks about moral issues and the way he behaves. Nor can we divorce the intellectual from the moral realm. One can suppress discussion about moral issues and values, but one cannot suppress the development of values and the formation of morals. Moral education goes on all over the school building – in the classrooms, in the disciplinarian's office, in assemblies, in the gym. It permeates the very fabric of teacher-student relationship. The school, then, cannot help but be a force for growth or retardation – for good or evil – in the moral life of the student. Moral education is an inevitable role of the schools. For the educator, it comes with the territory.[3]

This quotation I find to be accurate and insightful. It should give each of us pause: we expect teachers to be able to handle the complexities of moral education, including the difficulties of finding a common ground among parents who themselves are products of our pluralistic society and who very likely disagree predictably about what (and how) they want their children to be taught. A teacher, then, is supposed to teach the right things, the right way, to the right people, at the right time, against the backdrop of the complexity and ongoing quality of ethics and developmental psychology, the disagreements and dissimilar expectations among parents as to what is to be taught, the variety of religious backgrounds and expectations among the students, and the 'packages' of materials provided by the various governments and curriculum designers.[4]

So much is expected of teachers who may never yet have taken courses in philosophy, ethics, or religion and find in teachers' college that almost no time is spent examining the strengths and weaknesses of the alternative positions, clarifying concepts, and making evident the main hopes and aims of moral education of whatever sort. Rather, time is spent looking at the 'materials' and trying to find ways of making the transmission of such materials exciting, engrossing, and (apparently) relevant. The columnist Barbara Amiel records a telling response to the over-simplified 'packaging' of material for people who are undertrained and overstrained in the complex field of moral education in her editorial 'A Lesson in Oversimplification':

Taking computer-chip mentality to utter absurdity, our current school systems have decided that the most complex questions can be taught through preprogrammed thought. Ethics is packaged under the modern title of 'values education' (complete with charts listing the [ie, Kohlberg's] six stages of moral development in students to be checked off by teachers) ... A wise society would understand that it is far better not to try to teach jurisprudence or ethics than to simplify them into computer-chip games. It is better not to try discussing constitutional law or social morality at all than do it on a talk show for 45 seconds with a bright young host or hostess who wouldn't recognize an idea if it fell on them. It is an error to believe that this kind of education, whatever its political bias, does any good. The uneducated, healthy social and moral instincts of a population informed by tradition and religion are probably preferable to the misinformation of pop psychologists and multiple-choice ethics.[5]

Amiel's criticisms are directed against the watering-down of the centrally important subject-matter of ethics and values. The packages of materials, the visual aids and hand-outs all make it possible for a teacher who has never even encountered Socrates' difficulties, let alone come to grips with them, to teach the subject. In instance after instance, he or she chooses either to teach ethics as a 20/20-vision dogma (whether religion or 'science') or as a relativistic muddle! Teachers regularly get into trouble by indoctrinating, by simply teaching a tradition or a specific point of view, or by presenting pre-packaged materials as though they had the same standing as the theorems of geometry or the parts of the body in an anatomy course. In this they are no different from the participants in the Socratic *Dialogues* who had never thought deeply about the subject or who had assumed that what is taught, what is prepared for them as 'official,' is both appropriate and the best. All of this kills the critical spirit which I have argued is the single most important ingredient in an education. No wonder that the students do not come to see for themselves – often the teachers don't either. They simply pass information along, uncritically receptive of all teaching aids and work minimizers offered by the government and the curricula designers. It has often occurred to me that the only person who could benefit from a package outline of an issue or an area would be the theoretician whose work serves as the main source of the material. Anyone else is likely to rely too heavily on the resources and never come to see that it is a tentative attempt to reduce a great complexity, swarming with difficulties and unresolved matters, into a manageable unit. Only the creator of such a resolution can be counted on to be able to handle it, for he or she knows its limitations and can make live again the tension and excitement, the fears and frustration which led to its development. Of course, he or she is also the one who may need it least. Alas, those who need it most are those who can least benefit from it and are least likely to be able to handle it wisely, for they assume that it is gospel, cause it to be memorized in bits and pieces, use it to classify students and colleagues, and close their minds to alternative theories and critical reviews. This is the sort of thing that has happened to Kohlberg's theory, and so Amiel can correctly view Kohlberg's six stages as a shorthand approach to an unreflective decision about ethics. It is not what he intended, but it evidently is what has happened.

THE VALUES CLARIFICATION APPROACH

The other side of the question, the muddle of relativism or blindness taken as ordinary seeing, has been much more of a problem in the last decade or so.

Not only has our age been one of permissiveness (both at home and in the schools), but it has been at best a transitional age, with old values giving way to values not yet clearly defined or formed, or at worst the annihilation of old values with nothing to replace them. Our streets are dangerous, the elderly are beaten senseless 'for fun,' our lakes are filling with acid rain, the politicians and industrialists cry that the economy must come first, and, as if to prove the point, the neutron bomb is given a green light so that surviving micro-organisms can enjoy the museums and factories once occupied by human forms of life. These are not good times, and they appear to most of us not to be good times morally by whatever standards of judgment we are employing. But precisely at this time of breakdown of tradition and general worry about the state of the world, the most influential and widely used moral education curriculum has been one that is openly relativistic. The Values Clarification approach has been, for the past fifteen years, 'the most widely practiced in the American school.'[6] *Values and Teaching*, by L. Raths, M. Harmin, and Sidney Simon, published in 1966, has been the standard text for preparing teachers for and introducing students to the world of moral education. Sidney Simon is the key figure in the movement, but all the main characters are agreed that no particular set of values is to be advocated, no tradition is to be singled out as exemplary of the standard sought, for, according to them, no standard in common is either necessary or possible. What is aimed at is the stimulating of the students so that they will think about their own value-position and then set out to clarify that position for themselves with the help of discussion with teacher and peers, as initiated by certain classroom strategies and materials. To this point, the approach appears to be Socratic to the letter. One can even imagine a values clarifier admitting to students that if his approach numbs them by causing them to doubt all their previous beliefs about values, the same thing has happened to the teacher by virtue of having stung himself. The difference is that Socrates continued to believe in and search for a better answer to questions raised, moral questions in particular, and he let his dialogue partners, that is, students, know this; he pragmatically observed that unless you continue to establish standards for the better and the worse, then you will give up looking any further, will settle for what you have, or will consider the whole enterprise pointless, living from moment to moment, doing whatever you choose or feel to be right. Kathleen M. Gow, in her critique of the Values Clarification approach (often 'vc' to its adherents and critics – an interesting practice for it can serve to make one think that the label itself is so familiar, friendly, and established as to make critical questions out of place and unnecessary), calls attention to one of the classroom exercises recommended:

There is the *Values Clarification* exercise called 'Life Raft' which is designed, among other things, to help participants consider their own self worth. A group of ten students is told that they are at sea in a life raft which has a capacity for only nine people. One of the ten must be thrown overboard in order that the other nine may survive. Each participant in turn pleads his or her own case to the group, arguing why he or she should be chosen to survive. Following this desperate 'sales pitch,' a vote is taken and, by group consensus, the least 'worthy' is thrown out.[7]

Gow is right in her characterization of the Values Clarification approach, and it is instructive to note how subtle and seemingly minor are the differences between the vc approach and the various resolutions provided by the major ethical positions in both traditional and contemporary philosophy. To begin with, such bizarre but possible examples are common in introductory philosophical ethics textbooks.[8] What is different is that the professional study of ethics requires that you give a full account of the issues and the proposed solutions from the point of view of a systematic approach to the problem via the work of a great philosopher or a sophisticated school of ethics. Thus a utilitarian (like John Stuart Mill or J.J.C. Smart) might well answer the question in a way far different from a deontologist (like Kant or John Rawls), an egoist (like Thomas Hobbes or Moritz Schlick), or an emotivist (like A.J. Ayer or Charles Stevenson). In all these examples, however, great care would be taken to understand and evaluate the foundations of the system under investigation. A comparative evaluation would also be needed, and a final judgment would be required about the adequacy of the solution proposed. You are judged and graded on the comprehensiveness of your analysis, the accuracy of your interpretation of a great system, and the originality of your assessment of the quality of the proposed solution. These requirements are far different from the clarifier's approach, where the main responsibility, it seems, is to nod your head and remark softly, 'So you think that ...' Still, from a position outside the activities of the classroom and its requirements, the difference between the ethical philosopher and the values clarifier seems slight at most. The former comes to no final and irrevocable conclusion but simply evaluates and opts for one system/ theory – or theorist – over another, while the latter allows students to come to their own positions and conclusions after clarifying them and discussing them with teacher and peers. What distinguishes the two approaches, if I can lump all philosophers and their positions into something called 'an approach,' is that it is philosophy alone that sees ethics as a frightfully demanding discipline, enriched by a long and sometimes obscure history, enlivened by countless debates, and rendered 'sharp' and 'technical' by the quality of the debates, the subtlety of the distinctions, the rigour of the clarification, and the relentlessness of the analysis of both problems and solutions. The result is neither uniformity nor unanimity of opinion. But just as a physicist is hailed for the brilliance and insight of a new theory accounting for the 'facts' and leading to more fruitful results than its precursors in a long and difficult history of thought without necessarily being judged true in any final sense, so a great ethical theory may be more fruitful and better able to account for the 'facts' of human experience and aspiration than another, with the rider that while most physicists may actually come to agree at a point in history (for example, Kuhn's 'paradigm' model of science), most ethical theorists do not (*contra* Kuhn). The difference is important. Physics and the sciences generally seem to go from accepted position to doubt, to revision, to accepted position again, whereas the humanities move from a clustering of debatable positions to yet more doubt and revision, to a new clustering of debatable positions consisting of most of the old ones with perhaps one or two missing and one or two added. It is easier to say what a broom consists of chemically than it is to say what the 'perfect' or even a 'better' broom is. Factual analysis simply attends to what is in the material world, while value analysis must evaluate in the human terms of better and worse. The material analysis is enclosed, or at least more so, since it focuses on what a thing is, while the value analysis is open-ended in that it focuses on what will or might be, and all of these from one or several points of view. You may get a thing 'righter' in value analysis, but you ought to be cautious about aspiring too firmly to getting it 'just right' for all time. The line between senility and absolutist finality is very, very slight.

John S. Stewart, in evaluating Values Clarification in the schools, laments that 'vc has become some kind of sacred cow that is adopted largely on face value on the basis of its own claims with little or no examination of its educational soundness, philosophical justification, or alleged efficacy.'[9] How quickly a 'package' becomes a communiqué! It is interesting that Stewart's concern has to do with what is accomplished by causing the students to 'clarify' their values. Children who are having difficulty are not always to be aided by being clear about their situation, nor is a superficial value stance much the better for being a clear superficial stance. The tragedy of it all is that, in spite of the sensed inadequacies, 'most classroom teachers are either too busy or not adequately prepared to evaluate values education methods or approaches. But this area of education is too important to permit any theory or practice to go unexamined and unquestioned.'[10] Stewart hits hardest when he summarizes what he takes to be the superficial resemblance between vc and philosophical ethics: 'My analysis of values clarification begins with the claim that it is deceptively and dangerously superficial. One can easily be fooled into believing that many of the vc strategies really lead to an in-depth examination of one's values, when in fact one may have really done little more than look at opinions or feelings, and frequently on relatively trivial matters. One of the dangers involved is the conviction that values or moral education is really taking place in any significant way.'[11] By contrast, what I have been characterizing as the philosophical approach is an attempt at in-depth examination and a methodology for weighing the evidence, having first collected it, and evaluating the contending theories by contrast and comparison. Paramount in philosophical inquiry is the critical stance by means of which you study the problem and show the heretofore acceptable answers to be either wanting or in need of both clarification and additional supporting evidence before acceptance.

It is becoming too evident to need further emphasis here that Values Clarification has given moral education as a whole a bad name. But just as it would be unacceptable to reject the importance and existence of values on the grounds that one particular meaning of 'value' is wanting, and without considering the alternative possibilities, so it is unacceptable to reject the Values Clarification approach to moral education and then to reject moral education as a whole, without examining some of the major alternatives. The alternative to which we now turn, that articulated by Lawrence Kohlberg, is perhaps the leading one.

KOHLBERG

You will recall that Kohlberg's 'six stages' were specifically singled out in Barbara Amiel's negative appraisal of the present state of the moral development art and that her reasons clustered around the 'computer-chip' approach to pre-packaged materials, rendering the whole introduction to ethics a gross oversimplification, a kind of learning game in the classroom used to keep the attention of the young, who wish they were elsewhere. The moral education industry has grown quickly and widely, and the attempts to provide texts, films, tapes, and whole courses applying Kohlberg's approach have been so considerable in number and influence that one writer has written of the 'Kohlberg Bandwagon.'[12] Much of this probably has little to do with Lawrence Kohlberg, for, as was noted above, the people most likely to be able to handle 'applied' and simplified interpretations are the theoretic developers and their fellow theoreticians, but unfortunately the usual producers of popular or pedagogical accounts are journalistic simplifiers who seldom fully understand the ideas they sell and the implications resulting from these ideas. Thus, not only is the original source taken as gospel, but even the simplification rests on the assumption that the problems have been 'worked out' and the needed solutions are 'in hand,' resulting in a flood of applications now twice removed from the original theory and totally divorced from its cautions and struggles. But what is being advocated is another myopic perspective worthy of consideration – and philosophically 'consideration' translates as 'critical analysis and evaluation in the light of other alternatives.' Many who glance at and use Kohlberg appear to 'need' materials and answers so badly that they jump on the bandwagon as passive users. Many problems, which are not to be minimized, arise from passive, even apathetic use (and application) by such uncritical or poorly trained followers of the 'official' version of Kohlberg's theory, rather than from his theory itself. Many, but of course not all.

My own hunch is that much of the hostility surrounding the work of Kohlberg and the introduction of methods and materials based on it has arisen because of the implicit and sometimes even explicit 'authority' attributed to it. Kohlberg is seen as the front runner in the field, and his research has gone a long way towards putting his theories on an empirical basis – he has carefully collected his evidence and has sought experimental confirmation to bolster his claims. While he is clearly the leader in the field of moral education, and while he has provided hard evidence in support of his theorizing, it does not follow that Kohlberg ought to be viewed as the 'expert' in the field, or his pronouncements as authoritative. The truth is that his views are exploratory and his applications remarkably helpful. So is myopia remarkable and evidently exploratory. Peter Scharf makes the point well when he writes, 'To paraphrase a quotation by Winston Churchill, it [Kohlberg's system] is by far the worst pedagogical system in terms of its empirical and philosophical morasses, *except for all the others.*'[13] Thus, if Kohlberg were to be viewed as one theorist among others, or even as the leader in the field, but with all due reservation and critical attention, then his achievements would only come to be seen as the more significant for his having charted a path in what had become a wasteland. There is, of course, a fly in the ointment: the requirements of making up curricula for the classroom take Kohlberg's work out of the 'ivory tower' of philosophical speculation and gentle assessment and into the minds and homes of children right now. Any curricula development quickly takes the form of hard-setting plaster and carries the stamp of 'official doctrine.' This, I take it, is what causes philosophical nightmares for those of more traditional religious persuasion, for any attempt on their part to dislodge the new 'dogma' is greeted with accusations of being 'old-fashioned' or not being willing to consider the evidence in hand. For the myopic, of course, there is nothing sacrosanct and beyond further inquiry, nothing beyond doubt. To treat Kohlberg, then, as a new 'orthodoxy' is simply to swap one absolute for another, an older form of rigid authority for a newer one, or, in extreme cases, one form of oppression for another. The only antidote to this poison is dialogue which can operate within a pluralism of traditions and positions, demanding of each that they be clear, supported by evidence, systematically consistent, apprised of the facts and research of the day, and attitudinally exploratory.

KOHLBERG'S THEORY

Kohlberg bases his studies on the work of the Swiss psychologist Jean Piaget and the American philosopher John Dewey. The particular importance of the psychological foundation is that it allegedly provides empirical evidence and support for his theorizing. This is of no small importance, for it allows Kohlberg's work to be experimentally checked as well as empirically supported, and to make claims about the normal or ordinary pattern of moral growth and development which can be used as a guide to the progress of children and the effectiveness of classes in moral progress. It is little wonder that Kohlberg himself sees this innate 'standard' of moral assessment, this ideal of moral growth, as the distinguishing characteristic by means of which his views are to be kept distinct from Values Clarification and any other classes of relativism. Indeed, Kohlberg takes the relativists as one of his two major opponents. He calls himself a 'methodological non-relativist,'[14] and it is ironic that he is so often called a relativist by his critics. His other opponents are the authoritarians in moral education who deliberately attempt to 'inculcate majority values' without much, if any, critical inquiry.[15] The teaching of morality in a doctrinaire fashion is, for Kohlberg, a 'violation of the child's moral freedom.'[16] To make matters worse, it is all too often the case that the 'tyranny' of the classroom extends to more subtle 'indoctrination' through the ongoing everyday activities of the school. Children are expected, indeed required, to conform to the good management and law and order requirements imposed by the teacher. While this sort of discipline is obviously necessary, what makes it pernicious is the confusing of this sort of housekeeping, or purely pragmatic arrangement, with morality. Practical regulations should not be confused with moral rules. As the philosopher Mary Warnock, in her recent book *Education: A Way Ahead*, pinpoints the matter: 'If children are rebuked or even punished for breaking the school rules it must be made absolutely clear that it is not a moral offence which has been committed. Nothing is more confusing to a child, nor ultimately more damaging to morality, than to speak as though the breach of regulations about length of hair or kinds of permitted footwear were a moral offence. Nothing, alas, is more typical of a bad school than this kind of confusion.'[17] Yet how often is the confusion made.

Kohlberg's concerns, then, include both the obvious and overt attempts at moral education by lesson, direct study, and discussion of the issues on the one hand and the 'hidden curriculum' on the other. The hidden curriculum consists of the many ways in which the moral atmosphere of the classroom is established, the way in which children are treated and are encouraged to treat each other and their teachers, with the choice of maintenance of rules, why cheating or bullying or foul language is not allowed, whether co-operation is encouraged, when, and for which reasons and purposes, and so on. We teach morality by both lesson and example all day long, and what we talk about is no more important than the way in which we do it and the conditions of the room and the school where such learning and discussion go on. Who cannot recall a situation where the overt and the hidden curriculum were badly out of 'sync'? – a moral relativist teacher who, for reasons of good management, ruled his class with an iron fist and blurred the distinction between being morally wrong on the one hand and breaking a practical class rule, or even being wrong in answering an academic question, on the other; a teacher who spoke of fairness and justice but who each year had a 'pet' who did the special jobs and received special awards. My own daughter was confused and outraged by a teacher who imposed detention on the student who was last getting dressed after gym class yet who otherwise spoke of fairness and mutual concern.

Whether one is dealing with the hidden curriculum or with the actual teaching of morality through lessons and classroom discussion, it is Kohlberg's position that teachers must focus on the *moral growth* of the students. It is all too easy for teachers to keep their eyes fixed on the rules, the 'absolutes' of the classroom and society, and to ensure that they are enforced and thereby achieved as ends in themselves. If the goal is to assist the students in coming to see the worth and soundness of these rules, to explain to them both their necessity and their value, in a supportive and yet firm manner, then growth rather than the immediate achievement of absolute goals becomes the focus. Children have yet to grow into bright and moral adults; they are not yet adults.

The notion of 'moral growth' is, of course, vague, almost to the point of unintelligibility if left to speak for itself. Everyone is in favour of it, but disagreements about what it consists of, how it is recognized, and the means to its achievement are legion. But Kohlberg offers a meaning for moral growth and a standard or measure of that meaning, based on empirical studies in psychology. Kohlberg argues that the process of moral development, like the process of intellectual or cognitive development, can be described as the movement through distinct stages of awareness, with the later stage being more 'adequate' or better than the earlier. The sixth or most adequate stage is not reached by all people, or even by most, but it serves as the norm, the standard by which the earlier stages are judged less adequate and the goal of moral education for those who are able to achieve it. Kohlberg's six stages of moral development are empirical abstractions.[18] As such, they must not be viewed as the results of previous theoretical speculation about the history and development of moral theories, or as a dissection of a preferred theory of ethics. Rather, the stages are not hypothetical, nor are they deduced from some theory alone. They are inductive generalizations. They do not arise from a model of man, a theory of human nature, which serves as the major premise grounding and justifying any subsequent ranking of moral characteristics of men and women. As inductive generalizations, the 'characteristics' of a stage cluster together as they do simply because they cluster together that way repeatedly and predictably in the reasoning patterns of the subjects interviewed by Kohlberg and his associates. It is not unimportant to observe here that Kohlberg has been criticized for not taking sufficient notice of interview bias, that is, the power of hidden suggestion and expectation on the part of the interviewer, who may end up 'discovering' or confirming his own world view in the mouth and words of the interviewee.[19] The clustering which characterizes each stage is more than just random for Kohlberg, however, for stages are structured wholes or closely organized systems of thought. Indeed, each stage 'may be considered separate moral philosophies, distinct views of the social-moral world'[20] and as such are systematic attempts at logical argument and consistency in the face of the evidence as understood. It is also argued that the stages form an invariant sequence and movement is almost always forward, almost never backward. Furthermore, stages are not skipped but are passed through one after the other, and in order.[21] Kohlberg also argues that stages are 'hierarchical integrations,' so that the next higher stage 'includes or comprehends within it lower-stage thinking,' but the higher stage is opted for because there is 'a tendency to function at or prefer the highest stage available.'[22] A cognitive or a moral stage is a distinct mental structure, an internally organized whole or system of internal relations, by means of which information is processed, connected, and experienced.[23] Richard Peters succinctly traces the development in moral reasoning through the six stages of Kohlberg's analysis: 'Children start by seeing rules as dependent upon power and external compulsion; they then see them as instrumental to rewards and to the satisfaction of their needs; then as ways of obtaining social approval and esteem; then as upholding some ideal order, and finally as articulations of social principles necessary to living together with others – especially that of justice.'[24] Thus, when children are asked to decide and explain whether it would be right to tell on a friend in certain circumstances, they will respond with reasons which will reveal characteristic elements habitually associated with a specific 'stage' of moral understanding. They will emphasize punishment or reward at one stage, be concerned about their reputations at another, and only at a later stage concern themselves with whether it would be right for everyone to snitch on friends (or on anyone), or how they would like it if someone did or did not snitch on them.

The six stages of moral development, in addition to being empirical

generalizations and sequential and invariant, are also held to be universal. They are universal in that the last twenty years of research have
served to confirm that all people, from a wide sample of cultures on three
continents, move through the same stages.[25] Kohlberg claims that 'studies
show not only that the same basic moral concepts are used in every
culture, but that the stages of their development are the same in every
culture.'[26] From this he is able to prescribe how moral education is to be
achieved:

There are universal human modes or principles of moral thinking which progress
through an invariant order. In addition, there are differences in more specific
moral beliefs which are culturally or indvidually determined and are, therefore,
relative in content. Differences which can be seen in the basic structure of [sic]
moral thinking are differences in maturity or development. Accordingly, the
teacher may take the stimulation of moral development as the aim of moral
education. Such stimulation of development is not indoctrination; rather, it is the
facilitation of the child's development through a sequence which is a natural
progression for him.[27]

Kohlberg's emphasis on facilitation is important here. Adopting the
Socratic model of teaching, Kohlberg argues that the aim of moral
education is to help the child move through the stages and not get stuck at
a lower level which may appear both adequate and final to the child at that
stage. It is easy to become senile at any age, we have said, and moral
senility comes with the assumption that what one has come to hold is both
adequate and the termination of one's development. From the perspective
of a child who has just climbed his way to the Stage Two level of
understanding, the new height reached and its attending capacity for
resolving moral difficulties appears to have taken him very far indeed –
quite far enough, he would most likely say, for he has been able to replace
a 'wrong' answer, a clearly insufficient view, with a 'right' answer. But
when viewed by someone who is himself at Stage Three or higher, the
answer is inadequate and but an early stage in the child's moral progress.
Similarly, learning how to multiply fractions seems to be a breakthrough,
making mathematics both easy and powerful. One little dreams of the
wonders of algebra and set theory. Just as arithmetic is sufficient for simple
problems but not for complex algebraic problems, so the answers of Stage
One morality are generally adequate for resolving a problem as understood by a child at Stage One thinking but are not adequate for a problem
posing difficulties exemplifying higher-stage thinking. Indeed, the problems of algebra seem unimportant and fanciful to one who needs only to

divide a dollar bill into four equal amounts of change, just as the problems of universal justice seem irrelevant and most likely incomprehensible to one who must deal with the temptation to talk in class. The moral educator, then, must not talk at a level too far removed from the actual stage at which the child is currently thinking. To facilitate moral growth, Kohlberg argues, you should help children to understand the kind of thinking representative of the next stage, one level higher than their own.(Empirical studies suggest that children exposed to thinking one stage below their present level and more than one stage above showed much less progress than those exposed to thinking at the stage immediately above their own.)[28] In so doing, you help children to come to see the inconsistencies and inadequacies in their own lower-stage thinking, causing them to perceive a genuine moral conflict. For this reason, and in Socratic fashion, Kohlberg argues that the use of 'moral dilemmas' is necessary to stimulate children to doubt the adequacy of their present 'moral system' in coming to terms with the increasing complexity of the moral issues raised in the classroom and outside. When Socrates raised a doubt in the mind of a disputant about the adequacy of his definition of justice or virtue or piety, he was attempting to make him stretch, to see that his vision was inadequate, in the hope of finding a position which was in some sense 'better': 'If the child is challenged so as to perceive the contradictions in his own thinking, he will try to generate new and better solutions to moral problems.'[29] Then the teacher can work with the child in finding 'better' reasons, a deeper understanding, and a more adequate solution. None of this would be possible, of course, if relativism were the truth about morality. There would be no reason, except dogmatic or selfish ones, to get a Stage One thinker to struggle towards a higher stage, for it would be but a matter of preference if relativism were true. Here the position of Values Clarification would prevail. The object of classroom discussion would simply be to become clear and articulate about one's own value stage. There would be no reason to opt for another unless one simply preferred a change. But on Kohlberg's view, the higher stage is better because it is more adequate, that is, more able to cope with the complexities and requirements of moral life as perceived now by children who have been stimulated to see for themselves the inadequacy of their present 'theory' in coping with the issues raised.

KOHLBERG AND RELATIVISM

It is a curious and recurrent refrain in criticisms of Kohlberg's work to say that he is a relativist. Yet what is most important philosophically about the universality of the stages is Kohlberg's use of them to refute relativism. His work may, in fact, be seen as a passionate and sustained attempt to avoid relativism in moral education. He often refers to his theory as methodological non-relativism, and the congruence of multi-societal data allows him to leave cultural relativism behind very early on. For if the stages are universal, they are not universal simply because of coincidence of cultural or linguistic traditions. The universal invariants are not taught but are elicited through normal development. The model of moral learning, then, is Platonic: drawing out awareness of an already present capacity for 'seeing,' rather than forcing into the mind-bucket a series of rules, regulations, and moral norms to be processed and thought of as binding. And just as it is better to learn to walk than to continue to crawl both because of its rewards and because it is a normal progression in the development and maturation of the human being, so progress up the moral stages is pragmatically advantageous both in solving problems and in reaching one's full potential as a human being. In any case, Kohlberg contends that 'basic mental structure is the result of interaction between certain organismic structuring tendencies and the structure of the outside world, rather than reflecting either one directly.'[30] Therefore it is not quite right to say that the stages are simply drawn out of the child as though they were innately there in their full and final forms. Rather, the human capacities and their tendencies are both realized and modified by their application to and confrontation with the social and environmental conditions of the times, although the developmental results are classifiable within the six stages apparatus.

As an additional reflection on the cross-cultural studies which resulted in seeming universality in the description of the stages and their characteristics of invariance and sequence, Kohlberg writes that even religious instruction leaves untouched, and indeed progresses in accordance with, these findings: 'We have found no important differences in development of moral thinking between Catholics, Protestants, Jews, Buddhists, Moslems, and atheists. Children's moral values in the religious area seem to go through the same stages as their general moral values, so that a stage 2 child is likely to say "Be good to God and he'll be good to you."'[31] The Kohlbergian approach to moral education, then, is not to be taken as a dogmatic and anti-religious humanism arising in reaction against the world's religions, but as an analysis of what is taken to be the universal and invariant process of moral development in children and adults, religious or non-religious. As will be seen later on in this chapter, a seventh stage of moral development is now openly discussed by Kohlberg, and this seventh stage has many aims and characteristics in common with the great religions. Thus, Kohlberg's own call for comprehensiveness at the Stage Seven level is one that can be met by religions, speculative philosophies, ideologies, and any world or cosmically oriented position.

KOHLBERG AND THE NATURALISTIC FALLACY

Kohlberg attempts to define and empirically confirm 'a universal inner logical order of moral concepts, not a universal order found in the educational practices of all cultures, or an order wired into the nervous system.'[32] Precisely because he does not impose an order on human development but allows it to emerge and to demonstrate its own adequacy and superiority in solving moral requirements and demands, he is able to claim not to have committed the 'naturalistic fallacy' which has also been called the 'definist' (read define-ist) fallacy, a less misleading label. In fact, what he is doing is fudging. He might have been wiser to commit the fallacy outright and then give reasons for thinking that it is not really a fallacy at all. Otherwise, it is damning to the extreme to his theory to collect vast amounts of seemingly confirmatory evidence in support of the conceptual requirements of the stages of ethical development, while at the same time claiming no link at all between the facts of empirical observation and the value and moral worth of the higher stages over the lower ones that are claimed seemingly on totally independent grounds. As a result, how can you gain any insight from individual or societal facts about the moral reasoning of individuals, or the norms of the group or societies, which support the claims that certain ethical positions, for example, Kohlberg's higher stages, are better? Instead, what you are more likely to be doing is evaluating existing moral stances, and the people taking them, in the light of an already formed scale of 'parallel' moral values, held quite independently of the data you are supposedly analysing. And it does no good to say that what you are analysing is the conceptual necessities of moral reasoning, for the conceptual is as much an attempt to define the moral in terms of the non-moral (and therefore an example of the naturalistic fallacy) as anything else. More will be said about G.E. Moore and the naturalistic fallacy in chapter 4, but for the moment it is necessary to give a brief indication of the importance of this alleged fallacy to any contemporary discussion of morality. Technically, it is not evident that Moore himself characterized the main point or purpose of the fallacy as that of pointing out the difficulties inherent in moving from a purely factual or descriptive statement to a prescriptive or valuational one. From the fact that people do x, it does not follow that they ought to do x. But the move from is to ought was surely one of the things which Moore's focussing on the naturalistic fallacy called attention to. So-called 'definist' theories in ethics assume that ethical terms like 'ought,' 'right' and 'wrong,' 'good' and 'bad,' 'value' and 'dis-value' can be defined in terms of non-ethical ones, and that ethical judgments can be translated into factual ones. The claim is that values can be defined in terms of facts, 'Ought in terms of Is.' The assumption is a common one, and books and conversations regularly proceed on the assumption that there is nothing wrong with defining moral terms by means of non-moral ones: for example, that 'good' means the same as 'being an object of favourable interest or desire,' or 'the more evolved or developmentally later in time,' or 'that which is commanded by God,' or 'that which brings success and reputation.' As Moore pointed out, one can ask about any of these alleged equivalents, 'But are they really good?' thereby demonstrating that the force and distinctiveness of what is meant by 'good' is not encompassed by any or all of these meanings. Whether the translational equivalence is stated in natural (empirically verifiable) terms or in religious or ideological terms, the fallacy is the same, namely, the defining of the ethical in nonethical terms. Actually, Moore's account of the fallacy is stronger yet, for he warns against defining 'goodness' in any terms and in any way. Kohlberg's way around the naturalistic fallacy is to propose a theory of development which shows that the cognitively and ethically higher stages must come later than the earlier and less adequate stages because the later stages are logically and conceptually based and built on the earlier ones, arise from them, and result in the capability to resolve issues and difficulties heretofore often unseen and unresolvable. Kohlberg has become increasingly clear about which interpretations or forms of the naturalistic fallacy he does and does not commit and now boldly states that he does commit the fallacy by 'asserting that any conception of what moral judgment ought to be must rest on an adequate conception of what it is.'[33] It is increasingly clear that Kohlberg is not willing to commit the naturalistic fallacy, but only to flirt with it in maintaining that the empirical findings of psychological theory run parallel to, or are isomorphic with, the formal analysis of the apparently necessary and universal principles of normative ethical theory.[34] Kohlberg is careful, however, to attempt (even if unsuccessfully) not to claim more for this parallelism than his research allows. What it does not allow is concluding that the empirical confirmation of the developmental process through the stages from lower to higher is any basis at all for concluding that the 'Is' of developmental progress is also evidence for its 'Oughtness' or moral worth. Instead, Kohlberg affirms that 'morality is a unique, *sui generis* realm. If it is unique, its uniqueness must be defined by general formal criteria, so my metaethical conception is *formalistic.*'[35] You cannot get an 'ought' from an 'is,' for morality arises of itself and on its own terms. You get an 'ought' from an 'ought,' that is, from itself. To this extent, Kohlberg is faithful to Moore, for he is holding that morality is based on the conditions and requirements of moral thinking itself, but he does not also conclude, as does Moore, that that is the end of the matter. It is rather the psychological beginning, for once you know what moral philosophy requires, you can use it as a standard by means of which to measure and assess the moral developmental stage of anyone under consideration. The stages of psychological development may be judged as adequate or inadequate when compared with the present-day theoretical norm of acceptable moral reasoning. A claim of 'parallelism' is not a claim basing morality on the empirical facts. Morality is based on its own lights, rational requirements, and appropriate supportive feelings. To the extent to which Kohlberg does try to define moral terms and describe 'what morality ought to be,' he does commit the naturalistic fallacy.[36] However, as he correctly points out, so does everyone else who tries to characterize, and 'define' what ethics is. And using empirical evidence to support his moral conclusions is also to commit the fallacy. Only Moore avoided the naturalistic fallacy, for he stated that 'good was good, and that was the end of this matter.'[37] His insight and assessment effectively paralysed philosophy for decades.

THE SUPERIORITY OF STAGE SIX

What Kohlberg sets out to do is to show that Stage Six thinking is the fullest, most adequate, and rationally best account of what moral philosophy has thus far decided. 'Stage 6 is what it means to judge morally. If you want to play the moral game, if you want to make decisions which anyone could agree upon in resolving social conflicts, Stage 6 is it,' writes Kohlberg, on behalf of the formalists in ethics, himself included.[38] It appears that his attempts to demonstrate the superiority or increased adequacy of each successive stage over the preceding are fourfold. They are also a remarkably uneven lot.

1 Putting the cart before the horse, Kohlberg observes that 'all Stage 6 thinkers agree, all Stage 5's do not.'[39] This, of course, proves nothing,

unless one already knows that Stage Six reasoners are, in fact, superior to Stage Fivers, in which case one would simply show that what works in theory is confirmed by the empirical results as well. He elaborates: 'If the purpose of moral judgment structures is to yield choices on which all reasonable men could agree, then they should use Stage 6 rather than Stage 5 structures.'[40] The purpose of moral judgment is not merely to allow persons to come to agreement, or else the sophists were correct in suggesting that the point of morality is the settling of arguments and the resolving of differences of opinion. The purpose of moral judgment, rather, is to yield choices on which all reasonable men should agree. It is left, then, to show that the fact that they do agree is in accord with the logical and moral requirements of rationality and moral theory.

2 'All Stage 6's can agree because their judgments are fully reversible: they have taken everyone's viewpoint in choosing insofar as it is possible to take everyone's viewpoint where viewpoints conflict.'[41] The main thesis of 'reversibility' is amplified by Kurt Baier in several passages, which I have placed together for convenience and impact:

There can be no doubt that such a God's-eye point of view is involved in the moral standpoint. The most elementary teaching is based on it. The negative version of the so-called Golden Rule sums it up: 'Don't do unto others as you would not have them do unto you.' When we teach children the moral point of view, we try to explain it to them by setting them to put themselves in another person's place ... the behaviour in question must be acceptable to a person whether he is at the 'giving' or 'receiving' end of it ... anyone is doing wrong who engages in nonreversible behaviour ... The principle of reversibility does not merely impose certain prohibitions on a moral agent, but also certain positive injunctions. It is, for instance, wrong – an omission – not to help another person when he is in need and when we are in a position to help him.[42]

Reversibility is a key to understanding what Kohlberg is doing in his program of moral education, and I will come back to it in greater detail, and often, later on in the discussion.

3 In his earlier defence of the superiority of successive stages, two criteria were adapted from psychology and enlisted as central points of demonstration; these are differentiation and integration. In connection with the latter, Kohlberg argues that the formal criterion of reversibility 'entails other formal criteria in terms of which Stage 6 is best.'[43] The notion of differentiation is simply the degree to which moral values and moral

judgments are evident and distinct from other sorts of judgments and considerations, for example, from economic values, or the value of a person as a means only, or from purely formal logical judgments which may apply to items far more inclusive than moral concerns alone. Integration refers to the extent to which judgments cohere in a single and consistent (personal) system and yield a reversible (that is, symmetrical) result, equally 'fair' whether you are on the giving or receiving end of it. Such a judgment is both distinct and 'equilibrated,' that is, is a consistent and stable response to a distinctively moral consideration. Kohlberg sees these two principles as being parallel of the formal criteria of moral judgment, prescriptivity and universality.[44] It was R.M. Hare, one of the 'fathers' of prescriptivism in ethics, who most painstakingly articulated the nature and necessity of these two requirements of morality: 'Moral judgments are a kind of prescriptive judgments, and ... are distinguished from other judgments of this class by being universalizable.'[45] What distinguishes moral statements from most other kinds of statements is their prescriptive character. Like simple imperatives, prescriptive language commands, warns against, or in some other way guides choices or actions.[46] All evaluation, including moral evaluation, has as one of its distinguishing features its prescriptivity.[47] It is this element that has caused so much difficulty in the analysis of morality heretofore, for it contains within it the motivation, obligation, and imperative force to render a description into a command of powerful compulsion. Because we have to make choices and continually have to risk acting on these choices, we must evaluate and weigh the results of our actions: 'It is because I can act in this way or that, that I ask, "Shall I act in this way or that?"; and it is, typically, in my deliberations about this "Shall I" question that I ask the further, but related, question, "Ought I to do this or that?"'[48] Hare's prescriptivity is but another formulation of what is *sui generis* or distinctive about morality. It is differentiated, Hare and Kohlberg agree, by its prescriptivity.

Differentiation is the successive distinguishing of the moral from the non-moral and a fuller realization 'of the moral form,' Kohlberg writes.[49] For example, the value of persons at Stage Six 'has become progressively disentangled from status and property values (Stage 1), from the person's instrumental uses to others (Stage 2), from the actual affection of others for the person (Stage 3), and so on.'[50] In short, the distinctively moral point of view has come to dominate, is now readily separable from prudential, ideological, societal, authoritarian, legalistic, self-interested, and other claims and inclinations, and is seen as more binding because more rational than any other point of view. Therefore, a moral stage is more morally adequate and distinct if, and only if, it embraces a perspective which is anyone's.[51] We have moved from differentiation to integration, for the distinctiveness of morality demands that we apply our prescriptions generally and impartially, that is, universally and reversibly. As Hare stressed, the distinctiveness of moral language was not just its prescriptiveness but also its universalizability, that is, its capacity to be made universally applicable. Reversibility, the property of a perspective which can be embraced as 'anyone's,' includes within it the very moral differentiation which he seeks. Furthermore, as he himself observes, 'It is clear that universalizability is implied by reversibility.'[52] From reversibility comes the notion of universalizability, which is the other side of the coin: 'When we teach children the moral point of view, we try to explain it to them by getting them to put themselves in another person's place,' and again, 'The behaviour in question must be acceptable to a person whether he is at the "giving" or "receiving" end of it.'[53] Kurt Baier emphasizes the point by stating that non-reversible behaviour is simply wrong.[54] In any case, both Hare and Kohlberg would agree that universality and reversibility are necessary (though not sufficient) for us to judge any perspective, behaviour, and so forth as morally adequate.

Moral rules apply universally, then, to anyone in more or less similar circumstances. The moral point of view is above, or separate from, all other considerations except that of consistency of application from *anyone's* perspective. Jan Narveson drives the point home when he adds: 'Every effort to escape morality is a dodge, in fact, just as, and for the same reason as the effort to escape "rationality" is. We hear of people who profess to be against rationality, in some sense or other. The futility of this is transparent: all of these people enjoy words like "therefore," "not," and the rest of the vocabulary of reason, and could not state their views without them. But all that this shows is that the only way to do without rationality is to join the vegetables, which must perforce remain silent.'[55] The enterprise of morality, like that of reasoning, is inescapable given our need to evaluate, choose, and act with some hope of obtaining certain sorts of results rather than others. As Hare concludes, if we were stones, we might not need to bother about evaluation in general, or morality in particular, for they, unlike us, do not have to make choices and decisions about what to do.[56]

4 A view can be said to be more integrated when it completely correlates rights and duties, and presumably other correlative moral notions as well. Thus, 'At Stage 5, for every right, society has some duty to protect that right. Duties to other individuals, however, are not clearly specified in the

absence of either individual contract or social contract.'[57] Kohlberg then quotes from the deliberations of three nameless philosophers who were asked whether it would be right or wrong for a husband to steal an expensive drug which, it is thought, might save his wife who is dying of cancer (the Heinz example):

In Europe, a woman was near death from a very bad disease, a special kind of cancer. There was one drug that the doctors thought might save her. It was a form of radium that a druggist in the same town had recently discovered. The drug was expensive to make, but the druggist was charging ten times what the drug cost him to make. He paid $200 for the radium and charged $2000 for a small dose of the drug. The sick woman's husband, Heinz, went to everyone he knew to borrow the money, but he could get together only about $1000, which was half of what it cost. He told the druggist that his wife was dying and asked him to sell it cheaper or let him pay later. But the druggist said, 'No, I discovered the drug and I'm going to make money from it.' Heinz got desperate and broke into the man's store to steal the drug for his wife.[58]

One of the philosophers indicates that to steal the drug is not wrong, 'but it goes beyond the call of duty; it is a deed of supererogation.'[59] The second replies, 'If the person with cancer were a less close friend, or even a stranger, Heinz would be doing a good act if he stole the drug, but he has no duty to.'[60] Philosopher three correctly observes, 'The value of her (any) life is independent of any personal ties. The value of human life is based on the fact that it offers the only possible source of a categorical moral "ought" to a rational being acting in the role of a moral agent.'[61] Only philosopher three has allowed himself to universalize sufficiently to require of anyone, in a moral dilemma, that he decide with a position that is reversible. He chooses to perceive the situation apart from personal ties and accepts legal and personal obligations as important ingredients in his decision, but not necessarily sufficient guides. He has imaginatively put himself in the shoes and sickbed of another. Life itself is viewed as a fundamental value in the sense that it is a value/condition without which no other values are possible for a person. Moralists as diverse as Hobbes and Camus have been able to agree on this point. Still, is it morally right to break the law to try to save a life?

WHAT KOHLBERG IS REALLY DOING

The answer is really much simpler than Kohlberg suggests. Moral autonomy requires that you find out for yourself what is right and what is obligatory. Societal laws, other moral codes and pre-dispositions, and so on must all be submitted to this critical inquiry. If the life of the individual is fundamental in human valuation, that is, if people are of unconditional value, then a rule of society or the preservation of private property ought not to override such a value. Actually, it would be quite easy, on utilitarian grounds, to show that more happiness or goodness by far would be brought about by saving a life, exposing the druggist as greedy, and acting in accordance with one's own moral requirements based on the impartiality of reversibility and the generality of universalizability than by keeping the law. The point is not, however, one of utilitarian vs formalist thought. That is a red herring, an unnecessary detour which turns moral philosophy towards hypothetical struggles for supremacy, whereas contemporary moral philosophy has had a better time of it explicating what basic requirements any moral theory must meet. The matter has been well outlined by Kai Nielson, who argues first that 'morality has developed in such a way that it is now correct to say that in morality we are concerned with the reasoned pursuit of the interests of all rational or sentient agents.'[62] Indeed, 'there are certain moral truths that do not at all depend on the personal idiosyncrasies or cultural perspectives of anyone but would be affirmed by any rational agent apprised of the relevant facts.'[63] He then articulates three basic 'procedural rules': (1) proceed on the assumption that 'human welfare' and 'well-being' are defined enough to allow us to distinguish the bulk of acts which do and do not further these ends; (2) distribute as equitably as possible such values of 'welfare' and 'well-being' to all those significantly involved in a situation; and (3) assume the viewpoint of an impartial but sympathetic observer.[64] Rules (1) and (3) are the least controversial, the third being another formulation of Kohlberg's reversibility. The second takes us to a consideration of justice. But rather than try to show, on the basis of the empirical evidence of moral interviews, that formalism and Rawls have given the better or even the definitive answers concerning how one is to be just, it is enough to require that one be rationally committed to accounting for equitable distribution of goods. The concern with justice is not absent in most utilitarian theories, but the issue is whether a teleologist or consequentialist can satisfactorily account for the requirements of justice on his view. Stage Six morality, then, on this view, does not require that one resolve age-old moral deliberations, but only that one be hypersensitive to issues of justice and demand of oneself that considerations of justice be procedurally central. Perhaps this point can be fixed by citing a recent article by R.M. Hare, often described by Kohlberg as a formalist[65], yet one who is currently attempting to reduce the alleged distance between utilitarianism and justice:

> The normative theory that I shall advocate has close analogies with utilitarianism, and I should not hesitate to call it utilitarian, were it not that this name covers a wide variety of views, all of which have been the victims of prejudices rightly excited by the cruder among them ... In my review of Professor Rawls's book I said that there were close formal similarities between rational contractor theories such as Rawls's and ideal observer theories such as have been advocated by many writers and my own universal prescriptivist theory. I also said that theories of this [Rawlsian] form can be made to lead very naturally to a kind of utilitarianism, and that Rawls avoided this outcome only by a very liberal use of intuitions to make his rational contractors come to a non-utilitarian contract ... utilitarians have no need to fear the accusation that they could favour extreme inequalities of distribution in actual modern societies.[66]

The point of the above is not to defend utilitarianism against formalism but to focus the query 'What is Kohlberg doing?' in the battle of the ethical theoreticians, when his simple claim is that Stage Six moral reasoners deliberate on a higher moral plane than do those at lower stages. He does not have to resolve what is still unresolved amongst the protagonists themselves. He merely needs to show that more of the moral point of view is present in Stage Six reasoning and that moral notions and issues are more adequately conceived and handled. Unfortunately, Kohlberg has claimed that 'the purpose of this paper ... is to describe the Stage 6 natural structure underlying various theories like Rawls's and to justify the sense in which it is better than structures of reasoning based on the "more familiar" conception of the social contract and of utilitarianism.'[67] Until he backs away from such a claim, I suggest, he will fruitlessly embroil himself in exciting but most likely prolonged debates about the details of meta-ethics, whereas his strength ought to lie in wishing to show that Stage Six reasoning is empirically concerned with reversibility, universalizability, autonomy, impartiality with sympathy, human welfare, and justice. And clarity with respect to these (and no doubt other) central concerns would do a great deal to pin-point what teachers, parents, governments, and individuals ought to be concerned with in the classroom, the home, the nation, and themselves.

The key, then, to Kohlberg's arguments for sequential betterness of the stages is that they reduce to an argument for reversibility and therefore universalizability in moral judgments and include something like prescriptivity as well. This is simpler and far less controversial than elaborations of the more obscure categories of correlativity, equilibration, differentiation, and integration. Not only that, it lays bare what Kohlberg has been doing all along.

MORAL DEVELOPMENT

It might be possible to schematize, and thereby simplify, the major paths of moral development which Kohlberg has ably and empirically charted from Stage One through Stage Six. Consider the progression: from externality of criterion to internalization; from concern for self alone to reversibility and universalizability; from the dim flickering of moral awareness to a full-fledged concern with and adoption of the 'moral perspective,' irrespective of specific moral schools, traditions, or solutions to moral dilemmas. Relativism, the position that any moral or value judgment is as true for a given individual (or group) as another judgment is for a different individual (or group), is to be rejected because it is rationally inadequate and contradictory. Egoism, or self-interestedness, as a sufficient moral principle is inconsistent because it 'makes everyones private interest the "highest court of appeal,"' whereas one must mean by the 'moral point of view' a perspective 'which is a court of appeal for conflicts of interests.'[68] The rejection of relativism and egoism, when coupled with the demand of internalization, leads us to principled deliberation: 'If one has adopted the moral point of view, then one acts on principle and not merely on rules of thumb designed to promote one's aim.'[69] Furthermore, moral reasoning must be autonomous in that it depends on the process of justification and the requirements of consistency. To reason morally is also to reason philosophically and therefore critically. You can no longer stop with what you have always thought, or with how you feel, or with what society says, or with any other authoritative base. Something is good or right not because it is alleged to be so but because it can be argued for, that is, reasons can be given in support of it. Reason requires that you decide for yourself, autonomously. The teacher of morality is a resource person in your journey from scepticism and relativism to the study of ethics as a subject capable of yielding justifiable judgments, in your passage from egoistic self-interest to increasingly widening social perspectives until you seek universal and impartial ('ideal') decisions and the refinement of your reason and argument are such that you can make up your own mind rather than accepting authority or other external answers as though they were your own. You will have decided that 'being rational is being prepared, even

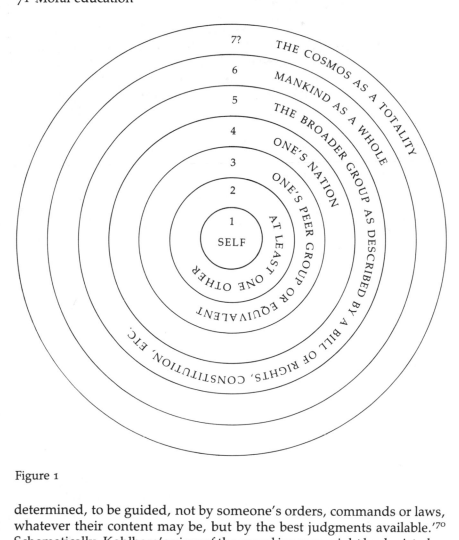

Figure 1

determined, to be guided, not by someone's orders, commands or laws, whatever their content may be, but by the best judgments available.'[70] Schematically, Kohlberg's view of the moral journey might be depicted as the stage by stage enlargement of what is to be included in our ethical deliberations (see figure 1).

RAWLS, UTILITARIANISM AND THE STAGES

Lawrence Kohlberg's incredible insight is that in moral deliberations there is something to measure and some way to collect empirical data. This insight, together with the refinements and the increasing array of confirmatory data, make him a successful pioneer in a field that has often appeared dark and hopeless. His difficulties, however, have resulted from a desire to place over this data an interpretive grid which would fit in such a way as to both explain the data and solve key questions in the history of philosophy. Let me try to show that this grid is an attempt to gain too much too fast and represents a straying from the original empirical data and its explanation.

Stage Five is repeatedly alleged to display utilitarian reasoning. I will ague shortly that Kohlberg by and large presents a caricature of utilitarian theory. What is pressing, for the moment, is to look more closely at the 'bag' of characteristics which I have extracted from his writings and which make up the description of Stage Five 'utilitarian' thinking. Moral reasoning at Stage Five requires any (or all, if possible – he doesn't give a minimum of them, or an ordering) of the following traits (arbitrarily numbered):

1 a legal point of view (though by itself this is more typical of Stage Four);
2 a social contract, implicit or explicit;
3 the possibility of changing law in terms of rational considerations of social utility;
4 critical examination or review of standards (ideally by society as a whole);
5 procedural rules for reaching consensus;
6 universal distribution of rights;
7 tolerance of differing values and opinions;
8 'The official morality of the u.s. government and Constitution'[71] (sic – see discussion below).

Without doubting that such ingredients occur in the responses of Stage Five individuals, you may well ask what central thread or available theoretical position would enable you to show a philosopher that these characteristics belong together because bound by a unifying principle or moral position? Would a philosopher recognize Kohlberg's depiction of this collection of traits as a clear and distinct utilitarianism? What, for example, is the official morality of the American government? I, for one, am at a loss as to where to begin! As for the American constitution, David Lyons aptly remarks that in addition to 'liberty and justice for all,' the constitution also endorses collective action in aid of 'a more perfect union, domestic tranquility, the common defense,'[72] and it will require some exceptionally fancy footwork to render these items obvious Stage Five utilitarian concerns. It is likely that the 'bag' of characteristics do regularly occur together, but the attempt to relate them to a constitution, an ideology, or even to utilitarianism *per se* is far too premature. Utilitarians require a more precise and unambiguous list and then a great deal of careful and painstaking reasoning to show what theories tend to encounter difficulties in keeping the prescriptive force and distinctiveness of moral terms intact, while formalists have the opposite difficulty of giving sufficient weight and place to human well-being and the goodness or value of the results of human choice and action. Justice and beneficence ought to go together in morality, but the greatest problems arise from losing the one owing to achieving the other. It does not appear that proponents of any theory have yet found a way to have both at once, let alone to act successfully on that achievement. Little wonder, then, that William Frankena wrote in *Ethics* that 'the clearest and most plausible view, in my opinion, is to identify the law of love with what I have called the principle of benevolence, that is, of doing good, and to insist that it must be supplemented by the principle of distributive justice or equality.'[73] Thus, rather than speaking of the superiority of one approach over the other, it is far more likely that a contemporary moral theorist will observe that something of both theories is necessary, and that what is needed in moral philosophy is a theoretical synthesis which accounts for and preserves both requirements, and which successfully resolves difficulties arising from their interaction. No such synthesis is yet available. Nevertheless, the characteristics of Stage Six thinking must account for both the utilitarian and formalist meta-theorizing and the continued search for a resolution through some sort of synthesis. Teaching ethics should demand that the teacher emphasize the inconclusive and, in this respect, myopic perspective on moral reality. It is not that the formalist position subsumes the insights of utilitarian thinking and then adds its own superior principles; nor is it that the utilitarian subsumes the insights of formalism. Rather, Stage Six thinking, if morally adequate in terms of the best thinking on the subject available at the present, includes the demands and insights of both utilitarian and formalist thinking. The conflicts and clashes arising from housing the two under the same conceptual roof demonstrate the excitement and frustration of contemporary moral myopia.

We may speculate why Kohlberg has never come to grips with the task of giving a painstaking definitive catalogue of characteristics of his Stage Five – it is tempting to speculate that it is because he finds his rough-and-ready conception of Stage Five clearly utilitarian in type. If so, and if we were as sure as Kohlberg is that Stage Six is largely Rawlsian formalist, then Kohlberg is on the brink of relating the major work in philosophical ethics in the past hundred years to his empirical findings, and in such a way as to show that his stages form a developmental progression, from which we may decide which is the highest, best, and most adequate, empirically and philosophically. That carrot would be a difficult one to turn one's back on. But vagueness similar to that surrounding the characterization of Stage Five is evident at Stage Six as well, at which the ethical principles can be described as:

1 abstract (formulated in terms of general concepts) – not concrete (in terms of specific acts or attitudes), that is, 'ethical principles,' not the 'moral rules' of Stage Four;
2 logically comprehensive (applying to most cases) or even universal (all cases);
3 reciprocal, consistent, or fair (applying impartially to all individuals);
4 self-chosen, that is, on one's own criteria, not the group's;
5 decided by intuition or conscience (as 'right' on the basis of the nature of the act or attitude) – not rationally 'calculated' (as 'good' on the basis of its consequences).

The principles include such concepts as:

1 justice of a judgment, that is, fair application of the principles involved;
2 equality of each individual;
3 rights of the individual;
4 worth of the individual as a person;
5 the 'right' (or 'wrong') as primary terms or elementary concepts – not 'good' (or 'bad').[74]

Kohlberg claims that these conceptual elements, characteristic of Stage Six, are clearly emphasized in formalist (that is, deontological) theories. But such concepts are also emphasized in utilitarian or teleological writings, where the good is supreme and the right (and the various rights) are derived from it. Perhaps one ought to add other more 'utilitarian' characteristics such as concern for the general welfare, goodness, happiness, and worthy ends of action, but they are not inconsistent with his Stage Six characterization and in fact do appear in his more lengthy accounts of Stage Six thinking and justification.[75] If the utilitarian elements are added to this 'bag' of characteristics, however, it will most likely burst at is seams, for it would include an array of things which any empirical naturalist would pick up at random in a knowledgeable walk through the field of normative ethical theory. The web of interpretation has become badly tangled. Nevertheless, it is obvious from the empirical findings, and as a result of contemporary debates among deontologists and teleologists alike at the meta-ethical level, that there are essential elements generally agreed upon in all adequate moral reasoning. We have already identified some of the ingredients which go to make up the essence of the moral point of view.

UTILITARIANISM RECONSIDERED

Part of what I take to be Kohlberg's confusion arises from his simplification of utilitarianism. For him it is self-evident that utilitarianism cannot be at a higher level than Stage Five because it is not able to deal with, or is unconcerned with, the 'bag' of characteristics of Stage Six reasoning. However, recent works by David Lyons and even by R.M. Hare serve to demonstrate with compelling force that the controversy about whether utilitarianism can account for justice and provide a place for human rights is doing much to expand and make precise the nature of utilitarianism. Lyons argues that John Stuart Mill had a theory of rights, and Hare holds that a utilitarian is quite able to account for the demands of justice within that theory. Reacting critically to the alleged superiority of Rawls' theory, Hare notes that Rawls' 'rational contractor theory' and 'ideal observer theories' are closely similar to this own 'universal prescriptivist theory.'[76] Without taking time now to define these positions, suffice it to say that Hare concludes that 'theories of this form can be made to lead very naturally to a kind of utilitarianism, and that Rawls avoided this outcome only by a very liberal use of intuitions to make his rational contractors come to a non-utilitarian contract.'[77] Developing his thesis further, Hare next maintains that the making of a moral judgment requires 'prescribing universally.'[78] He argues that this conclusion is not derived from elaborate game-contract hypothetical situations in the unlikely circumstances of Rawls' 'original position' but entirely from 'the formal properties of the moral concepts themselves as revealed by the logical study of moral language.'[79] Hare writes: 'The features of prescriptivity and universalizability' are the ones 'which I think moral judgments, in the central uses, all have. These two features provide a framework for moral reasoning which is formally similar to Rawls' own more dramatic machinery.'[80] As we have seen, Kohlberg agrees. What comes from this is an analysis of the formal requirements of morality in any developed and adequate form, akin to what we have been calling the moral point of view, which attempts to demonstrate that utility and justice are not necessarily, and certainly not obviously, at odds: 'First, it is sometimes alleged that justice has to be at odds with utility. But if we ask how we are to be just between the competing interests of different people, it seems hard to give any other answer than that it is by giving equal weight, impartially, to the equal interest of everybody. And this is precisely what yields the utility principle.'[81] In another paper, Hare concludes that 'formal justice is simply another name for the formal requirement of universality in moral principles on which ... golden rule arguments are based.'[82] If he is correct here, then consideration of justice and other alleged 'formalist' moral notions such as rights and obligations may be derivable from universalizability, which in turn is closely related to, if not actually derived from, reversibility (as Kohlberg argues). But then there is no prima facie reason for supposing that utilitarians or other consequentialists cannot account for moral notions without becoming formalists, since universalizability is a key notion for many, if not most, teleologists.

After remarking that non-utilitarians regularly weaken the utilitarian position by presenting fantastic cases based on little information and requiring enormous strength of principle acquired from some higher or ideal position,[83] Hare raises a major objection to most accounts of the trouble with utilitarianism, one of which is at the centre of the present discussion. Specifically, he maintains that to ask for moral decisions based on fantastic cases, while in possession of little or no factual information, is to ignore the importance of moral education in utilitarian theories.[84] That is to say, the utilitarian will not require of his children, or even of his friends, that they 'practise on every occasion on which they are confronted with a moral question, the kind of archangelic thinking he himself is capable of; if they are ordinary children, he knows that they will get it wrong.'[85] Instead, parents and teachers will wish to 'implant' usable principles which they will not wish to break without being prepared for the great psychic discomfort which will result, and whose breach by others will cause similar discomfort and moral indignation.

Additionally, parents teach their children that they will have to review such principles, learn to justify and, where necessary, improve on them, and come to deal successfully with conflicts among principles so that 'the result will be a set of general principles, constantly evolving, but on the whole stable, such that their use in moral education, including self-education, and their consequent acceptance by the society at large, will lead to the nearest possible approximation to the prescriptions of archangelic thinking. They will be the set of principles with the highest acceptance-utility. They are likely to include principles of justice.'[86]

We can be briefer with David Lyons' attempt to show that even the model utilitarian, John Stuart Mill, was far too complex a thinker to be fitted into what Lyons characterizes as a simplistic 'aggregate-of-goodness' theory of the sort which Kohlberg sometimes suggests utilitarianism to be. Lyons writes that Mill's moral theory, in particular his understanding of justice, does not even fit the caricature of 'aggregate-of-goodness' utilitarianism.[87] Rights, obligations, and justice itself are all essential to any conceptually acceptable moral theory, however. Lyons goes on to show that the tension between Mill's stress on the moral notions of 'rights,' 'obligations,' and 'justice' against happiness as the sole end of human action is never fully resolved.[88] On the face of it, Lyons' position seems to vindicate Kohlberg's insistence that formalist theories are superior because they explicitly require that rights and obligations must be included in a moral theory and that utilitarians must adduce such notions over and above the obvious consideration of the general welfare and happiness. As central and essential moral notions in formalist theories, they relate closely to the empirical formulation of the concerns and categories of Stage Six moral reasoning. However, they are also the concerns of Hare and Lyons, and paradoxically of John Stuart Mill as well. Lyons fixes the point which I have been making throughout when he concludes: 'It seems to me the solution to this problem is not obvious.'[89] If there is a major defect in Kohlberg's work, it has nothing to do with his empirical base but rather has to do with his choice of a meta-ethical stance as though it were obvious, or even necessary, for his theory to be 'complete.' This brief excursion into contemporary discussion is an attempt to make it apparent that an adequate philosophic basis for the understanding, justification, and application of basic moral concepts is not yet in hand and that the debate between formalists and teleologists is excitingly vigorous. It should be at least as obvious, therefore, that the professional philosophic hand has not come down on the promising head of formalism of the Rawlsian sort, or any other, to anoint it as the heir apparent to the title of 'more adequate' or 'better.' How much more fruitful it would be for Kohlberg to leave matters of such rich debate to the side, focusing instead on what is required in order to see whether it is in line with what Stage Six reasoners usually articulate. Were this stance to be adopted, Kohlberg's research would be far more accessible to the philosophically non-initiated, and the technicalities of moral philosophy could be reduced, by and large, to discussion and analysis of moral notions and their justification, much as Hare has attempted to do in his more recent attempts at clarification of his own utilitarian excursions.

In sharp contrast with the above discussion, Kohlberg's view of utilitarianism is at most basic, if not primitive: 'There is an ethical method of judgment, a moral point of view, which is not a mere instrumental or utilitarian calculation of the instrumentalities of means to ends or a quantitative maximization of observable satisfactions or pleasures. The moral point of view is not merely utilitarian; it implies principles of justice and impartiality.'[90] One would suppose utilitarians very naïve thinkers, indeed, to be concerned not with justice and impartiality but only with strict instrumentalities, calculating 'observable' (which I take it means obvious) satisfactions or pleasures quantitatively. In any event, whereas utilitarian Stage Five thinkers are simplistic, mechanical, and insensitive to issues of basic rights and justice, Stage Six formalists emphasize the value of the individual person and stress that no moral decision can be considered complete unless it takes account of and is in accord with principles of justice, fairness, and recognition of human rights and responsibilities. In fact, I think it to be the case that utilitarians would agree on all counts in the formalist characterization. The point at issue is whether the formalist can relate his concern with justice to the well-being of people in terms of actual consequences, while the utilitarian seems to over-emphasize the general happiness or well-being in such a way as to make it unclear how he can have his justice and his happiness too. As an aside, it is interesting to note how often Kohlberg himself retreats to a consequentialist/utilitarian argument in support of his formalist in-tuitions, making the above point about difficulties faced by formalists even more relevant to our critique of Kohlberg. In the often-quoted Heinz dilemma, Kohlberg himself appeals to straightforward utilitarian con-siderations in determining what one should do if operating behind Rawls's veil of ignorance.[91]

In summary, the thesis of this section is that all refined moral theories find questions of rights, obligations, justice, dessert, and so on to be of paramount importance in any comprehensive analysis. The issue is not whether they are important, but how they are to be defined, accounted for, and justified.

THE BEST AND THE ABSOLUTELY BEST

Kohlberg attempts to show that there is more to morality than simply counting each person as one in number and then acting in accordance with whatever will bring about the greatest amount of aggregate pleasure for the greatest number of those involved, or the least amount of pain, or the greatest balance of pleasure over pain. He is right, of course; matters of previous commitment, standing obligation, justice, and fairness must be considered and somehow dealt with. The problem is that Kohlberg often implies that, in addition to being able to rule out an array of 'inferior' answers as being lower stage and not yet fully representative of the moral point of view, he is also able to provide the 'right' answer. He has often placed before his classes at Harvard sample dilemmas which allow him to show what is necessary for a Stage Six answer to be adequate (and to show why lower-stage answers are inadequate), but the further temptation is to show how the dilemma is to be 'solved.' A recent example is 'Variation 1 – The Captain's Dilemma':

A charter plane crashed in the South Pacific. Three people survived, the pilot and two passengers. One of the passengers was an old man who had a broken shoulder. The other was a young man, strong and healthy. There was some chance that the raft could make it to the safety of the nearest island if two men rowed continuously for three weeks. However, there was almost no chance if all three of the men stayed on the raft. First of all, the food supply was meager. There was barely enough to keep two men alive for the three-week period. Second, a storm was approaching and the raft would almost certainly capsize unless one man went overboard. This man could not cling to the raft and in all likelihood, would drown. A decision had to be made quickly.

The captain was strong and the only one who could navigate. If he went over, there was almost no chance the other two would make it to safety. If the old man with the broken shoulder went, there was a very good probability, about 80 percent, that the other two could make it. If the young man went overboard and the old man and the captain stayed chances were a little less than 50:50. No one would volunteer to go overboard.[92]

What should the captain do?

Kohlberg argues cogently that it is not a moral solution to order the old man overboard. The preferred solution is to draw lots, for this jeopardizes them all equally and in Rawlsian fashion it can be shown that the old man's chances of surviving are raised from 0% to 50%, the strong man's decreased from 80% to 50%. The captain had to stay if any were to survive. The drop in survival potential for the strong man is offset by the greater potential given the old man, which is justified since it heavily increases the well-being of the least advantaged. Kohlberg argues that the lottery is the just solution. I think he is right. It is a just solution, but it seems equally moral on either formalist or utilitarian grounds. It is difficult to decide about resulting good without considering the fairness of the lottery and resulting survival potential, the effects of unfairness on an individual, particularly a Stage Five or Six moral reasoner, or the effect on the Stage Six captain of ordering someone overboard. Furthermore, are there not other possible moral answers as well? Kohlberg has ruled out the possibility of someone volunteering to go overboard, but in a real lifeboat situation it would not be unique for someone, particularly someone with a highly tuned moral sensitivity, to break the deadlock by jumping over. Again, out of sheer respect and empathy for the individuality and developing solidarity amongst the three passengers, the three might well decide to go down with hands joined and singing. Would these acts be any less moral? Indeed, it would not be hard to imagine them being singled out as examples of morality beyond the call of duty, but not beyond the call of moral reason. Of course, in addition to reason, it would take extraordinary courage, would evidence empathetic warmth and not mere intellectual recognition of the dilemma and its solution, and so on. But surely the solutions are fully moral. They are not universalizable in that we would not demand them of anyone, nor are they reversible for the same reason. Still, I would argue that reversibility and universalizability are minimum requirements of Stage Six morality, not maximum requirements. It is not that you cannot act in excess of these principles but that you cannot thwart them out of self-interest or expediency of some other sort. Stage Six morality ought to be viewed as clarificatory of what is required of one who is moral, but not of all that is required of one who is moral. It is not a straight-jacket but only the basic fabric. As many critics of Kohlberg have noted, there is undoubtedly more to morality than what is included in the Stage Six 'bag,' and Richard Peters' call for compassion is a good example.[93] It is very likely, no doubt, that we will all continue to discover, in living as well as in the literature, that there is far more to morality than we have heretofore dreamed of.

To tie Kohlberg's work to the success of Rawls and formalist positions would be tragic. To use Rawls and others to make clear what is required of one who is moral in the most adequate sense is exciting. Kohlberg acknowledges this, and has sharply observed, 'It may be true that Rawls' theory, or our own, may spring from the Western liberal tradition but this does not mean that Stage 5 or Stage 6 principles are Western rather than universal. Put differently, the validity of moral principles does not depend upon the validity of any particular theory justifying these principles ... Scholarly critiques of Rawls hardly put into question the principles of liberty and equality.'[94] Kohlberg's use of philosophy is not naïve. His work shows fully as much promise philosophically as it has already achieved in psychology. The caution expressed throughout this book is that philosophic potential tends to be actualized less quickly and only after debates of rather surprising magnitude. Even then, when the dust settles, one does not find philosophic victory, but a place in philosophic history along with competing victors and their theories. It is likely, therefore, that Kurt Baier's observation, which Kohlberg quotes for his own purposes as well, will prove to be operative in the normative realm: 'There is no a priori reason to assume that there is only one true morality. There are many moralities, and of these a large number may happen to pass the test which moralities must pass in order to be called true.'[95] In effect, Kohlberg's attempts to avoid relativism and even scepticism in the discipline of moral education may have caused him to approach too closely the more rigid and fixed absolutist and doctrinaire aspects of moral theorizing. Yet you do not have to declare yourself either a formalist or a utilitarian in order to avoid relativism. All that is required is that you get clear about the necessities of language and reason and the requirements of being moral in the first place. This is not easy. Morality has never been easy either to implement or to understand. The climb from relativism and egoism to attempted justification and more stringent rationality leads inevitably to greater degrees of generality and impartiality, stopping only at points short of the goal because of the internal fixation of growth and development. Otherwise, one must assume that the moral point of view will result in principles which are universalizable and reversible. Such a perspective will, where acted on with honesty and care, produce impartial and moral actions. What more could be asked of a theory of moral reasoning?

KOHLBERG AND HIS CRITICS

As ought to be the case in matters of philosophical importance, Kohlberg has many critics who have reacted to his work both sympathetically and unsympathetically. One of the more common criticisms is the charge that Kohlberg is really a hidden or crypto-relativist. Considerable concern has been expressed in many communities across North America that Kohlberg's approach will undermine the authority of the home, the teacher, the school, and the nation. In so far as the child is encouraged to develop the critical capacity to reflect upon all matters placed before him, then one can take the view that the aim of the exercise is to give the child licence to think (and do) as he comes to like. One of the most quoted and objected to passages in Kohlberg's work comes from his 'Stages of Moral Development': '[Another reason] for the legitimacy of the developmental approach to moral education is that the stimulation of moral development defines an educational process respecting the autonomy of the child, whereas any other definition reflects indoctrination. The constitutional issue arises from the point of view of the child's parent, who can object to the teaching of values other than the parent's own. Respect for the parent's rights is not respect for the child's autonomy, a more legitimate concern.'[96] Kohlberg's blunt admission that respect for the child's autonomy is more important than respect for the parent's rights has proved a 'red flag' alerting concerned parents and citizens to the seeming anarchism of Kohlberg and his followers. After all, it was the Values Clarification approach which also defended the autonomy of the child and sought only to help the child become clear and articulate about his own moral views. But now the Kohlbergian approach takes on an even more sinister form, for it admits that it actively teaches value stances which may well be in opposition to the teachings of the home, the churches, and possibly even the laws of the land: 'Kohlberg's Stage-6 person is autonomous, a sovereign being, apparently above the value of society's rules.'[97] While there is 'a certain appeal to us all' in being above the law (of the home, the classroom, or society), the fact is that it is not the place of the teacher or the school to 'undermine' these values. The reader will note that an old Athenian charge is being laid here – that of corrupting the youth and undermining the laws of the land. As has been said already, it is sometimes difficult to distinguish between those who appear to be destructively engaged in tearing down the norms and laws of society for motives of selfishness or treason and those who Socratically criticize in order to find 'for themselves' firm footings for their value stances. One of the risks of education is that exercise of freedom which makes every subject-matter, from values and ethics to politics and religion, fair game for the activity of critical inquiry. The educator must get his students to look at their opinions, prejudices, habits, stereotypes, and values, requiring both that they be clear about them and their implications and that they fairly judge the quality of the arguments in favour of and against them. He, like Socrates, is planting the seeds of doubt. The purpose of such sowing is not to undermine what is worth keeping but to undermine what is worth abandoning, to strengthen what is worthy of maintenance, to come to see this for yourself, and to articulate and defend your position by mustering the reasons and the evidence. Surely this is the *sine qua non* of the educated individual. Tearing down society or undermining the authority of parents is not. Improving society may sometimes require a critical thrust, but its purpose is improvement. Of course, what has just been argued is acceptable only within limits. What are the limits? There is no magic formula for deciding that, and active community discussion about this matter is both good and very likely inevitable. One obvious limit, however, is the philosophical requirement that it makes sense to be critical of the *status quo* of the individual or of your society if, and only if, you have some way of recognizing an improvement. Values Clarification clarifies; it does not improve by swapping one perspective for another as 'better.' Relativists and sceptics speak of change or of one system being preferred by them to another, but there is no place to rest a claim of 'better than.' Kohlberg has such a place, for his emphasis on universality and reversibility offers characteristics of 'betterness' that can be weighed and examined. Kohlberg provides full cognitive value, for his system aptly argues, musters the evidence for, and capably defends the 'betterness' of the higher stages over the lower stages. It may be that Kohlberg will be shown to be wrong, or perhaps his system will be significantly improved on, but there are no grounds for rejecting his view as a relativism, scepticism, or anarchism. Such views rest on the assumption that the only alternative to an authoritative claim of 20/20 vision is blindness. If Kohlberg is not an absolutist, then he is a relativist. The centrality and worth of educational myopia has been discarded and ignored. This is not to say, of course, that educational myopia must be accepted as the 'authoritative' view, for that, too, would be dogmatic. All that is required, educationally, is to observe that less than total and final confirmation, validation, evidence gathering, reasoning, and discussion have been and remain a vital part of the great disciplines, the humanities and sciences alike, from the earliest times to the present. It is authoritarianism and absolutism which must be viewed as 'exceptional' and remarkably 'rare' in producing either general agreement or confirmatory 'proof.'

What people often fail to see, as Kohlberg himself points out, is that to remove the criticality of freedom is to run the risk of viewing the teacher as 'the agent of the state or the social system.'[98] What is wrong with that is that it is undemocratic, and Kohlberg is a staunch defender of the democratic way in the schools and in our society. Not to be consistently democratic in one's approach to education and to the management of the classroom-learning environment is to move towards a position which, when perfected and made explicit, is representative of totalitarian states:

Conformity and respect for authority are called socialization, moral internaliza-tion, or conscience-formation by many psychologists and educators. As related to daily school practice, these aims represent effort to have children conform to rules of the classroom and the school. When these are made explicit as aims of moral education, we get a system of state-determined 'character education' such as is found in the Soviet Union. The moral curriculum is not hidden in Russian education, however. Rather, character education is considered the most important function of the schools, and teachers are trained to engage in a definite system of moral education directed toward fostering disciplined Soviet citizens (Bronfenbrenner, 1962). The Russian system is based on the notion that the teacher is the agent of the state or the social system, rather than being a free moral agent dealing with children who are free moral agents in a changing society.[99]

It all turns on what you think the responsibility of the educator is. Kathleen Gow, for example, writes that teachers are in fact required by law to pass on the approved moral values to their students: 'Our society has long recognized that the school plays a major role in the socialization of children. The school's mandate, as set forth in education acts across the u.s. and Canada is to commend to students the moral values and conduct that previous generations have approved: honesty, justice, courage, and service to others, for example. Pupils, the Acts have stated, are to be encouraged to pursue and prize these ideals for their intrinsic goodness.'[100] The present-day Education Act of the Province of Ontario, a document binding on all teachers in the public school system, makes evident in an even more specified way just what the teacher is expected to teach: 'It is the duty of a teacher to inculcate by precept and example respect for religion and the principles of Judaeo-Christian morality and the highest regard for truth, justice, loyalty, love of country, humanity, benevolence, sobriety, industry, frugality, purity, temperance and all other virutes.'[101] Given the phrase 'and all other virtues' tagged on at the end, there is probably not a thoughtful educator in Ontario who is not guilty of having 'critically examined' the meaning and appropriateness of some of the virtues listed, the supremacy of the 'Judaeo-Christian morality' over all the other religions and moral alternatives, or whether the list of other virtues is either evident or shared by most. On the other hand, it may be that the intended point of the legislation is not to stand in the way of critical inquiry but rather to support it as a means of coming to help students 'see' for themselves and thereby to create within society a cutting edge of teachers and students capable of recognizing abuses and making improvements in the existing moral understanding of the people of that province and beyond. John Anderson, a life-long defender of the importance of critical inquiry into all matters of educational concern, remarks that 'we can distinguish between the sort of training that develops judgment and the sort that destroys or discourages judgment.'[102] Referring to the teaching of Socrates, he adds that 'the position of Socrates is simply that this uncritical acceptance of tradition, this acquiring of Athenian virtue, is no education at all.'[103] Surely Anderson could be speaking for Kohlberg here, for both would argue that the educational significance of tradition is not its repetition, its being committed to memory, or its enforcement in the schools through discipline; the significance of tradition is that it is the prime 'stuff' to be considered anew by each student and afresh by each teacher who carefully examines and scrutinizes its clarity and the sufficiency of its support. Indeed, 'those who have come to terms with conflicting views and tendencies are far more vigorous and able upholders of a cause than those who simply follow authority.'[104] And should the critical examination reveal shortcomings or the 'official' calling of a vice a virtue, as in the case of the now famous Watergate scandal or the blind willingness of a Lieutenant Calley or an Eichmann simply to do what the official morality of the government or its agencies demanded, then it is the duty of the critic to rail against this misconception. Surely without this dimension a society has every chance of going stale and of going wrong.

MORAL DILEMMAS

The indispensability of 'moral dilemmas' as aids in the teaching of moral education should now be understood, if not agreed with. If there is anything to the claim that if 'subjects are not taught controversially, they are not worth teaching,'[105] then the stimulation of doubt and criticism is but an inevitable component of education (not training) and of teaching (not telling). Of course, what keeps this approach from being purely destructive is the positive end in view, namely, the coming closer to truth and the understanding of, and motivation towards, leading the morally good life. If you already know what this is, in detail and with final authority, then perhaps it is better to get on with it and to squash attempts at raising objections or entertaining requests for additional clarification. Such a stance is, however, rigorously totalitarian and certainly not educative as we have defined and described it.

Having said this, I think it should be evident that the sides have become too neatly drawn: Kohlberg is for freedom and his critics are totalitarians. I think some of them are, in fact, but most of them are far from it. The vast majority of his detractors are as opposed to totalitarianism as he is and, like him, view themselves as defenders of democracy. And a major reason for the misunderstanding between them has, I think, been identified by

Richard Peters, among others. Peters argues that the distinction between form and content in moral education must be kept at the front of one's mind. He notes that Kohlberg willingly grants that the content of moral (and other) rules, such as honesty, punctuality, tidiness, is learned by instruction (telling), imitation, and drill, 'aided by rewards and punishment, praise and blame.'[106] But Kohlberg is not interested in such habit formation, for habits are 'short-term and situation-specific.'[107] What Kohlberg wants is insight into the formation of moral rules, those fundamental principles, like freedom, fairness, truth-telling, promise-keeping, and the like, by means of which specific contents are judged to be moral or not. There is a great difference in the cognitive level of abstraction between simply following a rule about telling the truth and working out and articulating the reasons why telling the truth is, in general and in the long run, the right thing to do. I suspect that every thinking educator and parent would prefer to encourage the ability to reason out abstractly why telling the truth is the morally obligatory way of behaving, other things being equal. But such cognitive capacity is not yet developed in the very young and is not present in sufficient quantity for a significant portion of the population at any age. Developmental psychology traces the path along which people can develop, intellectually and morally, not must develop. Kohlberg himself warns that most people never rise above Stage Four morality.[108] The problem is, then, that if children or adults are not able to work things out for themselves abstractly in terms of moral principles, what is to be done in the mean time? How are they to be taught morality prior to achieving the capacity for higher-stage reasoning? Kohlberg attacks the 'common sense' approach to morality which teaches the 'bag of virtues,' that is, a set of approved traits such as honesty, responsibility, friendliness, service, and other values, on the grounds that such teaching does not constitute either a proper understanding of morality or the ability to take what is morally right in one situation and apply it to a different situation on another occasion.[109] Developing this further, he writes:

[The 'common sense' theory behind traditional moral education takes the position that] 'everyone knows what's right and wrong,' or at least most law-abiding adults do. Adults, then, know a set of facts like 'stealing is always wrong' or 'helping others is good.' These facts may be taught on the basis of the teacher's superior knowledge and authority, just as the facts of arithmetic are taught. Not only are children ignorant of moral facts; they are weak and easily tempted to lie, cheat, fight, disobey, and so forth. Children, then, need not only to be taught moral facts; they need to be taught to practice moral behavior and habits, and to be appropriately rewarded for moral behavior and punished for yielding to temptation.[110]

If you follow Kohlberg even part way, the 'common sense' approach would be a mistake for higher-stage people. It is a constant cause of resentment for a child to be treated like an infant. It is not evident, however, that the 'common sense' approach is equally wrong, or wrong at all for those who are at the beginning of moral development. Indeed, there should be no mystery about the place of 'telling,' of punishment and reward, of repetition for one who is at the beginning. If the stages are as distinct and exclusive as Kohlberg says they are, then children who are firmly at Stage One will not yet be able to understand even Stage Two reasoning. Thus, if all they understand is authority, then it is authority that they should get. Surely this follows deductively from Kohlberg's own writings. But it also follows that a teacher who wishes to lead students up and beyond their present level, that is, who is interested in the development of the person, must find some way of taking them out of their present stage and into a higher one. Kohlberg is, in effect, issuing the warning that it is all too easy to bog down at a lower stage of teaching and rest comfortably with an authoritarian classroom where everything is neat and easy and regulations are king. The qualified teacher, however, adds to authority the beginnings of higher reasoning in an attempt to sensitize and expand the capacities of the students beyond their present limited levels. Nevertheless, to the degree to which children do not understand anything but Stage One reasoning, authority is the only language of application, even though not of theory.

MORAL DEVELOPMENT

It is not easy to grow with children, and the tendency to treat them as we remember them is great. We stereotype children just as we do adults. It is easier to tell children what to do than to bring them to see the necessity for a certain type of action themselves. A parent has this difficulty continually with 'the baby,' however old that baby may now be. We also stereotype by assuming that because a child is in grade four, he or she must be able to understand normal grade four practice. This, of course, does not follow at all, for the child may be morally (and intellectually) behind the others developmentally. The great virtue of Kohlberg's work and its related applications and materials is that it (1) gives the teacher some way of ascertaining the actual level of understanding and development that the child is at; (2) provides a means of helping the child grow and catch up, that is, by exposing the child to the level of reasoning immediately above his or her present level; and (3) gives a clear and remarkably detailed account of the stages of development which lie ahead. If Kohlberg's work could be viewed simply as a schematic guide to moral growth, down-playing the 'ideals' of the higher stages as being either completely or adequately worked out, but emphasizing the importance of 'diagnosing' where the child is in order to determine where he or she should be going, his contributions would likely be recognized as enormous. Where the contributions come to be doubted is at the Stage Four level and beyond. I will elaborate on this point in the paragraph which follows. As a final comment, however, it is important to be clear about the fact that what I have just argued puts Kohlberg in the best light and makes his position seem easily able to account for the use of authority and the content learning of the virtues at the early stages. As Peters writes, however, things are not so evident in what Kohlberg himself often appears to argue:

There is a kind of abstractness and unreality about the approach to moral education which places exclusive emphasis on the development of a rational form of morality and which considers its content unimportant, dismissing it, as Kohlberg does, as merely 'a bag of virtues.' To start with, even at an early age, children are capable of doing both themselves and others a lot of damage. Hobbes once noted a sobering feature of the human condition which is that a man can be killed by a small child while he is asleep. Also the hazards to small children in modern industrial society are innumerable. So, for reasons both of social security and self-preservation, small children must be taught a basic code which, when internalized, will regulate their behaviour to a certain extent when they are not being supervised. There is also the point that a great number of people do not develop to a rational level of morality. For obvious social reasons, therefore, if the morality of such people is to be unthinking, its content is of crucial importance.[111]

Teaching is, taking both Kohlberg and Peters into account, a schizo-phrenic activity of incredible delicacy and acute judgment. It must make certain that the 'facts' and rules are taught as the necessary components of successful living from the very beginning, but these facts and rules must not be held so firmly as to block future growth. As the child develops the capacity to go beyond the simple formulations of early instruction, matters are further complicated and analysed and their implications amplified. At a certain stage, the whole edifice becomes 'fair game' for painstaking critical examination – whether in high school or university – and then again, over and over, for a lifetime of development and understanding. Throughout this process, it is imperative to acquaint the young with the obvious inevitability that they will learn more about some of the things being taught and will come to see them in different ways as they grow and go from grade to grade. While it may be necessary to enforce your rules strictly, you do not need to claim that the entire universe has instructed you as to the accuracy of your pronouncements. It is perhaps wiser to indicate that there is more to be said about these rules and facts, but that for now they will apply. I do not see that such a stand would undermine your authority or credibility; it would only enhance it.

HABIT AND CONTENT

The disagreements over the importance of learning the virtues and acquiring good habits are made most forcibly in the context of Kohlberg's own evidence that most people never reach the higher stages. Again, it is Peters who pinpoints the problem: 'Practically speaking, since few are likely to emerge beyond Kohlberg's Stages 3 and 4, it is important that our fellow citizens should be well bedded down at one or the other of these stages. The policeman cannot always be present, and if I am lying in the gutter after being robbed it is somewhat otiose to speculate at what stage the mugger is. My regret must surely be that he had not at least got a conventional morality well instilled in him.'[112] Kohlberg need not view his stage theory as a substitute for conventional morality, but rather as a guide to its development and a warning that it must be superseded by a principled and more abstract approach which, while in general support-ing the content of traditional morality, does sometimes attack it for its insufficiency. Conventional morality is, as the division into three levels of two stages each makes explicit, nothing more than the beginning and the middle of moral development and of morality. It is certainly not the end. What is at stake in these disputes is not only the proper conception of morality but the proper way of teaching morality. Kohlberg tends to view 'the young child as a philosopher,' as the title of one of his essays suggests. Peters hopes that the child does come to this but fears that there is a considerable period of time, often extending right through adulthood, when the child is far from the philosophic and thus needs to be taught in some other manner. Indeed, the eminent contemporary philosopher Mary Warnock doubts that morality has much at all to do with the powers of philosophic reasoning. She contends that the only way that virtue can be learned is 'largely by following a good example.'[113] She goes so far as to say that ' "moral lessons," with a syllabus consisting of the discussion and analysis of hypothetical problems and their solutions, or of actual social problems, have their place, and may be valuable and stimulating. But these lessons will go no way at all towards constituting moral education in the only serious sense, that of making children morally better. This has to be done by means of the example, the interventions and the consistent and deliberate moral policy of the teachers in the school.'[114] Alas, she gives no evidence for her position, nor does she come to grips with the quite large and varied body of evidence which Kohlberg has produced to the contrary. No one can claim that 'there is no evidence that such abstract discussion has any effect on conduct,'[115] for Kohlberg himself has published consistent results demonstrating significant advancement in moral growth as a result of exposure to moral dilemmas, as compared with groups under controlled conditions. Warnock has simply avoided the hard evidence or has dismissed it. I suspect, however, that her stand is the result of a view of the teaching of virtue which simply leaves no place for philosophic discussion about morality. It is not that she has ignored Kohlberg but that, in her view, he is not talking about the teaching of morality at all but only the study of morality:

For I believe that morality is not a matter of reason, nor therefore of reasons for the existence of certain rules. Such reasons are likely to turn on the consequences of observing the code or breaking it, and on calculation of what will or might happen if the code were generally to be broken, by people as a whole. Such calculations will not, I believe, by themselves influence people's behaviour. On the contrary, morality is essentially, and not just by chance, a matter of experiencing certain common, shared sentiments. No code will be seriously embraced unless a child believes in the rules, feels that they are right, and is motivated to obedience to them by the feeling that he would be ashamed to break them. To give reasons for the rules is not enough to generate a motive to obey.[116]

Philosophers will recognize here an old yet continuing debate between Plato and Aristotle. Plato and Kohlberg maintain that 'to know the good is to do the good,' while Aristotle, Peters, and Warnock want to say that even though knowing the good is important, doing it requires something more. Moral motivation to action requires feeling of some intensity and the development of habits of character. I will not now rehearse the seemingly eternal debate about how Plato may be allowed to have accounted for these objections by mantaining that 'true' knowing includes the total mobilization of the whole person – feelings, passions, appetites, and all, as well as reason. It is sufficient for our purposes to explore the importance of feelings and habits to moral education and to reflect upon the prominence, or lack of it, which they have in Kohlberg's program.

FEELINGS AND HABITS

To my mind, one of the most distinctive features of Far Eastern philosophy is the centrality of feeling or emotion in education. While there may be less difference between the ways of thinking of East and West than is sometimes alleged, there is little doubt that our own philosophic tradition, from Aristotle onwards, and probably beginning with Socrates, placed heavy emphasis on reason, often to the exclusion of other capacities of the human being. The Chinese, by contrast, have traditionally viewed the person as a complex of capacities, only one of which was reason. Furthermore, their consideration of the person as a complex but single entity places emphasis on the harmony and development of the person as a whole, rather than on the supremacy of one of the constituent parts. Thus, they would not regard a predominance of reason over feeling as the honing of a person's rational capacity to its ultimate efficiency, as we would, but as the warping of that person resulting from the underutilization of the other capacities of the person which are equally important to the whole. For that matter, there was and is, in the Far East, less tendency to divide the person into separate and distinct functions in the first place. The person is a reasoning-feeling-willing-acting locus. To reason is not to feel, but to reason without feeling is to be but a part of a human being, like playing a one-stringed violin. It is part of the 'nurture' of the person, then, to feed his reason-power, his feeling-power, his will-power, his acting-power, and most important of all, the harmony among all of those. Not to do each of these is to warp and distort. For our purposes, then, the question becomes one of deciding whether Kohlberg pays sufficient attention to the nurture of feelings, the will, and the translation of the lot into action, leaving harmony aside. Turning to Peter's criticism of Kohlberg yet again, it is helpful to find him criticizing Kohlberg's 'Kantian' approach to morality as being a one-sided view: 'There is no probing of the motives that explain ... actions, no assessment of the intensity or level of compassion which suffuses ... dealing with others.'[117] Peters and Warnock seem agreed that students raised on Kohlberg's brand of moral education might be able to reason at Stage Six but could still act selfishly, even ruthlessly, to further a cause or themselves. Or else they might be able to articulate the requirements of higher-stage thinking with precision but care nothing at all about putting it into action. To know the good is not necessarily to do the good. As Peters puts it, 'What is the moral status of a man who can reason in an abstract way about rules if he does not care about people who are affected by his breach or observance of them?'[118] Hume's emphasis on the 'sentiment of humanity' and the subsequent 'natural virtues' is cited by Peters as *prima facie* support for the nurture of more than the capacity to reason abstractly, even about morality. Even within the domain of reason, Peters argues that there is a 'cluster' of associated passions involved without which there would be no motivation to exercise reason itself: 'I am referring not just to the passion for truth, but also to other passions which are intimately connected with it such as the abhorrence of the arbitrary, the hatred of inconsistency and irrelevance, the love of clarity and order, and, in the case of nonformal reasoning, the determination to look at the facts. These passions both provide point to theoretical enquiries and transform the pursuit of practical purposes.'[119] Peters asks how children come to care about such matters, and also about how they are brought to care about the well-being of others. Warnock answers with the example model, and Kohlberg with the reasoning model, as we have seen. Yet Kohlberg does add to this model by advocating the use of the method of playing 'moral musical chairs,' of putting yourself in the other person's shoes. It is one thing to stress intellectually that morality requires a rule to be reversible so as to be equally fair and acceptable whether you are on the giving or receiving end of it; it is another to imagine what it would be like to be the other person. Whatever can be said of the former, it is the latter stance which is more likely to make an individual clear and passionate about the consequences of a rule for the other person. The Humean 'sentiment for humanity,' Confucian 'human-heartedness' or 'loving kindness,' Christian 'love,' Buddhist 'compassion' – all these are more likely to be developed by vivid imaginative role taking than by abstract reasoning. Also, Kohlberg's emphasis on the 'moral atmosphere' of the school comes close to Warnock's teaching by example and Peters' concern for the nurture of feelings. An exemplary teacher is one who not only thinks clearly but also feels deeply and instantiates both of these in his conduct in the classroom and without. Fine teachers in the moral realm do not simply know a lot about ethics; they demonstrate this knowledge not only by thinking but also by doing the right thing, and doing it humanely. It is little wonder, then, that Peters argues for a forced reconciliation between these two tendencies in morality in our long history. The form of morality is twofold, the first consisting of rational considerations based on principles, the second of 'roles, rules and the emotional life.'[120] The action in this debate takes place on the field of understanding where the 'demands of reason and the particularized promptings of compassion' struggle for their place. Be that as it may, 'these are both elements in the form of the moral mode of experience which we have inherited.'[121] Kohlberg appears to pay too little attention to one of these 'traditions' of our civilization.

ON CARING

The earlier discussion and chart on page 71 described the increasing inclusiveness of an individual's moral sensitivity, beginning with egoistic concern at one end and moving towards concern or care for the whole cosmos at the other. Kohlberg's controversial Stage Seven is an attempt to articulate the details of this broadest moral inclusiveness. The same old problem merely reappears, however, for what needs to be explained is how one can be brought – taught – to develop a feeling of caring and compassion for all existing things in the cosmos. The issue stems from the reflection that 'it is not a logical contradiction to say that someone knows that it is wrong to cheat but has no disposition not to cheat.'[122] A child might 'know what justice is, but might not care about it overmuch.'[123] In our culture, the great example of a rational 'coldness,' devoid of the warmth of the caring emotions, is that of John Stuart Mill. Mill is recognized as one of the geniuses of history, and his fluency in Greek, Latin, and other languages and his mastery of higher mathematics and the subjects of a basic education before the age of ten remain an educational showpiece of achievement. Born in London in 1806, by 1826 he had become a writer of considerable public note and was considered, by himself as well as others, to be a reformer. In 1826, at the age of nineteen, he entered a mental depression, a 'crisis,' from which he thought he might never emerge:

I was in a dull state of nerves, such as everybody is occasionally liable to; unsusceptible to enjoyment or pleasurable excitement; one of those moods when what is pleasure at other times, becomes inspid or indifferent; the state, I should think, in which converts to Methodism usually are, when smitten by their first 'conviction of sin.' In this frame of mind it occurred to me to put the question directly to myself: 'Suppose that all your objects in life were realized; that all the changes in institutions and opinions which you are looking forward to, could be completely effected at this very instant; would this be a great joy and happiness to you?' And an irrepressible selfconsciousness distinctly answered, 'No!' At this my heart sank within me; the whole foundation on which my life was constructed fell down.[124]

Mill reflected deeply upon his situation and, finding no way out of his unfeeling state, sought its cause. With the same honesty with which he admitted his uncaringness with respect to his highest ideals dealing with the improvement of mankind, he now maintained that 'the habit of analysis has a tendency to wear away the feelings.'[125] Feelings are the 'natural complements and correctives' for reasoning. He was but partially equipped to undertake the tasks he set for himself: 'I was thus, as I said to myself, left stranded at the commencement of my voyage, with a well-equipped ship and a rudder, but no sail; without any real desire for the ends which I had been so carefully fitted out to work for; no delight in virtue, or the general good, but also just as little in anything else. The fountains of vanity and ambition seemed to have dried up within me, as completely as those of benevolence.'[126] From this point on John Stuart Mill placed emphasis on creating a balance among the needs of the developing individual and affirmed that 'the cultivation of the feelings became one of the cardinal points in my ethical and philosophical creed.'[127] Mill's affirmation does not 'prove' him to be correct, of course, but proof is not the only business of a philosophy which hopes to deal with the questions of human life which have persisted through the centuries. Myopic insight is gift enough, and Mill has called attention to the importance of teaching the young to become sensitive, caring, compassionate, dedicated, involved, and concerned human beings. Kohlberg affirms the same need, but his methodology places emphasis on the 'analysis' which Mill came to see as one-sided.

LEARNING TO CARE

Kohlberg and Plato argue that you learn to act rightly by thinking clearly, looking for increasingly adequate systems of moral judgment; at least this is the major thrust of the reasoning approach. Aristotle holds, by contrast, that morality is a way you act in the world and that your activity is brought about and made firm by practice. Like a musician or a carpenter, you get better by doing, not by thinking about playing the piano or making mitred corners: 'But the virtues we get by first exercising them, as also happens in the case of the arts as well. For the things we have to learn before we can do them, we learn by doing them, e.g. men become builders by building and lyre-players by playing the lyre; so too we become just by doing just acts, temperate by doing temperate acts, brave by doing brave acts.'[128] Then, as if having discussed the matter with Kohlberg, he warns that unless you have been well brought up (and we might add, unless you have had a solid grounding in the virtues in your early school years as well), you are unlikely to be interested in moral considerations or have any means whereby to understand why anyone should care. All knowing begins 'with things known to us,' and the starting point of morality is to have had instruction in 'good habits.'[129] Otherwise, even the 'reason' for moral concern will leave you without a starting point, unmoved and uncaring. The 'Me' generation is not simply opting for a morality of selfishness because all the others have been found less appealing or wanting; it is regularly the result of not 'seeing' the moral issue in the first place, of never getting to the starting point of morality at all. In such a cave of egoism, you have no place from which to begin your development upwards. And while it is Socratically true that no growth will be possible without causing you to doubt the adequacy of your moral perspective, it seems equally true that no progress will be made even then unless you care about (1) being reasonable and looking for a better answer and (2) interacting with other people and with the environment of which you are a part. Every teacher and every parent can envision the difficulty of starting the process of your moral development if you feel nothing when crushing a live animal or inflicting severe pain on another person. It seems unlikely that you would be merely a lower-stage thinker; more likely, you would be cruel, insensitive, or angry. If you are a sadist, you are not merely a lower-stage thinker, but a person who has come to like the wrong things or who has no capacity for feeling or empathizing with another's pain and suffering. You would most likely be unmoved by the exercise of 'moral musical chairs' and could not easily deny being a Stage One thinker – it seems quite evident that you would be wrapped up in your own world and feelings. The point is that not all Stage One thinkers are sadists, or insensitive, or otherwise oblivious to other people's suffering; you might be merely arrested at the earliest, most primitive stage of moral development – the egoistic.

It is notoriously difficult to put into practice one's noblest sentiments and ideals. It is the stuff of every sermon that we are not very successful in living up to the high standards we conceive of, even understand, and aspire to. But are we always ready for the neighbour who needs to borrow a hammer late at night or the child who needs comforting? Indeed, there are no precise moral rules for dealing with most of life's situations, for they test our whole way of being-in-the-world and come to reveal our 'style.' It is morally sufficient, you might say, to pat the child on the head and hand him a cookie; it is morally exemplary to do more, either by showing him more caring than that or by taking the time to talk with him. It is difficult to say what makes you a more loving human being, or a parent who can 'radiate' and express concern and support, or a teacher who is warm and humane. It seems to be associated with your capacity for empathizing, or projecting that empathy, or both. So it is with the other virtues as well, and with the subtle qualities of character which distinguish one person from another. In this sense, moral education and character development have to do with the whole person, and the 'whole' in question is as complex, individualistically distinctive, and subtle as anything could be. No doubt this is at the core of Mary Frances Callan's concern, when quoting from Elizabeth Simpson's work:

In spite of its broad appeal, I, as an educator, am concerned with Kohlberg's emphasis on the development of cognitive processes for achieving moral judgment maturity. I view his approach for facilitating moral maturity as limited – limited in the sense that it focuses on reasoning to the exclusion of feelings and behavior. As Elizabeth Simpson states: 'Morality is fundamentally irrational– that is, differences in even such obviously cognitive phenomena as moral reasoning and judgment derive from essential personological [i.e. uniquely personal, yet basic to an individual] structures. Moral reasoning and behavior are a function of the *person*, and not simply of his capacity to think logically or to learn concepts and norms.'[130]

STAGE SEVEN

The irony of Kohlberg's advocacy of a non-relativistic position while being repeatedly accused of out-and-out relativism has already been remarked upon. There is a further irony. In so far as Kohlberg gets lumped together with the 'moral education movement,' he is repeatedly accused of being a militant secular humanist, whereas in fact he argues again and again that while morality is not to be based on 'divine command' theory, it is often, and rightly, intimately intertwined with religion and religions.[131] The 'divine command' theorists he rejects go back to Plato's *Euthyphro*, where Euthyphro the priest argued that something is good or moral simply and precisely because God said so.[132] But this is to commit Moore's 'naturalistic fallacy' and leave open – wide open – the possibilities for doubt lingering around this position. Do we really know what God says? Are we ever wrong in our understanding of what he says? Who is to say what he says – priests, drug takers, those who speak in tongues? Even though he says it, is it a moral rule that he is exemplifying, or is he doing what is wrong in order to test us? In the latter case what he actually says would be bad, not good, even though his ultimate purposes might be seen as good (if the test is too demanding, we might all fail in anguish – is this good?). As with God speaking to Job out of the whirlwind, however, we may never be able to discern his ultimate purposes, and hence may for ever confuse the bad with the good, and so on. But for Kohlberg to be opposed to the 'divine command' theorists in religion is not to be 'humanistic' by default. Even a cursory survey of types of religiosity will reveal that the divine command theorists represent considerably less than a majority and probably form a very, very small minority.

Kohlberg describes his moral point of view as akin to a 'natural law' perspective, affirming 'that human conceptions of moral law are not the product of internalizing arbitrary and culturally relative societal norms. They are, rather, outcomes of universal human nature developing under universal aspects of the human condition, and in that sense they are "natural."'[133] We must return to this quotation in a moment, for it contains the seeds of Stage Seven, but before that it is imperative that we look at Kohlberg's theory in the light of Moore's naturalistic fallacy. Kohlberg describes his 'methodological non-relativism' as 'the doctrine that certain criteria (importantly, reversibility and universalizability) of moral reasoning or principles are universally relevant. It means that, even if there are observed cultural divergences of moral standards, there are rational principles and methods that can reconcile these divergences or lead to agreement.'[134] Basic moral principles, then, like universalizability and reversibility, are universal. Relativism has been avoided, concludes Kohlberg, for universality amongst differing cultures has been found. But in what sense has the naturalistic fallacy been avoided? Part of the meaning of the naturalistic fallacy is that any attempt to immunize a moral claim from further criticism, alteration, or eventual abandonment is hopeless and misguided. It is, for Moore, always a fallacy to try to define 'good' in terms of anything other than itself, for you can always ask 'but do they mean exactly the same thing, and are you sure?' Obviously 'good' and its definition do not mean exactly the same thing, or else the definitional elements would not help in explaining what 'good' means. That very difference leads both to additional clarification and to continuing difficulty, for in attempting to justify your claim that 'good' means something other than 'good,' you must be able to supply reasons and evidence for your claim. But since Moore has argued that all attempts at defining 'good' are wrong because they are not exactly the same in meaning as 'good,' then it remains a continuously open question whether you have shown conclusively that your definition of 'good' in terms of something else is sufficient or correct. The case is never completely closed, and the openness of the possibilities of questioning and debate is for ever threatening. In other words, it always makes sense to question the authority and the specific nature of a moral claim, theory, or principle. For Kohlberg to suggest that he can commit the fallacy and yet get away with it[135] is to miss the point of Moore's challenge. Kohlberg argues that his universal principles of morality are 'outcomes of universal human nature developing under universal aspects of the human condition, and in that sense they are "natural."'[136] Moore, of course, would have a field day with this claim, for he would undoubtedly shout that it may well be the human condition, and may be the result of such interaction, but are the moral principles so derived actually good, or simply the ones that we have come to agree upon? All manner of principles have been agreed upon over the course of human evolution, only some of which might be claimed to be 'right' or 'good,' and only then on the basis of specific theories of what constitutes moral rightness or goodness. There is no doubt that Kohlberg does commit the naturalistic fallacy, and it is clear that he does not get away with it, at least in Moore's understanding of the issues.

It is really Stage Seven that makes it possible for Kohlberg to 'get away' with committing the naturalistic fallacy, for in the light of the purposes of this highest stage (1) you have no choice but to commit the fallacy, and (2) you don't at all mind committing it. You aren't bothered because the 'facts' of universal agreement in moral principles are supported by your faith in these principles being isomorphic with the structure of (ultimate) reality itself, whether God or Nature. In Kohlberg's own words, 'The natural law assumption that we endorse, however, is not the derivation of moral principles from factual generalizations but is, rather, the assumption that there are certain shared features of the natural order as known by science or metaphysics and of the moral order as known by moral philosophy.'[137] What makes the empirically derived cross-cultural generalizations more than bare facts about evolution and raw social correspondence is their grounding in the very structure of the cosmos. A final irony emerges at this point, however, and it is one that appears to even the score a bit. For if the Kohlbergian universal principles are based on the assumption of the laws of the cosmos and our correct apprehension of them, then the same questions asked of the 'divine command' theorists can now be asked of Kohlberg: Do you really know what the laws of the universe say to you? Are you ever wrong in your understanding of what they say to you? Who is to say what they say: politicians, scholars, drug takers, those who speak in tongues? The divine command theorist seems to be no better off and no worse off than Kohlberg. And even the appeal to the rationality of Kohlberg's account is only to put off the inevitable, for surely you can ask 'What good is the appeal to reason? Reason is so limited that the laws and structure of reality are only revealed through divine instruction and/or intervention.' How you come to decide which side you are on here takes us back to the very first pages of this book. There are many, many 'sides,' not just two, and the way you decide which path to follow and how to live requires the re-creating of your whole way of life and its assumptions. R.M. Hare articulates this point as well as anyone by saying that you can keep on giving reasons only up to a point – to the point of basic assumptions. Then, if you try to get another person to understand why you say what you do and hold what you hold, you can only go back through your whole life-view again in the hopes of getting him to see things your way. If the other person still doesn't see things your way and has a different set of assumptions about life, there is nothing more that you can say.[138] What Kohlberg – and the divine command theorists, and any other theoretician of perspective or way of life – must do is take you through the reasons, facts, and assumptions, in order to make you come to 'see for yourself.' If you do come to see for yourself, then you are able to defend the position and say why you hold it. This is not to say that you must hold to it blindly and in an authoritarian manner, but only that you will hold it as the best and most justified position that you have seen. To be open to the possibility that you may be led to change your views is to admit the possibility of doubt and error; it is not to be willing and eager to abandon your view. You have done much to help and improve what myopic sight you have and are not likely to give it up in favour of blindness by any name. In fact, your willingness to question your assumptions and way of life may but serve to enliven your support for it and advocation of it.

Stage Seven takes us beyond morality to the grounding or foundations of morality itself. Stage Six justice may be universal and rationally required, but it floats on mere psychological descriptive fact and need not motivate. Universal principles are more likely to motivate if you see that they reveal the very structure of the universe itself, or of God's design. The haunting question 'Why be moral?' just never goes away if you limit yourself to morality, Kohlberg claims.[139] Religion or ethics is 'a conscious response to, and an expression of, the quest for an ultimate meaning for moral judging and acting.'[140] Religion or ethics supplies 'additional social-scientific, metaphysical or religious assumptions' necessary to help answer questions which morality itself cannot answer and to motivate you by making morality part of the meaningful whole of understanding which you call your world-view. Whatever world-view you choose, whether theistic, pantheistic, or humanistic, what is necessarily included is an intuitive or direct grasping of the meaningfulness of your life and of the worthwhileness of the whole of things, of the cosmos.[141] Once you have found 'support in reality, in nature taken as a whole or in the ground of Nature, for acting according to universal moral principles,'[142] then you are freed from the paralysis of knowing what reason requires of you but not caring about it, or knowing what reason says but doubting that it is anything more than the rumblings of intellectual indigestion. The assumptions of religion and ethics give meaning to what you do and tend to assure you that what you do is both worthwhile in the total scheme of things and in accordance with the way things really are. 'The experience of despair calls into question the fundamental worth of human activity,'[143] and the assumptions of religion place us in harmony with the order, unity, and graspable structure of the whole of which you are a part and with which you are mystically identified.[144] Whether the union or cosmic identification of the mystical experience is religious or natural, it 'results from the cognitive ability to see nature as an organized system of natural laws and to see every part of nature, including oneself, as parts of that whole.'[145] If the assumptions and attitudes of identification are present, then it becomes as evident why you do for others what you would do for yourself, for there is no difference between yourself and others. The egoistic view of Stage One has exploded and expanded to become the cosmic oneness of Stage Seven: 'Mystical experiences that are religiously significant are those in which the oneness of being is disclosed and the subject-object duality is overcome.'[146] This is 'an emotionally powerful intuitive grasp of a reality that a metaphysics can only in a limited way express conceptually.'[147] It must be 'emotionally powerful,' for it requires the intense involvement of the entire personality, dedicated to the furthering of the worthwhileness of all that is included in this embracive whole. Such involvement of the whole person in support and appreciation of the whole world of existence is often characterized as requiring a unified self in harmony with a unified and harmonious cosmos.[148] You are taken out of your ordinary bounded self and set free to float in the boundless and nourishing cosmos. Here the full flowering and integration of intellect, feeling, and will may best be observed and experienced.

THE FLY IN THE OINTMENT

What seemed most lacking in Kohlberg's six stages, namely attention to the place of feelings and the motivation to enact the rational deliberations which one is capable of making, is presented in full in Stage Seven. Yet the result seems more artificial than necessary. It is only because the first stages are primarily concerned with judgment that feeling and will are not considered centrally important. Pedagogically, the intellect, the emotions, and the will ought to be nourished all along the stages, for fear that otherwise they may be stunted or atrophied when needed. Worse yet, since so few reach the higher stages, a methodology which explains the importance of the integration of the capacities of the whole person only later on may be much too late for most to ever appreciate or encounter. The hunch you have that the higher stages must be taught, at least as models, however foggily understood, becomes critical here. If, as teacher or parent, you begin to acquaint lower-stage people with higher stages of thinking, feeling, and acting, then surely you are at least preparing them for the higher stages by keeping the vision of excellence before them as an ideal or model to emulate, however poorly and partially at first. This brings us to the last point to be considered about Stage Seven: the status of acts of supererogation (that is, acts of sacrifice 'beyond the call of duty,' and therefore not actually required by morality, even though given the highest praise and respect).

Kohlberg makes a strong case for Stage Seven not being an alternative to Stage Six thinking but a necessary addition to and support for it.[149] Justice is not abandoned but grounded and reaffirmed. To go beyond the requirements of Stage Six justice and to act out of love, or agape, is to go beyond what is morally required. 'Acts of agape cannot be demanded or expected by their recipients but are, rather, acts of grace from the standpoint of the recipient.'[150] In the captain's dilemma discussed earlier,[151] someone might volunteer to jump overboard, and this might be done out of love, much as a saint is one who has sacrificed happiness, and even life itself, in the service of others. But this 'extra' is not demanded by justice. It is over and above what justice requires of you, namely to be treated as an equal among equals, with the fairness of the principles and methods of selection not in question. Now acts of grace they may well be, but to distinguish them from what might be included in discussion of the first six stages is strange indeed. This strangeness has not been lost to Kohlberg's critics, who have noted pointedly that what he provides is a minimum morality, whereas what has enlivened religion and the ideals of society through the ages is a higher view of the moral individual who goes considerably or consistently beyond the bare minimum. In this connection, Hastings Rashdall in *The Theory of Good and Evil* offers a distinction between the requirements of duty and the 'claims of a more abounding charity.'[152] Acts of supererogation are acts in which one does more than duty requires in the ordinary or minimal sense of 'duty.' It is always a person's duty to act in ways most 'conducive to the general Well-being.'[153] Duties are termed 'absolute' when they refer to 'rules of conduct which the general Well-being requires to be observed by all men under given external circumstances, irrespectively of the subjective condition or character of the agent.'[154] For many people, however, morality does involve consideration of character as well. Even Kohlberg admits that considerations of 'ethics' and not just of morality require that one consider the ideal, unified, harmonious self.[155] Thus, a consideration of all the relevant circumstances of an action and its actor includes internal as well as external circumstances. Internal circumstances include the specific moral (ethical), religious, emotional, and intellectual qualities of the moral agent. Rashdall concludes that acts of supererogation are not required of everybody and certainly not of everybody equally, but because of the specifics of character and vocation, they may be nonetheless required. 'Acts or omissions which the general good only requires under certain *internal* circumstances or subjective conditions may be termed *duties of Vocation*.'[156] In social periods where the minimum is advocated as being all that morality requires, the moral ideal has been reduced for 'all men to one of mere respectability, and tended to discourage acts or careers of exceptional self-denial and devotion.'[157] Kohlberg is to be commended for dealing with the question of supererogation in ethics, a subject not often discussed in formal ethical theory in contemporary debates. The problem is, however, that it appears to come to his system as an afterthought, as a final stage which includes material that can't be handled elsewhere in his system.

It is worth repeating that the reason why Stage Seven may seem to be a tag-on at the end of the system is that it was left out of the system all along but should not have been. If the issue of moral idealism is part of morality, then to redefine morality and ethics so that the latter does include supererogatory acts while the former does not is both arbitrary and revealing. A dictionary will not confirm that Kohlberg's distinction between morality and ethics is either served by precedent or well accepted in the discipline. The distinction is his, and so the defence must be his, and his alone. I am suggesting that it is an announced distinction, not a well supported one, and that what it reveals is an attempt at the end of a systematic analysis of a field to include what was left out but should have been included from the very beginning.

STAGE SEVEN NOT A 'STAGE'

It is only by excluding the material of Stage Seven in his theory of the six stages that the material may be seen to be a seventh stage, a separate stage, at all. Consider the following as evidence for my position. A child at Stage Three of moral development who abides by the biddings of peer-group pressure risks her life to save a friend. When asked why she did so, she continues to reply that she did not want to be without her friend and so couldn't let her die, and that she would not be able to face her parents and her church friends had she not attempted to save her. Whatever her announced reasons, she performed an act of supererogation by risking her own life and so would be judged a heroine in most societies. She did so not because of any metaphysical theory, or because she saw the distinction between morality and the further duties of ethics, or even because she grasped the foundations of the teaching of her church. She did so because she had a robust conscience or awareness of her own requirements, because she was able to identify with or even love her friend, and because she had come to accept the higher ideals of the teachings of her church. Even loving her friend dearly might have been enough to 'explain' why she did what she did. This is not Stage Seven 'thinking.' She might have acted simply because her parents, her friends, and her rigid church had all impressed on her that not to go beyond the call of duty in such cases was to fail utterly, to be condemned to eternal Hell and to 'sin' so badly as to be unworthy of continued association with her compatriots. Such a position may be a caricature, but it might well, as in the present example, achieve the grasping of an ideal and provide the motivation for performing an act of supererogation. Stage Seven may be that stage at which the reasons for and justification of one's entire religious, moral, and ethical position become conscious, that is, both clear and articulated, but the ingredients of such philosophical system-building have, by necessity, been there all along.

In chapter 1, discussion of R.M. Hare's work led to the view that all conscious selection displays preferentiality and that all preferentiality demonstrates a perspective, a point of view, a web-of-meaning, a way of life, an assumption or two without which it would be impossible to pick out anything from the infinitely rich source of information provided by and through experience. Surely it is one of the tasks of philosophy to point out that even at the more primitive levels of human understanding the so-called 'common sense' and presumably 'given' facts about the world are selections resulting from assumptions, usually unquestioned, about the world, the self, and the nature and status of the experience given. Philosophical and scientific talk of 'straight sticks apparently bent in water' and 'sounds in the woods with no one around to hear' are meant to challenge the common sense view. Similarly, to speak of the earlier stages of moral development is to imply a perspectival context, that is, a system of assumptions and principles by which you select and perceive the world, others, and yourself. This is a philosophy of life, a metaphysical system, however ragged and simplistic. Egoism is a perspective based on assumptions or principles of selection and producing a particular view on the world. All stages, then, have Stage-Seven-like components, but these components are rarely sufficient for mature analysis; they are regularly implicit rather than explicit and often unsystematic and incomplete. In a way, to bring morality into education is to embark upon the quite typical philosophical task of investigating and clarifying the assumptions, beliefs, and principles of competing ways of life and views of the world. Generally you are able to leave behind a rather impressive collection of inadequacies, clichés, and unexamined commonplaces which heretofore had stood firm. But there comes a time when what is left is a range of well-argued-for positions all of which are worth listening to, and from among which you will have to choose a 'preferable' view by means of which to order and understand your place in the world. It is even possible syncretistically, that is, by conflation, to choose aspects and ingredients from several of these 'great' traditions. It is less than apparent to me, however, that because Stage Seven thinking appears to Kohlberg to be Spinozistic, or Teilhardian, or mystical in some defined sense, it is not also Confucian (a far more legalistic and tradition-oriented view), or more typically Christian (or religiously orthodox), or Marxian and therefore avowedly anti-religious humanistic, or typified by the fundamentalism of contemporary Islamic orthodoxy. In other words, if Stage Seven provides the context, broader justification for, and widest understanding of the place of morality and man in the cosmos, then any metaphysical, religious, and broadly philosophical system may be employed. Not all systems are equally sound or acceptable. Some systems are simplistic, easily caught in contradictions, militantly irrational, and sometimes even 'immoral' from the perspective of even Stage Two morality. These and all other candidate systems must be judged in part by the requirements of whatever moral perspective has emerged, and be rejected if found wanting. But if the moral requirements are in place, and the tradition or perspective is the product of the wisdom of time and clear thinking, then there is probably no conclusive place to stand from which to make final pronouncements as to which view is the right and final one. To ask which is right and final is to demand 20/20 vision, in which case there would probably not be the need for such a long analysis, or even for such a long chapter in the first place. Philosophical questions do not usually get resolved, but they serve as catalysts for inquiry of the kind which, if sustained with care and concern for one's own integrity and the well-being of others, including other creatures and things, may well lead to ideals of living, loving, and acting which equal and even surpass the myopias thus far attained by mortals. Indeed, there is no conclusive evidence that human nature is a completed process. But that is the subject of the next chapter.

3

Paralysis and choice

There is a possible negative consequence to cognitive and moral myopia; if you regard your answers to vital questions as tentative, that is, less than absolute and final, then unfortunately you may become indecisive, wishy-washy, or even volitionally paralysed. If your best answers can only be seen myopically, and if the most you can achieve is a temporary moral resting place soon to be demolished by more information or by a competing position, then perhaps it would be better to forget the whole exercise and just live intuitively. This is the alternative solution proposed by the existentialists. More than any other philosophical movement in this century, existentialism has identified the need to mobilize yourself in aid of whatever values and objectives you have chosen. Unlike the positive appraisal given above, the existential criticism of myopia has been steadfast in maintaining that one form of myopia is like another, and that the only way to avoid paralysis is to make a decision, to choose the kind of person you wish to be and the kind of world you want, and to work steadfastly towards creating them. The existentialist emphasis is on choice, responsibility, and unflagging determination. While it is true that most existentialists would have little sympathy for the myopic vision here maintained, or for Kohlberg's theory of the nature of human development as a norm for human growth, nonetheless their latter positions are strengthened by the insight gained through their emphasis on choice, will, responsibility, and overcoming despair. But even if that were not the case, the force of the existential tradition in this century makes us 'confront' the criticisms of traditional philosophy and attempt to relate existentialism to education. To whatever degree educational theories embrace existentialist views, I contend that the encounter will prove highly provocative, in terms of both what is accepted and what is jettisoned or attacked.

One major emphasis of the last chapter can serve well as the opening emphasis for this one: moral philosophy, like living itself, concerns your whole person and your chosen way of life. Reason is not the sole constituent of decision making and human character; in fact, for many of the existentialists it is the weakest of our assets and possibly even a significant liability.

My purpose in this chapter is not to present existentialism for acceptance or rejection. Rather, I will concentrate on factors considered within the existentialist tradition which may prove illuminating in the 'myopic' educational philosophy here presented, and perhaps in the philosophy of education in general. I will begin with a brief overview of existentialism, if only to warn you that the tradition is so much less than a seamless web that it may be inappropriate to term it a 'tradition' at all. Many of the so-called existentialists have denied the appropriateness of this designation for themselves, but the label continues to be applied. However, such resistance to a label within the 'school' makes it apparent that an easy and all-encompassing account will be difficult. 'Existentialism' is, nevertheless, a term which has been used to encompass religious, non-religious, and anti-religious thinkers, Christians and Jews, and is applied without even the slightest blush to Shakespeare and the Book of Job.

Existentialists generally affirm a non-rational dimension to philosophy and stress concrete experience rather than abstract speculation. They are apt to emphasize your subjective discovery of your own self rather than an objectivity of self that identifies traits shared by all or most individuals. Rather, you are urged to find your own moral path and goals in life. At the same time, the world of nature and society itself is said to hold no answers to cling to but only confusion or even absurdity. 'Absurdity' is almost a preoccupation among existentialist writers. For quite different reasons, it is also a key notion in the vocabulary of the sceptics and scoffers who reject the search for standards and find no ground for moral firmness, and for Kohlberg's Stage Four-and-a-half (see page 205 below) individuals who, as part of their movement from the conventional morality of Stage Four to the post-conventional Stage Five, appear to regress to earlier ways of thinking. The rebelliousness of teenagers, the seemingly destructive criticism of sophomoric university students who call all things into question, doubt the wisdom of the 'establishment,' and view all authority and guidance as the exercise of totalitarian power – these attitudes seem to be a common prolegomenon to their 'seeing' the compulsiveness of the universal and reversible characteristics of the higher stages.[1] It is as though you have to live with absurdity and go through it in order to rise up and see Stage Four as inadequate and Stage Five or Six as more adequate. What is at issue here is not whether to accept Kohlberg's account of this stage transition, but whether to recognize the absurdity of man-made laws, moral cliches, or a 'bag' of virtues in general. It is not my point that existentialists are somehow 'stuck' at Stage Four-and-a-half, for that would be to assume that the Kohlbergian system was itself able to fix the norms of morality beyond most disputes. I have attempted to concentrate on Kohlberg's powerful myopia, not his alleged 'absolutism' of rigid stage definitions. I have given reasons to suppose that Stage Six is not clearly better than Stage Five, and have entertained the possibility that, for some well-argued positions and for people at the lower stages of moral and intellectual development, a Stage Four morality may be all we need to keep us from each other's throats. Moral philosophy as an abstract discipline or influence comes much later in the school career than do those teachings, shared lessons, and hidden influences geared to stimulate you to consider with passionate concern the pros and cons of your possible alternative actions. What the existentialists add to moral philosophy is not merely the insight that you accept your experience of absurdity but the total analysis of the human situation which affirms that you accept (not rationalize or explain away) absurdity as experienced (not conceptualized), and that you see this experience of absurdity as a platform for moral growth. As a person at Stage Four, you are in rebellious despair because of absurdity, while as an existentialist you are coming to discover your own authentic way of being moral because of that same absuridity. You can make absurdity a positive insight and not just a negative or destructive reaction against the 'lies' of those in authority.

As if to underscore further the existence of competing myopic views, there are both religious and atheistic existentialists. Both wings of the school agree that you are in a desperate situation as rational man. You have been thrown into an uncharted world with a reasoning capacity that adds as much confusion as it resolves, and a nature which is largely only potential and hence not a standard for the living of your life. The extent to which you agree with others as much as you do is more likely the result of brainwashing or the early development of habits and the putting on of blinkers than an expression of the stages through which you must have passed in your development. The real questions have to do not with how customary life goes on but with what you find when you re-examine the wisdom and laws of your society, culture, and traditions and the assumptions about yourself. The religious existentialists generally affirm that, while God alone can help you, a finite human being, out of this desperate situation, the matter is one for each of you to settle with the God of your choice. Even then, the act is one of faith or individual will and not one of reason or natural inclination. In short, since there is no hope without God, you must believe in order to hope, even though there may be no ground in reason or nature for that belief. Sören Kierkegaard said that you believe precisely because it is absurd to do so and hopeless not to.[2] Nietzsche, by contrast, announced the 'death of God' and placed the point of belief within you, who are endowed with the god-like power of creating your own values, moral dicta, social structures, and even laws of reason.[3] He represents the atheistic existentialists, who find it unnecessary to posit a God to help man beyond the abyss of absurdity. Either way, existentialism is the philosophy of the individual as free agent wandering alone in an unknown and often unsympathetic universe, an agent whose powers of reasoning not only are insufficient to chart a way to a suitable clearing but tend only to further entangle the branches and tendrils through which he is walking. Reason leads us from the toil of farming to the use of toxic chemicals as fertilizers, insecticides, additives, and preservatives in the embalmed produce which reaches the market; from spears for defence to Neutron bombs – the story is familiar. You will note that the existentialist is attacking the claims of 20/20 vision in particular, although he would also claim cynically that myopia is but another name for 'blindness' dressed up to give the appearance of sight – a pair of glasses without eyes.

PHILOSOPHY AND REASON

Only in modern times has Western philosophy insisted that it is exclusively the science of reason. Earlier, philosophy was variously conceived as the handmaiden of religion or the systematic exposition of a way of life and not just as a way of thinking. Plato patiently led his students to a realization of their own innate knowledge and included in his concept of wisdom both the right moral and aesthetic feelings and the socio-political commitment to return to the cave to the aid of those still living in shadows. With philosophy you knew how to live, love, and die. One of the leading interpreters of the existentialist movement, William Barrett, has written that existentialism has more in common with the

Oriental philosophies than with most Western ones, at least in so far as it requires commitment and relevance to the whole of human living, and to the whole person, rather than simply to human intellectual life: 'Even today the motive for an Oriental's taking up the study of philosophy is altogether different from that of a Western student: for the Oriental the only reason for bothering with philosophy is to find release or peace from the torments and perplexities of life.'[4] Philosophy must not be abstract and impractical; as Kierkegaard put it, it must not be like a great castle that reaches to the sky while, in reality, the creator of that magnificent edifice lives next door in the humblest of shanties.[5] The point of comparing the many philosophies of the past with castles you couldn't really live in is that they actually divorce humanity from reality – your reality and that of the universe – by claiming certainty where there is nothing more than assumption. These certainties are then imposed with the authority of law and of sacred and binding moral imperatives, clamping human beings fast to an unchanging view of themselves and their world. The turning of assumptions and hypotheses into necessary truths is a fabrication that leaves you trying to live that illusion, trying to conform yourself and your way of life to the 'model,' however poor the fit, and however sincere your insights to the contrary. You are left poverty stricken in the more realistic shanty of failure and anguish, frustration and hopelessness. This difficulty is the result of a fundamental misconception. The nature of humanity and the world is viewed as fixed and discoverable; in truth, argue the existentialists, humanity and the world are in dynamic flux, constantly being made and remade, not discovered.[6] Human nature can change, and it does; not only can the world and its laws change, but they do. Attempting to tie down the world with your understanding, you find your 'laws' and proven facts crumble regularly with the changes and discoveries in the laboratories and the market-places, from year to year and century to century. The nature of humanity is to become, that is, to actualize an indefinite potentiality. You are what you are not because you had to be but because you chose to become (or perhaps became by habit) who you are, in the kind of world you have been taught to see. Yet your nature is not just your present actuality but an indefinite possibility of becoming something else, of becoming other than you are now. Your true nature is not your present being, but your capacity to continually become. Humanity is not that which is at the moment or has been up until now: it is what its constituent members will choose to become, individually and collectively. Mankind's essence is always becoming, not any fixed and confining nature or ideal way of being a man or woman. This last claim might well, if adopted uncritically, prove a nightmare for a moral educator who wanted to do more than passively nod his head at the self-discoveries of his charges; but it is not a nightmare for one who wishes to use existential analysis for more senior students, who might wish to augment their own perception of the moral point of view with insights into the place of the will, of choice, and of responsibility in moral thought and practice. When viewed simply as a call for openness in moral inquiry, the existentialist warning is not that a rational or informed morality is impossible, but that any other morality ought to be viewed as a becoming, resulting from an exchange of one myopia (rational or moral) for a better one, on the basis of the evidence given.

THE CENTRALITY OF CHOICE

The all-important decision is: who or what do you wish to become? You must choose your project – that range of aspirations, values, likes and dislikes, abilities, fears, and hopes that makes you decide how you will live. How you live determines who you are. For you are what you do, and what you do is ultimately determined by your project, and your project is not predetermined or necessarily thrust upon you but chosen. It may be that most people simply accept becoming who they are expected to become, but that, too, is the result of a choice not to choose for themselves. Merely to affirm that God made us with certain innate and necessary traits is to deny our nature as becoming, our freedom, our potential. To speak of the necessity of history is to turn human beings into objects, like sticks and stones, instead of developing agents who are capable of choosing and projecting their own natures and futures. Most of us simply flow with the crowds, with expectations, custom, the majority mores and morality of the time, and in so doing abandon our freedom to choose for ourselves except in choosing not to choose for ourselves.

How did the misconception arise that our nature is fixed rather than dynamically in process? It grew out of theological and rationalistic assumptions about the orderliness of nature and principles of human nature as provided by a divine architect and made evident to you through revelation or reason itself. Nature as a whole is an open book which our innate reason is capable of understanding and which is governed by fixed and immutable laws. Scientific understanding is progressive, and the only limits to complete understanding of nature, both the world's and our own, are time and human ingenuity. What grounds do you have for accepting such a view of man? On the negative side, it was Nietzsche who announced that 'God is dead.' In itself, of course, this statement simply matches the corresponding theological assertion that God is our creator and sustainer. Lying behind Nietzsche's outrageous and startling proclamation, however, is a theory of human knowledge and its limitations.

THE LIMITS OF REASON

In order to claim with justification that reason does in fact lead to correct information about things, you must show, first, that reason does not distort what it apprehends and, second, that convincing evidence shows a one-to-one correspondence between what appears to be the case and what is in fact the case. We can only know what we know in the way that we know it, and thus we can never show by some other standard or means that things are in fact the way they appear to us to be. We are trapped within appearances; at best, we can only assume that the way things appear to us is the way they really are. The assumption, however, is unjustified; it is akin to shouting that God exists. What proof is there? For Nietzsche, definitive rational or empirical evidence cannot be given either way. Instead, the argument rages on through the ages. Furthermore, there is convincing evidence that what comes to you through your senses and intellect is not passively received, but rather actively interpreted and even distorted. You can be deceived by your senses, see the world differently under the influence of drugs or illness, conceive alternative geometries to tantalize your mind, and reach a stalemate about which moral perspective is the correct one. From such instances you could easily reach the conclusion that the prime object of human inquiry is not the external world at all but the internal world which conceives of the world as a whole and seeks to organize it by its own created laws and principles. The prime object of human inquiry is humanity itself, and reason can only yield objective knowledge within the limits of agreed-upon premises and within consciousness. You can argue that the laws of reason are intuitively certain and evident, that is, axiomatic. What this assertion really comes down to is that you have come to hold them and nothing that anyone says will make you give them up, for they are the starting points and the foundation for all further evidence. This being so, no evidence can be given in direct support of them. This argument is not quite candid, however, for in order to be able to talk and reason after affirming axioms, you must have the starting points of axioms, postulates, and certain rules of language and logic if you are to understand and be understood. But Nietzsche's primary target was the purveyor of supposed 20/20 vision who argued that because you presented axioms, apodictic scientific laws, and firm moral and religious teachings, it was because these things were bright and clear, thanks to God, or the power of reason, or both. Nietzsche's argument is that these rules tell you what you must do in order to communicate and understand an otherwise chaotic body of experience and mental activity rather than what reality is like in itself. You are studying and classifying how you in fact organize what you are aware of. You are not thereby studying the world as it is in itself, or your own fixed and immutable nature. You are studying the view, the world as you have come to see it, and you have come to see it this way because of a view of yourself which, while originally chosen and projected, is now second nature and apparently fixed. Your view, that is, your way of looking at the world, of thinking, of organizing, is a complex habit, often helpful, but equally often blinding. Your view causes you to distort your thinking and your experience, your hopes and desires, your way of perceiving and treating people, making the whole set of attitudes little more than a sophisticated reflex action. It is mere conjecture to suppose that your habits and organizational patterns yield knowledge of reality-in-itself – a conjecture built into your presuppositions to give them clout.

ON SCEPTICISM

Even for the existentialist, the point of the foregoing is not to create a pernicious scepticism or to paralyse; rather, it is to show that reason has not necessarily led to correct views about things but is itself employed by human choice in achieving answers to questions. What is important is not that you discover what you really are or what the universe is really like, but that you decide how you will live, what you would like to become, what you will explore, and what principles you will apply in your ruminations about, and interaction with, others and the world. All knowledge is value-laden and expresses human preference. It does not follow from this that one preference is no better or worse than any other, although Nietzsche and the existentialists often seem to be pushing for such relativism. In general, though, the aim seems to be to break the power of rational assumption and the hold of the doctrine of a fixed human nature in order to free you to reflect anew upon your own deep hopes and aspirations and upon the principles by means of which you come to organize your world and yourself. In the process of doing this, what is most evident is that an often underemphasized aspect of all knowing is the actual willing or choosing of a framework for such knowledge. What is central in all knowing and doing is what is central in all feeling and willing – your own principles and perspectives, your web of meaning.

THE SELF

This centrality of perspective or view is just what the existentialists wish to claim. The question 'What is the self?' is not to be answered intellectually but to be lived. The answer cannot come in any other way, because the real significance of the question is not what the meaning of life is but what the meaning of life will be. Furthermore, it is not a question about human life in general but about some particular life – my life or your life, for instance. The meaning of a life does not pre-exist but must be created, chosen, and then continuously re-created, again and again. You must find this meaning or project for yourself alone. The meaning of a life is not to be thought about merely in the abstract, is not the same for you as for me, is not a question to be answered the same in the present as in the past, let alone the future. Similarly the question 'How should I live?' is not to be answered by thinking, by using your intellect to discover immutable and self-evident principles, but by living, by becoming passionately involved in life rather than existing passively. Your essence does not come before your existence. You are not born a baby adult who slowly comes to discover what you are from birth. Instead you come into the world with nothing predetermined before conception, and very little afterwards except some physical and character traits. You have no fixed end or purpose, no absolutely fixed character or program of personality development. Your essence consists of the way you choose or project your existence, and not the other way around. Your essence is not given but comes to be made, that is, is created as you exist. Your final essence is determined only at and by the moment of your death, for then no further project is possible for you – you become who you have been. But as long as you can affirm a project anew, you are not who you have been but who you will become.

The existentialist emphasis on freedom can now be understood as resulting from your entry into a universe of uncharted mystery and surprise, with nothing to turn to except a partially effective capacity for reasoning and a will of enormous power but without much instinctive direction or guidance. But what you do in your encounter with the wilderness is your own responsibility for all of that. You are the one responsible for what you have become – not God, or nature, or mother, or society, or anyone or anything else – for all these influences can be shrugged off if you choose to do so. It is up to you to decide what your project will be. Of course most of you put off deciding and flow comfortably with the crowd, with the prevailing opinion, with the approved and the established.[7] Certainly you are free to do so. You are always equally free to abandon the easy route and choose one of your own. The choice is yours, as is the responsibility. This individualistic approach is enticing and no doubt serves as an important antidote to the mass philosophies that surround you on all sides. Yet radical freedom and the resulting extreme degree of responsibility has its price, the first ingredient in which is anguish and despair, the second scepticism, and the final 'giving up' might well be as drastic as suicide. How are you to decide what to become? To glory in your freedom is possible if, and only if, you can find some clear way of exercising it profitably or correctly. Such operational standards have been abandoned, it would seem, and so you are left to decide, without guidance, what is profitable, moral, and worthy. You are forced to choose, but what you choose is less important than the fact that you choose. This awful realization – that choices are made while you teeter on the edge of a midnight-dark abyss – results in despair, hopelessness, and meaninglessness. You are incapable of answering the questions you ask, except by choosing, but the choice is blind. Your choices, however, are grounded in your project, which itself is grounded only in your life and dangles by the tiniest thread of hope that the choices will prove to be the right ones for you in particular circumstances, even though you cannot know this beforehand and may not even be able to recognize it as such afterwards.

THE WORLD IS DENSE

The second ingredient in the high cost of freedom is the apparent incomprehensibility of the world. The natural world appears dense, even alien – and certainly unhelpful – rather than hospitable and inviting. You are simply thrown into a world at birth without any innate guidance to fit the puzzles and problems of life which appear constant and lethal. As José Ortega y Gasset describes the situation, hope seems unlikely:

Without our previous comments, we are shipwrecked in a world we neither built nor thought about. We did not give ourselves life, but we find it at the very moment when we find ourselves. Anyone carried asleep to the wings of a theatre, and then thrust suddenly and awake before the foot-lights and the public, would be struck by a similar flash of illumination. When he finds himself there, what is it that he finds? Without knowing how or why he got there, he finds himself plunged into a situation which is difficult; the difficult situation demands that he comport himself decently in the public appearance which he neither sought, foresaw, nor prepared. Fundamentally, life is always unforeseen. No one announced our appearance before we stepped onto its stage – an always concrete and definite stage – no one prepared us for it.[8]

And no one could have prepared you for your existence. Codes of behaviour, social norms, laws, religions, and science are all myths designed to give you something to grasp as you are dashed to and fro by life's currents. Or they are anaesthetics designed to numb you to the horrible abyss of nothingness that stands for ever before you. Either way, they do not really make your lot intelligible or the world understandable. That can only be done by each of you individually, using whatever guidance you can muster from within and by choosing, by sheer will, a path in the dark wilderness of dense underbrush for which you are willing to take total responsibility. Such hopeless, blind choice is the existential predicament of the human situation. How, then, can you decide what is morally right or wrong in particular situations?

CONCRETE MODELS

If you require that existentialism provide crisp principles for valid ethical decision making, you miss the point. You must speak of a real individual's choice, perhaps your own, and not about abstract people in abstract situations confronting semi-human stereotypes. To suggest what you should do is to go too far and hide the personal, involved, highly responsible, and ultimately free choice that any authentic decision requires. What you can do, however, is point out those conditions under which authentic selfhood may be expressed and responsible choices made. No doubt this explains, in part, why the philosophical novel is chosen as the medium by which to convey much existential thought. Reading about an individual embedded in a particular situation forces you to enter into the anguish and strain of decision making and to understand, if not to share, responsibility for the results. The novel does for the reader what the method of dialogue does for the participant; it forces you to take part in the proceedings. In general, you are not handed a correct answer but are made aware of several non-authentic solutions that are commonly accepted as being moral. The ethical models are put forward as being worthy of emulation in spirit, not necessarily in deed. Models will vary with those involved and with circumstantial differences. It is the strength and the quality of character displayed which is the constant. Yet how are you to act ethically when held in the vice-grip of ambiguity and paradox? On what basis are you to choose values among the countless varieties discerned, now and in the past? All hope of finding answers to these questions vanishes unless you distinguish between the existential analysis of the human situation and its solutions. Recall Job, sitting on his dung heap, his family and fortune, reputation and confidence stripped away. What remained was a pathetic old man, with running sores covering his exposed body, who retained enough 'self' and deep subjectivity to shout at the universe and at his God that he was innocent, as righteous as he knew how to be, and willing to confront God, in whom he steadfastly believed, face to face, in order to plead his own case. Had he been allowed to plead his case before God, he would have asked two questions: 'Why do I suffer when I have done nothing to deserve it?' and 'Why does anyone suffer?' These questions about evil seem to reduce to the issue of disorder or chaos. In a world created by a just and good God, how can suffering fall upon the innocent and the young? Why are fortune and health so indiscriminately apportioned that the good often perish while those judged by human standards to be evil thrive and continue to inflict injustice and suffering on so many?

This analysis is clear. You live in a world whose wheels appear to grind inexorably and indiscriminately fine or coarse. The laws of human beings are not always upheld but are frequently dashed by the workings of time. Job is the symbol. He sits and suffers and, by human standards, is innocent. Of course, reading the Book of Job, you know perfectly well that Job is innocent, but you also know about the wager between God and Satan that requires Job's righteousness and steadfastness to be tested. This is absurd. If you were to maintain belief in a God who would kill and maim in order to test one of his 'children,' rational understanding of your place in the cosmos would henceforth be impossible. The solution offered in the Book of Job is to place your trust in God, whose wisdom alone can create order out of apparent disorder. Human understanding is always so limited as to be like trying to solve a puzzle with many of the parts missing. Indeed, when God does speak to Job from out of the whirlwind (from chapter 38 on), he reminds him that since Job knows nothing of creation, was not present when the foundations of the world were laid down, and is unable to account for the presence of the seemingly ugly and unnecessary behemoth and leviathan, he is certainly not going to be able to sort out or answer questions of righteousness, justice, personal worth, and the role of suffering in the world. It may only be a test, but only God can know that. Your only hope is to give up false hope and pride and turn to the only source of correct answers. You can know only if God tells you, and he will tell you only if you turn to him in faith.

THE PERSON

The most human scenes of the Book of Job concern the attempts of others to comfort Job in his agony. The central insight is that comfort can be given only if you reach for the sufferer as a person and not as 'guilty' or 'evil.' Thou-ness, or the accepting of the other person for what he or she is, is non-judgmental, at least in so far as you abandon the easy categorization or stereotyping of another in favour of direct contact with a self every bit as unique as your own and just as worthwhile. You are required to sympathetically enter the perspective and outlook of the other person in order to understand his or her feelings, fears, hopes, project, and centre of being. The existentialist stress on individuality and solitary choice is not meant simply as a pointer to your own ultimate isolation as decision-maker but as an indicator of the profound depth in and the requirement of responsibility as applied to every individual. The inner core is unique and inviolable, but it may be freely given, as it is when you treat another as unique and ultimately worthy (potentially, at least). Ortega makes this point with great power when he describes a scene by the bedside of a great and dying man.[9] Four people are present – wife, doctor, reporter, and painter – but only the wife sees the dying man as the unique and worthy self with whom she has been identified through the give and take of their life together. Using 'emotional distance' as one possible yardstick for measuring this solidarity, Ortega writes: 'For the wife of the dying man, the distance shrinks to almost nothing. What is happening so tortures her soul and absorbs her mind that it becomes one with her person ... A thing can be seen, an event can be observed, only when we have separated it from ourselves and it has ceased to form a living part of our being. Thus the wife is not present at the scene, she is in it. She does not behold it, she "lives" it.'[10] Here the emphasis is on the knowledge of the other person which is gained subjectively, not objectively; by feeling, not reason; through identification, not distancing (that is, stepping back to get a less emotional perspective). Empathetic imagination has taken the place of rational rules. Intimacy has overridden law and authority. And while you may not have yet wrestled with the relationship amongst these ingredients to see whether they might all be able to have a place in morality, the existentialist is pointing out that subjectivity, intimacy, appreciation of uniqueness, empathetic identification, and the capacity to feel, to choose, and to remain steadfastly responsible for your own thoughts and actions are regularly undermined by dependence on law, authority, regulation, concern for the consequences of your actions at the expense of the tone or spirit of your actions, and the easy excuse available to one who on psychological grounds simply is not to be blamed for what he or she has done. The inside of morality can wither and die, leaving only the external shell to wear you down to uniform size and texture.

ETHICS AND RELIGION

The religious solution is one solution to the human predicament but it is not the only one. As will be recalled, within existentialism there are two schools, the religious and the atheistic or non-religious. Speculatively, the Book of Job might have ended without God's appearance in the whirlwind, with mighty Job reduced to oozing sores, sitting on a dung heap challenging a hypothetical God to make sense of his plight. Referring to or implying a cosmic silence following Job's protest would have been no less a theological statement by the writer of Job, but his stance would then be humanistic. While humanism need not be atheistic, and indeed during the Renaissance and Reformation periods was decidedly not, the humanism of the present century has often denied any significance to traditional religion and has made human capacity the measure of value. Nietzsche and Jean-Paul Sartre are two of the leading figures in the history of this anti-religious human-centred humanism. The announcement made in the silent space where the whirlwind might have been is that 'God is dead' or that there never was a God. The theological orientation of humanism is directly the result of having to overthrow theology in order to make room for the development of human capacity. Does God answer you as Job? Or is there just silence? That is left to you to decide. But that there are Jobs who suffer tragically is plainly evident in our own century in Nazi Germany, the napalmed forests of Vietnam, and Idi Amin's Uganda. One of the great insights of existentialism is that moral matters are a concern of primary importance whether or not one is religious. There is no doubt that religions have been major sources of moral concern and insight, but the openly atheistic or non-religious stand of some existentialists makes it equally evident that a concern for ethics is not diminished one iota when you are left on your own. Indeed, it has been argued by thinkers from Plato to the present day that it is of fundamental importance to get clear about the foundations of ethics, apart from its religious entanglements and supports, as a necessary step in clarifying and justifying your moral stance. Plato, in the *Euthyphro*, asks whether something is pious, or, in our context, good, simply because God says so, or whether God says that something is good because it is good.[11] As Kai Nielsen and A.C. Ewing have pointed out, if something is held to be good simply because God wills it and for that reason alone, then the claim that in willing it God also confers goodness upon it has no basis. Rather, the appropriate conclusion is simply that 'God wills it because God wills it,' and this is to add nothing in fact to recognition of God's having willed something in the first place.[12] You may still ask whether what God wills is good as well as God-willed, here used only of a thing 'willed by God' (including anything 'commanded by God'), not of a person 'having a will like God's.' To the extent to which you can answer that question you have an independent and separate standard for determining what things are good, quite apart from which things are willed by God. And it is not enough to say that because God is himself perfect goodness, then whatever he wills must be good, for unless you already had a meaning for goodness apart from Godlike or God-willed, it would be circular to say that God is himself good; you could only affirm that God is Godly[13] or has Godliness. It is necessary, then, for an independent content or meaning for goodness to be maintained for there to be any meaning to the claim 'God is good.' Otherwise, all that one has said is 'God is Godly, namely, Godlike or God-willed,' or 'God has the quality of himself and what he wills.' Nor can it be claimed that it is the case that 'God is good' is an analytic truth, one that can be got completely by definition. Nielsen provides the following example to make the point: 'Jane says to Betsy, after Betsy helps an old lady across the street, "that was good of you." "That was good of you" most certainly does not mean "that was God [Godly in our terms] of you." '[14] Nielsen concludes that 'God is good' is for him a 'truth of language,' that is, a partially defining characteristic of God which must have a meaning arrived at independently of God and then applied to God, whether as the perfect being, or whatever.[15] 'We could have no understanding of the truth of "God is good" or of the concept God unless we had an independent understanding of goodness.'[16] And if one of the things that we mean by God is that God is good, then in order to use 'God' correctly we must already understand how to use the word 'good.' Therefore, an 'understanding of goodness is logically prior to, and is independent of, any understanding or acknowledgement of God.'[17] Of course it may be easier, even safer, to turn to God's authority in deciding what ought to be done morally, but your understanding of the goodness of God's commands as good is logically prior to your understanding that they are God's commands. And in answering a query about why God's will is taken to be good, you could and should refer to the criterion of goodness by means of which God's goodness is determined and then affirmed.

If you continue to deny the adequacy and accuracy of human reason in dealing with such matters and go on to question even the laws of logic, then it follows that there may be no basis at all for calling God's commands 'good.' You just decide to place yourself under the authority of God's commands not because they are reasonable, or apparent, or experientially evident, but because you have faith in God and place yourself in God's hands. It may well be absurd to do so, it may be beyond reason, it may leave unsolved why he would allow evil to exist in a world, and so on. As Kierkegaard would note, however, it is precisely because it is absurd that one takes the leap of faith, beyond and in spite of reason and experience. But then you cannot say that 'God is good,' but only 'I have chosen to place my life in God's hands, for him to do with what he wishes,' and 'I believe that he is good.' For you to be certain that God was good, that all things would work out, and that you are better off for having taken the leap would be to deny the absurdity and turn it into a calculated and rationally profitable gamble. There is no guarantee that things will work out; there is only the unguaranteed decision itself, based on trust and faith.

EXISTENTIAL TENSION

A series of tensions are inherent in the existentialist stance outlined to this point. A tension arises as a result of the confronting of a contradiction. So long as the contradiction persists, the tension will persist, like a stretched rubber band. This tension is my explication of existentialist anxiety (*Angst*). You must commit yourself by taking the leap of faith even though you can be said to have no reason for doing so. You must choose what to do without having any guarantee that what you choose is right, but you must still do it wholeheartedly. You must interact with other people and look for better ways of so doing without any grounds for assuming that they share a perspective on the world which is at all compatible with your own. You must choose your projects with no way of knowing whether they will interfere with someone else's project or will yield a path through the wilderness which is any better than aimless wandering. Not only are these tensions real and understandable, even to be expected, but for the existentialist these tensions are to be encouraged and preserved. To deny the fact that you perceive the world and your place in it as perplexing and absurd is to whitewash this truth by covering it up with claims about absolute truth, the order and harmony of nature, the revelations of unchanging wisdom, and so on. Perhaps Albert Camus emphasizes the fact of absurdity in everyone's experience with more candour and insight than any of the existentialists. He argues that the human situation must be viewed as a twofold reaction to the world and your place in it. First, there is the experience of the absurd, that is, the givenness of density, or chaos, or orderlessness, or alienness, of never having anything like total success in trying to make rules and laws or giving final answers to any matter in question – the lingering doubts, the inadequacies, and the recognition of your finiteness; and second, there is the (equally compelling) nostalgia for unity, the insatiable desire and demand for order, understanding, and cosmos. Here, for Camus, is the greatest and most important source of tension: the recognition of your inability to make complete and fixed sense of the world and your insatiable desire to continue to try to do just that. However constantly and predictably your hopes for understanding and guidance are dashed, equally predictably and zealously you try again. That is, you try again so long as you are a healthy existentialist, able to look into the face of darkness with firm courage and determination. But no sooner have you claimed this and taken assurance from the claim that there is such firm guidance than you experience matters which raise new and profound doubts, as if you were an inexperienced tyre repairman trying to stuff an inflated inner tube into a tyre. As often as you tuck one side in, the tube keeps popping out with renewed force somewhere else. Neat solutions are no less incomplete in the worlds of academic learning, religion, and morality.

For Camus, to be an authentic existentialist, healthy and honest, you must keep alive both elements of the 'notion of the absurd': the contradiction between the experience of disunity or chaos on the one hand and the nostalgia for unity or cosmos on the other must be stretched tightly, absurdly, between the extreme ends of a single taut bow. You are the bow, and your effectiveness as a human being requires that the balance be maintained. Suicide, a collapse of this tension, arises from fixation on one or the other element, destroying the balance. Thus, if you fixate on the disunity of the world, you may be led to the intellectual suicide of scepticism, or to physical suicide out of despair and utter meaninglessness. If, on the other hand, you fixate on unity (at the expense of the experience of disunity), you may be led to intellectual suicide (for example, religious optimism, philosophical system-building, or social ideology and propaganda) or even to physical suicide on behalf of your ideals. The healthy existentialist, however, must keep alive both terms of the paradox: unity and disunity must be held on to, and both affirmed and denied simultaneously. As an individual, you must hope and struggle while knowing that victory and complete success will remain for ever out of reach. To deny either the experience or the nostalgia is to deny your humanity.

Perhaps the most powerful image of the preservation of this tension or paradox is to be found in Camus' *Myth of Sisyphus*.[18] In this reworking of an ancient Greek myth, Sisyphus is a king of Corinth condemned by the gods to push a great rock endlessly up a steep mountain in Hades. With bleeding hands, muscles screaming with fatigue, and sweat running from every pore, he shoulders the rock to the mountaintop again and again, and each time stands aside to watch his burden tumble back down the slope to the very bottom, where he began his labour. He trudges back down the slope only to begin the painful ascent all over again. What is significant about Sisyphus is that he symbolizes the human situation. You never get to the top, to your ideal destination, for no sooner is a theory or a reform in effect than new evidence or circumstances or concerns come to light and begin to erode the truth or significance of what has just been established. 'Progress,' the final improvement of mankind, 'the revelation of historical necessity,' even God's truth – all are built on shifting sands, for the winds of doubt and new considerations are always blowing. Even if you are religiously orthodox, you cannot easily achieve conviction or convince others that your way is meticulously correct in the light of conflicting views and interpretations within your sect or denomination, let alone within your religion as a whole, or even with other religions. You can ignore these differences or simply minimize their importance, but then you are unduly stressing the nostalgia for unity at the expense of the experience of disunity. It is equally inappropriate to reject religious claims for unity of belief, however, on the assumption that there is too much disunity in the world.

Unlike the rest of us, Sisyphus is condemned to an eternity of struggle and cannot find a way out. Instead, for Sisyphus and the absurd man or woman, the solution lies within. If you can recognize the futility of life and its goals and at the same time consciously choose to live your life with vigour and undaunted determination, then you will have created a path worthy of your strength and talents; you will have the only happiness available to human beings who have confronted the experience of the absurd. You will hope without the help of eternal assurances, act without guarantee of external guidance, and love without the promise of fulfilment or constancy. In this you will be exactly like Camus's Sisyphus, for while you are not eternally condemned by the Greek gods, you are condemned by the lifelong human situation to accept inadequate or ill-fitting answers to life's questions. You must begin over and over again, and there is little likelihood that you will ever get it right. As with sweeping the kitchen floor, it is a mistake to suppose that you will sweep it once and for all. Rather, you will sweep again and again in the hopes of keeping the dirt and dust down to a manageable level. The tension becomes unbearable only when you take as your aim the destruction of the tension itself, that is, when you try to eliminate the absurdity and disorder in favour of perfect order. Otherwise, you live as you love, without the assurance of continuation. Love, in order to be love, must be freely given and not constrained, and deeper and certainly truer for being freely offered moment by moment. While the pledge is to love 'till death do us part,' you cannot be sure that changed circumstances will not make this serious pledge inappropriate, irrelevant, or impossible to grant. You can promise to stick it out, but you cannot promise to continue loving. You can say that the tube fits the tyre but you cannot totally ignore the protrusions and lumps. At all events, it is the honesty which is the recognition of the continued existence of the tension which forces Sisyphus inwards, and introspection reveals that he is happy. He is happy because he has admitted the truth of his situation, accepted the inadequacies of his understanding, and yet chosen with passion to continue to walk down the mountain, to live and to love, we might say, without any external purpose such as the lure of progress, or the support of external approval and assurance. All that you have is the passionate desire and willingness to do the best that you can. But why is Sisyphus happy and not filled with anguish and despair? He has lost a benevolent universe designed for humankind and has been plunged into one which is inhospitable, absurd, and 'dense' (that is, strange and inaccessible). Like him, you have gained direction of the only worthwhile sort – you have been forced to look for your answers, ideals, and strength within. What is worth doing must come from your own subjectivity. You must decide, act, persevere, and take what you get, being responsible for it. Happiness is not something given, nor is it deserved. It is a state of inner determination, acceptance, and dedication to your project.

WHAT TO CHOOSE?

You may feel anguish in wondering whether any old project will do, or whether there are any limits to your choice of projects, any means for evaluating your alternatives. On this issue, Camus's character shines forth with brilliance. Basically, he argues that you must take life itself as the fundamental value. It is the one constant value, for without life no values of any kind may be had. Furthermore, there is no way of consistently affirming your own life at the expense of others, for if life is to be preserved in one case, all other things being equal, it must be preserved in others as well. In short, in accordance with the universalizability of the principle of the preservation of life, you must seek to protect all human life. Next, since human life is the basic value, and since you are to protect it generally, can you then give reasons for holding other values as basic or at least required? Camus says you can't give good reasons, except for those negative values, like violence, that contradict the preservation of life. Therefore, all other values must be based on a Sisyphian determination of self, a choice without guarantee yet taken with full responsibility. Camus's solution is humanistic, for he maintains that humanity itself is the setter of values and that humanity alone can present a solution to the despair and nihilism of the experience of absurdity. As a social being in contact with other freely choosing individuals, you may find that you react like them to your own situation. Since you wish to enhance life, your own and that of others, as well as to protect it, you attempt to ascertain the values of other people. At any point, in any group where like-minded men and women express a solidarity of ideals and values, there arises an inter-subjective standard or system of standards. To remain part of the solidarity you must choose to live those values for as long as the solidarity remains, choosing and rechoosing them at each moment, and at the point of each and every action.[19] When the solidarity is absent or diminished, a new position or system of values is required in view of the new situation, and fresh solidarity is required. In a world of change, no position lasts unchanged for very long, and the rebel as existentialist is a perpetual example for each and every one of you who is candid about yourself, others, and the world.

SOCIAL SOLIDARITY

What distinguishes Camus from Nietzsche and Sartre is his attempt to move from the individual to the group by the addition of the notion of solidarity. In so doing, he proposed an ethic that grows out of his analysis of the absurd, an ethic consistent with the meagre hope arising out of your encounter with the 'density' of the world and the flimsiness of human myth making. The price is, of course, high, for happiness is obtained against a background of alienation and despair. Subjective guidance, even when communally oriented, may be but collective arbitrariness. You make your choice together with some or all of your fellows for a time only, and then you regroup and rebel again. Job turned to God; we must turn to each other. But none of us knows. In solidarity we live and die, and in rebelling together we become aware of what it means to exist morally – for and with others.[20]

According to Camus and other existentialists, you will not find moral solutions in neat formulas or in utopian states where the uniqueness of the individual is reduced to that of a gear in a machine or is defined by the bare commandments of tradition. Instead, realizing that there are no pre-packaged answers to human problems, you will find insight only through much guesswork and prodding of the blackness of yourself, others, and the world. Still, you may follow some commandments as rules of thumb, that is, as the best indicators of what has led to the achievement of certain goals or the realization of values in the past. Just as the means that previously brought success may no longer work in changing or changed circumstances, so what once was deemed an end may no longer satisfy you or be judged valuable. Even so, you may find this view of morality and of value formation accurate in so far as it describes how most people set about to live but unconvincing as an account of what morality ought to be. However passionately a group adheres to its collective goals, it may destroy or limit the well-being of others or distort what tradition says about morality and the common search for values. Even with the clear emphasis on allowing the uniqueness of other positions to flourish, so long as the basic value of the protection of human life is respected, it is hardly necessary to point out that different moralities and ways of life repeatedly conflict. How is a solution to be sought? On what principles? Who is to decide? Who is to have the power? Indeed, you may even question the extreme emphasis on the experience of the alienness and density of the universe. Why is it that only disorder is said to be actually experienced? Have you never experienced any order in the world or in yourself? To affirm the existence of disorder does not require that you deny the existence of any order at all. That is the 20/20 thinking of either/or absolutism. Thus, there may be evidence in support of a middle position which can accept the existential challenge that answers may not be final and that the world is filled with surprises and disappointments, without denying that human experience has also rewarded those who have seen deeply and well with the help of rules, principles, laws, and other organizational tools which do make the world less chaotic and the self somewhat structured and consistent. However limited and precarious knowledge may be, it is not simply chaotic and haphazard – there is order, even though that very order may become rigid and block more adequate ways of seeing from emerging. What I am suggesting here is that Camus did not follow his insight into tension far enough. In the remainder of this chapter I want to add what I think Camus left out and apply this modified result to education.

CAMUS REVISED

Let me begin with a diagram. Figure 2 is Camus's position and his account of the notion of the absurd. As far as it goes, it is helpful, but it doesn't go far enough. I want to argue that it is inaccurate and evidently distortive of both human experience and human reasoning. Camus's paradox is not exhaustive of the paradox of the human situation. First of all, human life provides ample evidence of the experience of disunity; doesn't human experience also regularly provide ample evidence of unity? We send rockets to the moon and beyond, perform open-heart surgery, biochemically produce new forms of life by 'genetic engineering,' and claim evidence in developmental psychology for patterns of ordered growth. None of these examples have the aura of the absolute about them, and all are not only being questioned at the present time but regularly undergo refinement and basic change. To deny perfection, however, is not to deny all order. Even in the moral sphere, however difficult it is for you to act and find yourself short of your envisioned goal, you surely do not need to conclude that since you have fallen short of your goal you should abandon moral rules and guides altogether. Just because you don't get the floor clean once and for all does not mean that you have to stop sweeping. What Camus takes as the fact of the experience of disunity, I would take as one of the facts of human experience. The other major fact, whether religiously or humanistically explained, is surely the experience of unity. It is not merely a 'nostalgia,' that is, an intellectual superimposition on the experience of disunity. It is as much a direct experience as that of disunity. Otherwise, our empirical attempts at experimentation and confirmation in science would be pointless. Equally, the existentialist claim that science is riddled with inconclusiveness and paradox would not be found in the

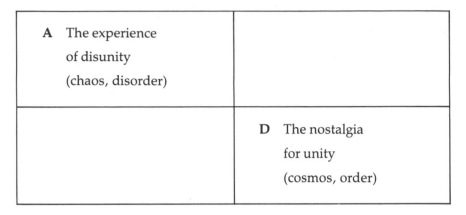

Figure 2 The notion of the absurd 1

experience of scientific experimentation if it were but a 'nostalgia.' While it is hard to say whether there is more experience of unity than disunity in the world, there is ample evidence that there is experience of both. You can deny the existence of unity only if you mean by it perfect, eternal, immutable unity. But this is to deny but one meaning of unity. This is a play on words. There are countless examples of regularities in nature, in human development, in societies (as Gallup polls make evident), and in the fruits of thousands of years of moral speculation and action. To deny the existence of unity is to go too far. You may well find final answers rare, if not impossible, but you also gain information about the world that approaches sufficient regularity for prediction. And while the law of induction is itself in philosophical dispute, neither Hume nor anyone else in his right mind would conclude that, since there is no final and authoritative proof that the future will resemble the past, to walk in front of a bus is therefore as wise a choice as not walking in front of a bus. What we conclude, instead, is that it is wise to respect the apparent regularities of the universe until there is sufficient reason to suppose that they no longer apply. To doubt the philosophic foundations of induction and regularity is not to abandon them either in philosophic theory or living practice. Thus our figure 2 is expanded to figure 3.

On my scheme, what distinguishes the nostalgia for unity from the experience of unity is the simple fact that the latter serves as the apparent 'given' for the former to draw upon and to refine yet further. The starting point of 'systems' is, as Aristotle pointed out long ago, the fact that the world tends to sort itself out.[21] That is to say, acorns grow into oak trees

A The experience of disunity	B The experience of unity
	D The nostalgia for unity

Figure 3 The notion of the absurd II

and not sometimes into swans and sometimes into elm trees. Human beings begin as children, become adults, and then grow old; the process is invariant although not always completed or error-free. The nostalgia for unity is the result of the human insistence on knowing much more than is readily apparent, on finding the reasons why things are regular in the way that they are, and in altering the regular processes or enforcing them against other influences, in the interests of agriculture, medicine, and the vast variety of technological activities of the modern world. The nostalgia for unity is the desire for delving beneath the surface in the interests of finding further regularities and opportunities for prediction of, and actual control of, the processes of man and nature.

PHILOSOPHIC DISUNITY

Alas, this nostalgia itself can run to extremes, not only overriding the caution that comes from the actual experience of disunity, but annihilating as well what I now propose as the fourth ingredient in this tension – the nostalgia for disunity (figure 4). What is this alleged nostalgia for disunity? Perhaps the name is excessive, and therefore it may be unwise to term it an actual desire for disunity. Nevertheless, the Socratic *elenchus*, or perpetual questioning of held positions, at least gives the appearance of a nostalgia for disunity. Socrates was accused of making the better argument the worse and the worse the better, with the clear implication that he would never accept anything as claimed but always gave reasons to expose the disunity concealed within the surface unity. To deny the

A The experience of disunity	B The experience of unity
C The nostalgia for disunity	D The nostalgia for unity

Figure 4 The notion of the absurd III

nostalgia for disunity in this Socratic sense is to ignore the demand for vigilance in criticism of any positions in order to determine how well they stand and to discover where you will stand yourself. It is also to turn a deaf ear to the educated critic or scientist who actively seeks negative instances or flaws in reasoning as part of the method of assessment, confirmation, and proof. The nostalgia for unity must never be allowed to run wild without a compensating intellectual desire and commitment to pick that thesis bare and claim no more for it than it allows. The substance of this position has already been taken up in chapter 1.

TENSION AND EDUCATION

The relationships amongst these four tensions which are part and parcel of human existence may serve as a possible model for educational assessment. If any of the four sources of tension are either absent or undernourished, it is likely that the teacher can help you by over-emphasizing precisely that dimension. For example, if you are only aware of the chaos of the moral realm and have come close to the position of the sceptic, it is well for the teacher to strive to point out the evidence for regularity and the importance of having a somewhat fixed and well-reasoned moral code. On the other hand, if you have a fixed, watertight moral perspective you will very likely gain more from a breath of disorder and a turn to the puzzles and complexities of moral theory. Whether you turn to the side of experience or of nostalgia depends entirely on whether you are making a claim about the empirical facts of the world or about the strengths and weaknesses of theories and principles. Whether you emphasize unity or disunity depends entirely on the degree to which you appear to be leaving out of account those dimensions which would keep the tension of inquiry and discovery alive. Of course, if you deny that there is any need to continue the search, either because there is nothing to be found or because what is being sought has already been found, there is little more to say. But, then, the question of learning becomes a pseudo-question and the issue is one of memorization and training alone. And while it is the case that such training and memorization will probably occupy much more of the child's time at the beginning under any educational scheme, the aim of educational methodology as a genuine search for understanding and discovery must be to leave such memorization increasingly behind. Thus, the aim of this proposedly four-sided tension model of instruction is simply to make certain that none of the elements is entirely forgotten anywhere along the way, with the eventual goal of having all four in vital interaction. The teacher should stand in the centre of this tension, just as you, the student, must eventually place yourself in order to balance the tensions. The art of teaching is the art of keeping all four elements alive and in some sort of active balance. A balance or harmony is usually achieved by offering an overdose of the opposite or contrary ingredient. The eventual aim, however, is a continual dialogue of a self-imposed and self-sustained kind among all four elements in the square of tension described. You come to check your nostalgia for unity automatically by recalling the experiential evidence of disunity, and by critically examining the logic and context of the alleged unity (that is, by exercising your nostalgia for disunity). Your nostalgia for disunity, however, is moderated by your experience of unity, which in turn is qualified both by your experience of disunity and by your nostalgia for unity, which in turn … While the process need never end and in practice never does, you are not left in the hopeless position of having to live without ever knowing exactly how. This leads us back to the question of paralysis.

COMMITMENT

If it is the human lot to be humble about what you know, and even about the details of what you claim to have had revealed to you, then there is constant and continual need to check, re-examine, rethink, and reapply what you know, think, feel, hope, and do. The boundary between commitment, without which there can be no facts and no grounds for a decision, and absolute commitment to a position from which there can be no change is very narrow indeed. Perhaps this is the reason why good people and good education often go astray, as we noted in chapter 1. Commitment is necessary to avoid paralysis. Passionate commitment is required in order to be fully imbedded in your world and your life. Irrevocable commitment is to be avoided, however, on the grounds that you do not really know very much about the surprising cosmos of which you are a part, and because of the ever-real possibility of human error, mis-hearing, or mis-seeing, or mis-understanding, and because of the constancy of change in the process of living a life. As an apt learner, you are able to commit yourself frequently, regularly, but rarely, if ever, irrevocably. Above all, you retain throughout life the willingness to explore new perspectives even at the risk of leaving behind cherished opinions. The risk is real. The alternatives may well be beyond number and are verifiable only tentatively and partially, not absolutely, and at the expense of a great deal of peace of mind. It is the task of the teacher, on the view here presented, to act as a constant renewer of the active tension among the four elements of human understanding and human knowledge (figure 5).

While the model recommends that you and the teacher stand in the middle of these tensions, this is not to suggest that you take a middle or 'wishy-washy' position. Indeed, in order to maintain the proper tension, you must have become militantly critical or exhaustively thorough in mustering the evidence for experiential order. The final goal is not to end up with a single right answer, you will note. That is, for all intents and purposes, educationally beside the point. The point is that growth in understanding will best come about, continue, and become self-sustaining when the student is encouraged to keep alive that dialogue of the mind in its interaction with real experience. The art of teaching is the art of encouraging, developing, and causing to become self-sustaining just this kind of mental, emotional, and behavioural activity which is typical of a mind, a soul, a body, and a citizen who is alive.

NATURE AS HOSPITABLE

Emphasis on the nostalgia for disunity alone, however, does not take us very far in finding a ground for valuation and social agreement in decision making. It works only as a continuing caution. The experience of unity, on the other hand, is a more significant source of values. If the world is not totally dense and alien, then you can and ought to turn to it regularly in

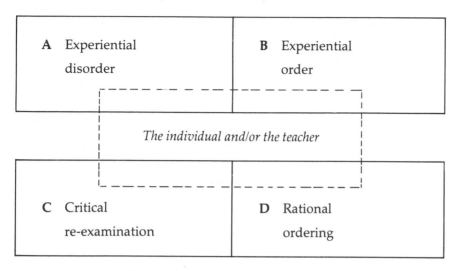

Figure 5 Elements of human learning

order to grasp whatever guidance you can from those glimpses of apparent order available to you.[22] Indeed, even Camus finds profound meaning in the simple pleasures of the warm sun and surf in Algiers and in the personal interchange without which there could be no mutual concern and shared delights.[23] Your basic response to the world need not be that of estrangement and fear. Surely this is one of the great excesses of much of existentialism, and Sartre is perhaps the worst example of this. What is worthy of note here is that estrangement is only one of several perspectives on the world. The Chinese and the Japanese, for example, look on the world as a source of joy and support, of harmonious activity to emulate and adapt to. Westerners, on the other hand, are struck by the similarity between this feeling of kinship and identification with nature and Kohlberg's Stage Seven thinking, which describes in detail imaginative empathy as being embracive of the entire cosmos. This is the language of mysticism, where mysticism simply means the capacity to lose yourself in the greater whole around you, to become one with it. Even from the perspective of modern science, you have evolved out of primoridial ooze, and that evolutionary past is still genetically yours, including an affinity for what you have come from. You are different from the plants and animals but cannot be indifferent to them. Your environment is inextricably theirs and, as contemporary ecologists are warning, your needs are remarkably similar. Those who argue that, as part of nature, you must set your values accordingly may well provide guidance in determining where modern societies must place their priorities through a show of solidarity aimed at environmental and social protection and ultimately the survival of the species and its world. Pollution, world economy and world government, industrialization and its controls, birth control – all are dense issues, less because of the chaos of the world than because of the obtuseness of human beings and their society. To deny your place in nature or to foul and destroy your own nest is to close your eyes to the experience of unity and order which nature itself offers you. To deny your place in nature, which can kill but which more often supports and provides the ground for human existence and so much human enjoyment, is to be blinded by the experience of disunity or by the oppressiveness of a rigid imposition of an 'ism' or ideology which allows you to take control blindly without knowing where you are heading or why.

The four-part tension diagram is one way of responding to the challenge provided by existentialists. It is a qualification of the existential-ist emphasis so often put in extreme and powerful ways. The 'cry' of existentialism is still fully operative, however, warning that you are a finite creature, unable to resolve your moral or intellectual dilemmas with the sort of assurances that you desire, yet often psychologically willing to hide that fact under the guise of science or religion or a philosophical system or a claimed ideological necessity. Knowledge becomes not a state of achievement but an unending process that yields fool's gold more often than wealth. Even the positive solution offered by Camus stands as a partial solution for those who hold views generally opposed to the existentialists, for he insists that you apply your whole self not only to social matters, but even to the universal interests of human life and human value everywhere. For Camus, solidarity is the origin of valuation and morality. Values are made, not discovered – yet they are discovered in the sense that it is only through your social consciousness, your social affirmation of people with similar preferences and dislikes, that you come to know what is worth defending at a given time and place in history. Much like the chart under discussion, one reason why freedom is more important at one time in history than at another is that sometimes there is so little of it that a cry in its favour arises out of solidarity with Mankind. At other times and places, it is peace, or law and order, or integrity, or the curbing of violence that becomes the central issue and concern. You magnify a virtue, a vice, a problem, a solution, to the point of addiction – addiction to a heavy dose of a remedy originally administered to regain a healthy balance. It is a common mistake to continue the unusually heavy dose, making it an ongoing prescription, even after health is restored. To be addicted is, of course, to court illness and disharmony. A heavy dose, too much of even a good thing, necessarily breeds an imbalance, if made a normal part of one's routine.

CONCLUSION

A recurrent charge against existentialists is that their viewpoint turns each individual into an isolated island of values and interests, not only unwilling to interact with other islands but actually fearful of doing so. Camus has provided an original critique of this position and suggests instead a way of allowing value to transcend the individual, horizontally, that is, by embracing one's fellows in solidarity, thereby bursting the boundaries of the walled-in self. He denies the possibility of vertical transcendence, that is, of gaining divine or supernatural assistance, where a 'higher authority' tells you what to do and which values to cherish. Instead, he advocates horizontal authority where you choose your own values on the universal ground of the protection of human life and of those life values affirmed through social solidarity. Like Camus's rebel, you will gladly die to protect those values deemed inviolable; in this you transcend the egocentric limits of the individual, but only horizontally in embracing more people than yourself. Once you know what the limits are and that these limits are universally binding and that the values which you affirm are more general than your own life, the moral concern has emerged with energy. But it has also been noted in this chapter that more is available to you than a moral nostalgia (hope) in the face of an experiential chaos. The world of nature and the inner structures of your consciousness are at least available as a source of some order. Even the very human activity of assigning value is structured and predictable, and its orderliness enables you to intend good or evil for yourself and others. Otherwise, if it were a matter of chance alone, 'then no one could, with the best will in the world, learn how to do anybody else any good – or for that matter, how to do him harm.'[24] As has been argued already, utter and total chaos is not necessarily the only alternative to perfect order and certainty. A more mature wisdom may require you to recognize both your limitations in achieving certainty (cosmos) and your differences from others. You are unique in history and possibility, yet you are from the same stock as other humans and from not totally dissimilar cultural backgrounds. It is not enough to single out either the differences or the similarities. Both aspects must be kept in tension. The moralist must take a stand, but not one that is uncritical. The teacher must instruct, but not without consideration of the unique background, capacities, aspirations, and cultural values of the student as individual. One of the teacher's most important tasks is to bring or keep alive, or even strengthen the tension in the student: to create it if it does not already exist; to strengthen it if it is not robust enough; to keep it alive if it is. Robust tension, however, can be as evident in the moral sceptic as in the dogmatist or ideologist. In this sense, the teacher of morality is a Socratic gadfly, a beneficial source of irritation beneath the surface of complacency. Also, the very activation of tension in others reactivates the tension within the teacher, and possibly deepens it. The goal of such tension, such critical inquiry, is vigorous exploration, heightened interest and concern, and an integration of self resulting from the deepening of self-consciousness. At the same time, morality requires that you be concerned with the most general principles of human behaviour possible and in ways which extend far beyond the confines of the self to include each and every one whom it concerns, impartially and justly. Such constancies and preferences are grounded as much in the order of nature and of human nature as they are in the nothingness and arbitrariness of existence in a wilderness. Perhaps it is because Camus and the other existentialists have been, in general, unable to accept or to identify with this unity in the world and in the self that the emphasis on anguish, despair, dread, fear, and trembling and the nausea of existence has remained the dominant and characteristic existentialist perspective and stance. Had they been more able to emphasize both sides of the paradox of experience, the disunity both of the world and of human beings, they might have been able to speak more regularly of happiness, of feeling at home in the world. Had they emphasized both sides of the paradox, they might have been moved to joy, and not despair, whenever a course was charted which was so well integrated with the environment, and so supportive of the life and values of the community, that the temptation would be to ignore the actuality of despair and meaningless-ness altogether. Nevertheless, a joyful encounter with your fellows and with your world need not come at the expense of the denial of disorder and uncertainty, but may occur both in spite of and because of it. Joy is as much a result of continued growth in understanding and novelty as it is a response to that which is comfortably established and predictable. The miracle is that, while the tension of contradictories remains unresolved, joy nevertheless arises and flourishes.

4

Values and intrinsic value

The ends or goals you choose determine your character and, in large measure, the quality of that portion of life for which you are directly responsible. A value is something you use to subordinate one end-in-view to another in determining what is prized and what is done. The importance of this fact for ethics is brought out by W.G. Everett, who characterizes ethics as 'the science of comparative values because every moral choice is a selection of a greater or a less value, positive or negative, according to the nature of the choice as good or bad, better or worse.'[1] Thus, a great deal of what you are as a person hangs on what you select as valuable and disvaluable. In view of this you would suspect that open and animated discussion about values would occupy a great deal of your time and energy, and that the subject would prove so gripping and important that you would be drawn to it again and again. The facts, however, point in the opposite direction. To discuss values and their selection is a risky business, too private and revealing for easy dialogue. Politics, religion, and sex, it is said, are all value-laden subject areas, not easily mixed with polite and relaxing social interchange, for to discuss them is to risk disagreement and anxiety. To explore human valuation in schools is acceptable for many if and only if the boundaries are so clearly marked out beforehand that the possibility of genuine free-spirited exploration is ruled out. You begin with a map of the ground to be investigated, with landmarks carefully designated and summarized. There is little need to actually look to see where you are treading. Whereas I argued in chapter 1 that you ought to embark upon a philosophical inquiry as though you were exploring an uncharted sea for the first time, in practice valuation and morality are taught as though they constitute a fearful philosophic subdivision which disallows either the freedom or the excitement of independent discovery, for fear of shipwreck. Indeed, since you run the risk of offending and shocking by speaking openly or even hypothetically of morality, it is usually kept under wraps, out of the way of everyday talk, and always within prescribed limits and expectations.

Ironically, fear may bring into being a state of affairs far worse than that brought about by taking away psychological constraints. Fear can make of healthy ambiguity seemingly 'clear' evidence that you are warped in character, somehow lacking in moral sense, and to be watched carefully if not altogether avoided. Such a reaction is not totally wrong-headed, of course, for there are limits beyond which we must not let people stray and act, and there are lesser limits as well which we must point out to children and use various means to enforce 'for their own good.' But just because you take a firm stand and commit yourself to certain moral values, that doesn't require you to shut down dialogue or consider moral change or improvement an impossible heresy. A wide range of choice in lifestyle and personality growth may still exist, within broad limits, with dialogue and the process of valuational sensitization assisting. It is my observation that we have lost the ability to be comfortable with values and with moral discussion. Yet comfort does not imply sloppiness or frivolity. On the contrary, it can convey an attitude of vital interchange in an atmosphere of relaxed and yet intense purposeful inquiry. You leave behind all pretences and share inquiry into the vital core of personal existence with other individuals who actually encounter each other's ideals and feelings without fearful deafness or defensiveness. An idealized interchange of this sort might be imagined between two spiritual masters who, like children awaiting an adventure story, are both eager to hear the fantastic tales of where the other has been and what he has learned. There is excitement without threat, exploration without the desire to win points or the need to convert the other. Each hopes that the other will speak first, for it is the other's vision that is sought and the ensuing cross-fertilization which will make new growth and fresh insight spring into being.

FOCUS ON AMBIGUITY

One of the strongest reasons for valuational and moral inquiry results from clear recognition of the confused and complex state of the art itself. If anything, the perplexity felt about the general possibility of knowledge is even further heightened in the sphere of valuation and moral knowledge.

Recognition of that fact may lead to acceptance of more open, more enthusiastic, and more comfortable valuational and moral dialogue. In what follows, the complexity of ethics will be discussed and some of the disagreements illustrated in an attempt to make it plain that discussion ought to thrive because this oldest of arts is still in the throes of intellectual adolescence. While the more limited focus of this chapter is on the meaning and function of a single moral term, 'intrinsic value,' the point of the analysis is to show how great are the complexities and disagreements, even among the 'experts,' with respect to this single notion within the vastly more complex sphere of ethics. The conclusion that I draw from this attempt at the analysis and the disambiguation of this term is that moral discussion ought to be engaged in against the backdrop of high-level disagreement and ongoing inquiry amongst specialists who are far from agreed about the fundamentals of morality, let alone about the details of the entire system. But again, to say that they are not agreed, and that significant ambiguity exists, is not to throw up ones hands in despair. On the contrary, the struggle for clarity, system, and evidenced support of positions has led us to the point of refined distinction and the sustained defence of competing perspectives. While it is unlikely that ambiguity will be eliminated, or that one view will soon emerge as the agreed upon and correct one, the sensitization which takes place as a result of exploring the high points in the field is itself of great benefit. To question seriously what justification there is for egoism or scepticism probably does more to make one a careful thinker, and a thoughtful doer, than would any number of frontal assaults on egoism or on an irresponsible scepticism. Indeed, the thoughtful egoist and sceptic will very likely prove to be considerably more other-directed than most party-line conventional moralists. To be deeply concerned with morality is the essential starting point in the study of ethics, and such deep concern requires recognition of problems and ambiguities. Solutions will represent best responses to such problems, and will be enlivened by genuine concern and honest searching.

This chapter, then, is a focused beam of exploration designed to reveal the complexity of disagreement and ambiguity existing throughout the serious study of ethics. For a teacher or student not to be aware of this theoretical vulnerability is to encourage the rote learning of moral rules and social role playing, as though these are obvious and firmly established and justified. Not only does such an attitude yield rigidity, but the superficiality of memorization and the weak motivation gained from the mere authority of others are but a paltry image of what genuine search and moral discovery can achieve. Ethics ought to be of passionate concern to everyone, and a continuing inquiry of such major excitement and importance that it is second to no other.

VALUE DISTINCTIONS

Several technical distinctions need to be made to ease entry into the discussion of value and its kinds. The distinctions which I will make are not the only ones which could be made, nor are they made in the only acceptable way. Indeed, the major purpose of this section is to call attention to the amount of disagreement about even one of these terms. In the meantime, however, I will propose rough-and-ready divisions within the generic term 'value,' about which there is as much controversy as to correct meaning as any other. The ordinary beginning is to divide values into 'intrinsic' and 'extrinsic.' While there are many definitions of 'intrinsic,' it is perhaps sufficient to refer to such values as being worthwhile or valuable in themselves or for their own sakes (even though nothing might be thought to be valuable apart from some human or other consciousness).[2] In any case, intrinsic becomes more clear when contrasted with extrinsic value. The extrinsically valuable is that value which, while not valuable in itself or for its own sake alone, is valuable because it leads to values which are valuable for their own sakes (that is, intrinsic values). Even within the extrinsic classification, however, there are additional classifications to be made. Something may be of 'instrumental' value because it is a means to something which is intrinsically or extrinsically valuable, and if the latter, to something, eventually, which is of intrinsic value. For example, money is instrumental to providing food, clothing, and shelter, which are themselves instrumental to good health and happiness, which, it might be argued, are valuable in themselves. Then there is a kind of value which C.I. Lewis calls 'inherent,'[3] or resident in objects. These values are referred to by some as objective values, but Lewis is uneasy with claims to objectivity. Instead, he calls a property 'inherent' which is generally agreed to be resident in objects and which, upon presentation to a normal human being, reveal more or less predictable intrinsic or extrinsic values.[4] Inherent values are value potentialities, becoming actualized value experiences only upon presentation to a conscious being. Both inherent and instrumental values are extrinsic values.

'Contributory' value is the last value-kind to need definition, and it is somewhat elusive. Together with instrumental and inherent values, contributory value fills out C.I. Lewis' threefold classification of extrinsic values. Whereas all intrinsic value is characterized by immediacy, contributory value, like all extrinsic values, may be seen as a means to, or more properly a contributor to, having intrinsic values. Contributory value is not that value which results from a particular arrangement of individual values, each of which is intrinsically valuable. Because of its importance to the whole of which it is a part and which is a whole of intrinsic value, a contributory value is not just an instrumental value. If the whole were not itself of intrinsic value, then the part here termed contributory could better be labelled instrumental. But instrumental values are not parts of wholes which are themselves of intrinsic value. Only contributory values are ingredients in intrinsically valuable wholes. They are necessary parts of intrinsically good wholes, and only of wholes which are of intrinsic value. It is not what they lead to or are instrumental to that is important, but what they are necessary ingredients in that distinguishes them from other extrinsic values. Charles Baylis, whose book *Ethics* provides an unusually good account of the kinds of values, uses the example of a carburetor in an attempt to make plain what contributory values are: 'A good carburetor contributes to whatever value the engine of which it is a part has, even though it would be of little or no value sitting on a shelf by itself.'[5] This example is both confusing and wrong, because the whole of which it is a part is not necessarily of intrinsic value but is instrumental to the satisfaction which will result if the engine does perform as desired. The carburetor is a part of a means to an end and is not a part of an end which itself is of intrinsic value. Only experiences can be of intrinsic value, not automobile engines. Since the carburetor is not a part of a whole which itself is of intrinsic value, it is an example not of contributory value but of instrumental value. To summarize, then, contributory value is the value of a part of a whole, which whole is of intrinsic value. If the whole is not of intrinsic value, then the part is not of contributory but of instrumental value. If something is not a part of an intrinsically valuable whole but a means to it, its value is instrumental but not contributory.

INTRINSICALLY VALUABLE WHOLES

No doubt what has now become obscured is what sort of a whole of intrinsic value we might imagine for which a necessary part might justifiably be termed 'contributory.' Lewis' answers are almost all related to wholes of experience, Gestalts, or passages of a lifetime. He emphasizes the importance of the mutual qualification of the part by and of the rest of the whole of which it is a part, and this process results in the mutual alteration of the value of each and of the whole.[6] The most telling example is that of a young boy working for money to buy a ticket to the circus: 'The small boy may work long and hard for the price of a circus ticket, but his labor will be infused throughout with the value-quality of vivid anticipation; and his later satisfaction at the circus may also be enhanced by honest pride in having earned his own enjoyment. Here the one experience qualifies the other not only causally and instrumentally but also directly and in the manner of ingredients in a temporal *Gestalt*.'[7] Here one experience adds to a later and greater whole of value quite above and beyond what was first experienced in the labour of earning the money for the ticket. The anticipation of attending the circus added to the quality of the labour. Putting these characteristics of contributory value together, we find in Lewis an excellent account of what he means by the term:

The value of an experiential whole may be affected not only by the values immediately found in its separate and included moments but by the relation of these moments of experience to one another. It may be that a life which begins badly but ends well is better than one which begins well but ends badly, even though the ingredient experiences which make it up should be as nearly comparable as could well be imagined and should differ only by what is involved in the different temporal order of them. It is by this kind of fact that the value realized in any whole of experience will reflect the character of it as a temporal *Gestalt*.[8]

Two final points need to be made on this technical front. First, both the good and the bad, the valuable and the disvaluable are values. Wherever you speak of intrinsic value, there is the corresponding notion of intrinsic disvalue, or of instrumental, inherent, or contributory disvalue. Second, it is well to distinguish between instrumental values and the values of utility. Lewis writes of something having utility when the value ascribed to it makes no claim (and implies no decision) about the genuine value of whatever it is instrumentally useful in bringing about.[9] Thus, you might say that a particular laboratory procedure exhibits utility in bringing about certain results even if you have no idea at all of the value, instrumental or intrinsic, of the result it brings about. But it is still instrumental in bringing it about. Such values are the values of utility.

THE STATUS OF VALUES

A nearly predictable result of exposure to ethics and the study of values in college and university is the sort of confusion and frustration that Meno must have felt after having conversed with Socrates about whether or not virtue could be taught. To make matters worse, the *Meno* concludes ironically that you may possibly live a virtuous life by a kind of lucky intuition or divine inspiration.[10] Plato's heart is obviously not in this thesis, and he uses it here and elsewhere to warn that those who do not struggle with reason and evidence are likely to end up with a position that is just this impoverished, haphazard, and utterly indefensible. Twenty-five hundred years later the debate is no less intense and inconclusive. Still, much has happened in ethics. Scholars are much clearer about some issues and concepts than ever before and have 'good reasons' for rejecting certain kinds of actions as based on wrong-headed, inconsistent, or at least inconclusive arguments. Feeling the lack of better arguments, you need not reject imperfect ones which will lessen your myopia any more than you should let discouragement over inherent imperfections in the automobile deter you from making improvements in it.

Stephen Pepper, in his monumental work *The Sources of Value*, defines value 'in the broadest sense' as 'anything good or bad ... pleasures and pains; desires, wants and purposes; satisfactions and frustrations; preferences; utility, means, conditions, and instruments; correctness and incorrectness; integration and disintegration; character, vitality, self-realization; health; survival, evolutionary fitness; adjustability; individual freedom, social solidarity; law, duty, conscience; virtues, ideals, norms; progress; righteousness and sin; beauty and ugliness; truth and error; reality and unreality.'[11] It would appear that there is nothing left out; you can take a value stance, positive or negative, towards anything in human experience. Everything can be coloured by human valuation. The problem is 'how to bring order and clarity into this apparently heterogeneous mass of subject matter,'[12] especially in the light of the wild disagreements about whether values are subjective or objective, empirical or non-empirical, and so on. Aside from these perplexities, valuation has been active in human life and thought from the beginning. C.I. Lewis says of this: 'The sense of good and bad ... is primordial to conscious life at large. Indeed it would be plausible that mere feeling of euphoria or dysphoria is the most ancient form of consciousness. Though what is humanly experienced with these qualities has become complex, as the human mentality in general has become complex, still the distinction itself remains basically the same; and the sense of good and bad is something which man brings forward from his prehuman ancestry.'[13] Human or pre-human, the sense of the valuable and disvaluable is both obvious and hopelessly baffling. Again quoting Lewis: 'The problem of characterizing the immediately good is a baffling one; an irritating one even; because, in the first place, everybody knows what it is; and if anyone should not, we could hardly tell him.'[14] And anyone who doubts that the issue of characterizing or defining 'value,' or the 'good,' is a thorny one should reread Plato or simply undertake a quick look at twentieth century Anglo-American ethics.

G.E. MOORE

It was the English philosopher G.E. Moore who, more than anyone else in this or perhaps any century, stung the 'experts' by announcing that all previous attempts to define 'good' were failures and that most of these failures resulted from (1) confusing good in general with specific goods, and (2) from supposing that 'good' could be defined at all. With the publication of Moore's *Principia Ethica* in 1903, the entire history and status of ethics and value theory had to be rethought. Appropriately, in chapter 1 of *Principia*, Moore inquires into the subject-matter of ethics, seeking a more basic description of ethics than the 'consideration of human conduct.' After all, sociology, psychology, political studies, cultural studies, and so forth may all consider human conduct, thus removing the uniqueness of this criterion as a single distinguishing characteristic of the subject called ethics. Even more important, 'other things, beside conduct, may be good.'[15] If good conduct shares the property goodness with other good things, then an adequate consideration of good conduct would also include an examination of good in its most general sense. But mistakes of this sort might be precluded 'by considering first what is good in general.'[16] If, broadly speaking, discussion of what is good and what is bad is the subject-matter of ethics, then until you know the meaning of the word good (and the word bad) in its generic sense, you cannot hope to understand ethics. Furthermore, it is not safe or wise to compile a list of virtues or vices, things good and things bad, the valuable and the disvaluable, until the central issues and terms have themselves been examined and defined. The meaning of good and the meaning of bad are of fundamental importance to ethics, and questions arising out of these meanings are the most fundamental in all ethics. A mistake with regard to the definition of good or bad entails a far larger number of erroneous ethical judgments than any other. Thus, without a firm foundation, made possible by correct answers to the fundamental questions, systematic knowledge cannot be expected to result from the rest of ethical deliberation or from the teaching of ethics. In fact, until the answer to the question 'What is good?' is known, it is impossible that 'any one should know what is the evidence for any ethical judgement whatsoever.'[17]

Catching our breath for a moment in the wake of Moore's initial challenge and sustained analysis, let us remind ourselves that Moore's search for a generic definition is not to deny that the vast numbers of things, people and experiences, ideas and ideologies, and so on are very different and that the sense of value or goodness attributed to them may also vary widely: 'Directly findable value is not so much one quality as a dimensionlike mode which is pervasive of all experience. There is not one goodness and one badness to be found in living but uncountably many variants of good and bad, each like every other most notably in being a basis for choosing and preferring.'[18] To make matters more confusing, it seems, according to C.I. Lewis, that whatever term we apply to this variety, whether 'goodness,' or 'value,' or 'pleasure,' must include such diversity:

If 'pleasure' or any other name is to serve as synonym for the immediately and intrinsically valuable, then it must be adequate to the wide variety of what is found directly good in life. It must cover the active and self-forgetting satisfactions as well as the passive and self-conscious ones; the sense of integrity in firmly fronting the 'unpleasant' as well as 'pleasure'; the gratification in having one's own way, and also the benediction which may come to the defeated in having finished the faith. It must cover innocent satisfactions as well as those of cultivation; that which is found in consistency and also that of perversity and caprice; the enjoyment of sheer good fortune and that which adds itself to dogged achievement. All this in addition to the whole range of the sensuously pleasing and the emotionally gratifying. And the immediately disvaluable has its equal and corresponding variety. Such immediate goods and bads are ill compressed into any single term or pair of terms.[19]

And yet that is exactly what Moore demands of us. His logic is simple. If all these varieties of values can be called values or goods, then they must have something in common, or else it is a horrible mistake to call them by the same name. He rejects the idea that there is nothing tying this diversity together except the arbitrary stipulation of a common label, and persists in his attempts to identify and isolate the common quality. Is it pleasure? No, for things can be valuable without being pleasant. Is it to be preferred? No, for some things are good even in an age which does not see that this is so. What, then, is good? Reflecting back on Moore's answer to his own question in the light of history, it is fair to say that his answer was as disappointing as his critique of the entire previous history of ethical theory was devastating. Good means good, said Moore, and added conclusively that that was the end of the matter![20] Good is indefinable, unanalysable, simple, and unique.[21] And all attempts thus far to define and analyse good have resulted in clear failure. Should anyone doubt this, argued Moore, just apply the 'Open Question Test' 'Whatever definition be offered, it may be always asked, with significance, of the complex so defined, whether it is itself good.'[22] Good does not mean the same as anything else – not pleasure, not 'more evolved,' not 'demanded of us by God' – for good must be intuited as itself, and as depending on the characteristics of those things called good.

BEYOND MOORE

Part of the justification for dealing with Moore here is that his status and his success as a critical philosopher in our century make it evident that the intensity of the debate amongst the professionals in ethics has not decreased since the time of Socrates. Ethical disagreement and ethical inquiry are as intense as ever. The continuance of the debate is not evidence for the sophistic conclusion that, since people cannnot seem to agree about the good and the bad, the right and the wrong, then relativism is the only honest position to hold. If such a conclusion is apt, it is not obvious and would have to be argued for on its own grounds. There are philosophers who argue cogently and vehemently for such a position, but not on the grounds of its being the obvious one.[23] The most that can be claimed is that such a position remains a live option, a possibility. In fact, something like a malaise of hopelessness settled in after Moore's work, and ethical theorists sought to free themselves from Moore's assertion that almost everything up to now was mistaken and from his intuitionism which seemed to reduce ethics to an 'either you have it or you don't' position. Worse yet, if you had it, there is little that you could do to demonstrate that you had it except to cause the other person to see things from your own point of view. If the other person still failed to see what you saw, you would have no recourse but to try again, with nothing new to offer or to retract in the knowledge that you were right in any case. It is little wonder that the position called 'emotivism,' first appearing in the scholarly journals in 1923, seemed to be an accurate summation of the actual results in ethical theory in the first third of our century: 'The peculiar ethical use of "good" is, we suggest, a purely emotive use.'[24] By

1936 the emotive theory had ripened to the point where A.J. Ayer, in his monumental work *Language, Truth and Logic*, could write:

In admitting that normative ethical concepts are irreducible to empirical concepts, we seem to be leaving the way clear for the 'absolutist' view of ethics – that is, the view that statements of value are not controlled by observation, as ordinary empirical propositions are, but only by a mysterious 'intellectual intuition.' A feature of this theory, which is seldom recognized by its advocates, is that it makes statements of value unverifiable. For it is notorious that what seems intuitively certain to one person may seem doubtful, or even false, to another.[25]

Little wonder that J.O. Urmson remarks that 'the emotive theory of ethics has its origin in epistemological despair.'[26] As has been stated, that despair resulted from the success of Moore's attack on all previous attempts to base ethics on any properties other than goodness and on the failure of his own intuitionism which, as Ayer notes, justifies nothing, and thus leaves the intuitionist claim open to attack by everything and everybody. Ethics becomes the power of conviction, of persuasion, of getting others to see things your way, or at least forcing them to do things your way. Ethics is persuasion and power!

There is much more to be said about twentieth-century Anglo-American ethics, more to be said about ethics on the continent, and indeed there are 'more positive reasons for accepting the emotive theory than these general epistemological considerations.'[27] But even without saying more and without detailing the more recent and lively debates between the utilitarians and the formalists, for example, it is evident that the teaching of ethics must consist heavily of exposure to the problems and confusions, the perplexities and the seemingly equally justifiable alternative answers and the cries of despair and claims of subjectivism, relativism, and scepticism. There is no easy answer to any of these issues, not even to that of defining the most basic term of ethics – value or goodness. However, while the teaching of ethics must provide room for ambiguity and a wide range of alternatives, it does not follow that the situation or the subject-matter is in a hopeless state. Rather, as in any other area of human inquiry, it is well to instil a tolerance for ambiguity and inconclusiveness which is tempered by the recognition that significant insights have, nevertheless, occurred. In fact, in order to see the greatness of achievements you must first comprehend the depth, complexity, and sweep of the problems in question to which the alleged achievements are proposed answers. Knowing that you do not know should only intensify the desire to know more, not decrease it. You may give up the search, on the other hand, if you are at either extreme of the scale of the certainty of knowing: the sceptic has no hope of ever finding out and the absolutist has no need or reason to look. The *daimon* in you has both hope and need.

VALUES AND INTRINSIC VALUE

While value, in its most general sense, may be said to be anything good or bad, it is imperative to keep clearly in mind that not all values and instances of valuation are moral concerns. Terms like value, good, bad, right, and wrong can be used in both the moral and the non-moral senses. For example, something may be of economic value, like a used stamp for collecting, without necessarily being of any ethical significance at all. Or a child's arithmetic quiz may be right or wrong, but not morally so. In spite of this built-in imprecision in the way in which we ordinarily use these words, I am going to use value as the more general term, referring to all kinds of value, including moral value, and words like good, bad, right, and wrong as indicators that the discussion has turned from values to ethics *per se*. I do not thereby deny that something can be said to be good or bad without the intention of signifying moral qualities. I simply wish to adopt the convention of distinguishing between value in general and moral value in particular by making words like good and bad morally specific and not valuationally general.

The more obvious value distinctions are those of intrinsic, extrinsic, and contributory values. As an instructive test case revealing the state of the art of value theorizing, let us look at the meaning of intrinsic value, often regarded as the central valuational and ethical term, to illustrate the degree and nature of the complexity and disagreement involved in contemporary ethical and meta-ethical debate.

Having already witnessed the difficulties encountered in the attempt to define value in the twentieth century, it is understandable that Pepper asks 'How [is it possible to] guarantee that different writers on "value" are discussing the same subject?'[28] Now, to make matters considerably worse, it will become evident that the 'intrinsic' in intrinsic value is as varied in meaning and function, making intrinsic value a philosopher's nightmare. Several decades ago John Dewey observed that '"intrinsic" as applied to "value" is so ambivalent as to be more than question-begging.'[29] The focus of Dewey's concern is the common meaning of 'intrinsic value' which refers to that value attaching to something apart from its relation to anything or anybody else in the universe and apart from any consequences resulting from it. To hold that something has intrinsic value in this sense is to hold that something would be so valuable even if no one were to know it, or value it, or even if the whole world were in agreement to the contrary. In Dewey's words, 'The extreme instance of the view that to be intrinsic is to be out of any relation is found in those writers who hold that, since values are intrinsic, they cannot depend upon any relation whatever, and certainly not upon a relation to human beings.'[30] Dewey thinks that the argument reduces to absurdity, for if one were to reserve the term 'intrinsic' for whatever properties or qualities are non-relational in this extreme sense, the final result would be that 'there are no intrinsic qualities whatever, since it can be shown that such intrinsic qualities as red, sweet, hard, etc. are causally conditioned as to their occurrence.'[31] Since all properties are known by human beings and are, therefore, in relation to human beings, such relation cannot serve to differentiate between intrinsic and non-intrinsic values, if intrinsic means out of relation to human beings. Even G.E. Moore, who once argued that the only safe method of deciding what has intrinsic value is to imagine them as though they existed 'quite alone,' in a universe isolated from human beings for ever and apart from all possible consequences which might result from the existence of things of intrinsic value, came to abandon this position later on, as we shall see in a moment. Moore's 'isolated universe' example was given succinctly in his *Ethics*:

By calling one effect or set of effects intrinsically better than another it means that it is better in itself, quite apart from any accompaniments or further effects which it may have. That is to say: To assert of any one thing, A, that it is intrinsically better than another, B, is to assert that if A existed quite alone, without any accompaniments or effects whatever – if, in short, A constituted the whole Universe, it would be better that such a Universe should exist, than that a Universe which consisted solely of B should exist instead. In order to discover whether any one thing is intrinsically better than another, we have always thus to consider whether it would be better that the one should exist quite alone than that the other should exist quite alone.[32]

In *Principia Ethica*, where Moore first applies the method of isolation, he concludes that a beautiful universe is of intrinsic value, that is, is better than an ugly universe, even if there was not and could never be any sentient creature to value it as such. Apparently objective existents can be of intrinsic value and will be of such value in any circumstances and possible universes, real or imagined, whether or not anyone can ever become aware of them. Later on, Moore wrote that 'things,' 'existents' cannot and do not have intrinsic value by themselves alone, but only in so far as they form part of the conscious experience of a sentient being. 'Quite alone' comes not to mean absolutely alone and isolated. Dewey was right about this, and Moore came to agree. Quoting the later Moore:

One thing, I think, is clear about intrinsic value ... that it is only actual occurrences, actual states of things over a certain period of time – not such things as men, or characters, or material things, that can have any intrinsic value at all ... If we want to estimate rightly what would constitute an intrinsic improvement in the state of things in our imagined year next century, and whether it would on the whole be really 'good' at all, we have to consider what value it would have if it were to be the last year of life upon this planet; if the world were going to come to an end, as soon as it was over and therefore to discount entirely all the promises it might contain of future goods.[33]

In the above passage we find Moore not only rejecting his isolated universe example and redefining the sense of 'quite alone' to refer not to things or states of affairs apart from conscious experience but also helpfully emphasizing the basic distinction between intrinsic and extrinsic value. An experience is of intrinsic value when the value attributed to it inheres in the nature and quality of the experience itself, whereas its extrinsic value would consist of the value of those consequences resulting, at least in part, from its existence. My joy may give someone else pleasure and may even bring me other good results as well (a better reputation, a gift, a new friendship), but all of these additional benefits are extrinsic or resultant values. The intrinsic value of my joy lies in its own nature, 'quite alone' and apart from any other consequences following from it. We have a curious result from all of this to consider. Moore came to admit that all values, intrinsic and non-intrinsic alike, must have relation to human beings (or at least to sentient creatures) and their experience of life. Yet this is precisely the position which Dewey himself adopted in rejecting the term 'intrinsic value.' Dewey argued that if intrinsic only means what Moore and others said it meant when speaking of values possessed by things out of relation to all experience had by human beings, then the term has no practical significance since we cannot know of anything out of relation to us and apart from human experience. Even if such eternal values should exist, we could not know of them as such, for to know of them is already to make them relational. Out with intrinsic value, argued Dewey. What he should have concluded was that this single meaning of intrinsic value was wrong-headed, and he should then have gone on either to provide another definition which was suitable for his purposes or to analyse the term further to see what other meanings there might be in ordinary usage. One such alternative meaning, as we have seen, was that offered by the later Moore: intrinsic value is that value which attaches to an experience apart from consideration of any further consequences which might follow from it. Intrinsic value is the value of an experience 'in itself' and quite apart from all other future and tangential considerations.

SOME MEANINGS OF INTRINSIC VALUE

Had Dewey considered other meanings of 'intrinsic value,' I think he would have encountered several of importance. Let me briefly list several candidates for consideration, without making any claim that the list is complete:

1 The Oxford English Dictionary defines intrinsic as 'situated within; interior; inner.' In accordance with this definition, 'intrinsic value' refers to value which is part of the nature of that to which it is attributed. 'Inner' is here contrasted with 'outer,' and 'interior' with 'exterior.' Thus, 'intrinsic' refers to something as it is in itself, irrespective of outer or other circumstantial or environmental conditions.

2 'Intrinsic value' may also be taken to mean 'objective value.' In this sense, the value of a thing is dependent on the intrinsic nature (in other respects) of that thing, and remains so long as the thing remains what and as it is. Whether intrinsic value is itself a part of the nature of a thing is a different issue and probably pertains more directly to the first meaning of 'intrinsic value' given above. The main point of this second meaning is that the object itself serves as the source of consistency and constancy in correct value attribution. To the extent to which our apprehension of things is objective, our apprehension of intrinsic value can be objective. It may be recalled that Lewis opts for the term 'inherent' value rather than objective value. He also classed it as an extrinsic value, since only experiences can be of intrinsic value.

3 John Dewey argued that 'intrinsic value' means absolute, unchanging, eternal, and timeless value, independent of any change or decay, fluctuations in circumstance, or relation with human beings. This meaning we have commented on in more detail above.[34]

4 Some have held that intrinsic values are self-justifying values. Such values are self-evident. John Laird writes that 'an intrinsic good must

justify of itself, because everything except itself is excluded by definition.'[35] Laird continues, 'A moment's pleasure, fleeting, sporadic, and
forgotten, would be an 'intrinsic' value; but many philosophers would
refuse to call it a 'self-justifying' value on the ground that nothing
episodic and impermanent should be dignified by this name.'[36] Laird
himself agrees with this restriction and argues that values may be said to
be self-justifying when imbedded in a system or set of values whose
special authority is not derived from some other authority. Following
Laird, then, the term 'self-justifying' will refer only to values related to
some organized system of values (for example, morality, science, art,
religion), and not to value experiences had out of such relation to value
sets and systems. However, such a conclusion is less than obvious, and
when we turn to the work of C.I. Lewis in more detail it will be obvious
that what Lewis term 'intrinsic value' is precisely value not imbedded in a
system at all but unmistakable (and to that degree self-justifying) as such
by its own nature alone.

5 Intrinsic values are often thought of as ends of action. Dewey, for one,
rejects intrinsic values in this sense, for he maintains that no values are in
themselves appropriate ends of action, since, in order to determine what
ends are to be brought about attention must be paid to the means available
for achieving those ends, to the total consequences which would follow if
they were to be brought about, and so on.[37] Moore, too, while recognizing
the primacy of intrinsic value in ethics, does not hold that judgments
about what things are of intrinsic value are sufficient for deciding what
ought to be done. There are two basic questions in ethics, he tells us, and
care should be taken not to confuse the two: (1) 'What kind of things
ought to exist for their own sakes?' and (2) 'What kind of actions ought we
to perform?'[38] And questions about what ought to be done involve
consideration of what things are related as causes to that which is good in
itself, and further require consideration of both short- and long-range
consequences resulting, in part or whole, from the existence of that
original intrinsically valuable state of affairs. Ethical judgments, then,
involve empirical judgments about those causal ingredients and laws
which apply at a given time, thereby yielding, in conjunction with
prevailing circumstances of the moment, certain results. It is Moore's
contention, thus, that 'not a single question in practical ethics can be
answered except by a causal generalisation.'[39] On the other side, it is no
less true that 'all such questions do, indeed, also involve an ethical
judgment proper – the judgment that certain effects are better, in
themselves, than others.'[40]

Thus, the conclusion reached here is that a judgment regarding the value or goodness of an action or a state of affairs – that is, an 'ethical judgment proper' – will not, by itself, and in isolation, tell you what you ought to do, or in the ethical sense, what you ought to value. To decide what is ethically 'good,' or obligatory, or 'right' requires in addition (1) an empirical account of the actual prevailing circumstances as relevant, (2) an empirical account of the anticipated causal effects which might be expected to follow from the action, and (3) a listing of the main alternative actions open to one, and a comparison of the expected results, in the short and long run. Ethical judgments are much more than judgments about which of two experiences is the more intrinsically valuable: pleasure is, in itself, more valuable than pain. To one needing his appendix removed, however, short term pain is 'better' than the agony of death. It is better to let children gain pleasure from playing in a sandbox than stop them from gaining such pleasure, unless the sandbox is in the path of some sort of frequent danger. Then it is better to cause the children to cry great tears and move them to safety. The pleasure of playing is better, in itself, than the displeasure resulting in tears, in itself. When linked to the circumstances and the causal laws of the time, however, sand play is hardly comparable to the risk of death. Ethically, it is far better not to do that which is, in itself, far better intrinsically. If this is so, then the 'intrinsically valuable' is obviously not, by itself, an end of action, but only an important ingredient in deciding what is to be an appropriate and wise end of action.

6 'Intrinsic value' is sometimes used to mean what I choose to call 'basic value.' 'Basic value' refers to those values which underlie all others but are themselves underived from any other values. Basic values are not values because of what they lead to, but because of what they are in themselves.

These alternative meanings of 'intrinsic value' do overlap. A self-justifying value, for example, was one which 'must justify of itself, because everything except itself is excluded by definition.' Similarly, in definition 1, it was stated that 'intrinsic value' is part of the nature of that to which it is attributed, 'irrespective of outer or other circumstantial or environmental conditions.' It is likely that one could reduce the list of meanings to two or three by carefully collecting together compatible and even synonymous meanings. My point is only that these different terms are used, and that the emphasis is not quite the same in any two of them. While 'basic values' may be said to be 'self-justifying,' what is to be emphasized is that they serve as the basic or fundamental starting points of any valuational enterprise. The fact that, in order to be basic, they must be self-justifying is no less necessary, but less focussed upon.

One important difference between Laird's notion of 'self-justifying' values and 'basic values' is in itself sufficient to serve as a distinguishing characteristic. 'Basic values' are self-justifying in themselves, even if 'episodic and impermanent.' They are self-justifying in themselves, and not because of a system or set of values to which they belong. Value of this kind is self-justifying in the sense of being rock-bottom, given as evident, the primitive ground, beginning, or starting point of all valuation. Just as we earlier inquired as to how it was possible to 'get knowledge gathering started,' to gain a foothold against scepticism and blindness, so now the question is, how does valuation get started? Are some values self-evident, and those because of which all other things are valuable? My answer is yes, and of course it should come as no surprise to learn that even this is a bone of contention in contemporary philosophical debate. Whereas I want to argue that what gets valuing going is the preferring of, or selecting of, some states of affairs as worthwhile in themselves, a 'primordial sense' which stops the infinite regress of the open-question test as applied to valuation: one values money, extrinsically, for what it will buy, and the goods bought for the pleasure they bring, and the pleasure they bring for ... 'For what?' 'Why is pleasure valued?' It just is, or as a child would say, 'because ...' However convincing my position might seem at first, consider the following passage from Paul Taylor's *Normative Discourse*: 'a world where all values were extrinsic, the value of one thing depending on the value of another whose value in turn depends on the value of something else, ad infinitum,'[41] is neither impossible nor unimaginable. However, concludes Taylor, such an approach would produce a world which was less than ideal, for it would be a world of 'practical people' who had learned that some activity would bring about certain results, but who had no reason for bringing about those results rather than some others.[42] Comforting though this qualification by Taylor is for my position, Monroe Beardsley argues that it is unnecessary and that there need be no 'basic values' at all:

But this is a caricature of a world in which all values are extrinsic. For, in the first place, the question whether people 'do anything for its own sake' is not at all the question whether there is intrinsic value; the world without intrinsic value (that is, our world) is a world in which people may often do something for its own sake, and may experience many enjoyments, but they cannot justify doing something for its own sake by simple appeal to enjoyment. And in the second place, a world in which all values are instrumental would be precisely a world in which every correct value judgment could be supported by a reason, and so there would always be a 'reason for getting one thing done rather than another.'[43]

What demands our reaction is the claim that a world of extrinsic values alone would not suffer because of the lack of intrinsic values.

Turning to Moore again, we find him maintaining that intrinsic values are non-derivative or basic in that all legitimate uses of 'good' or 'value' must have reference to them and are derived from them.[44] All non-intrinsic goodness depends on there being something which is not instrumentally good, contributively good, or good as a means, but good in itself or for its own sake. In order to be able to state meaningfully that anything is good or valuable, there must be something which is good or valuable in itself. There must be a basic and foundational starting point. C.I. Lewis makes an important distinction, of help to us here, between 'value' and 'utility.' If there were nothing of value for its sake alone, then there would be no genuine value of any kind whatever, for there would be but an infinite regress of things which have utility for bringing about something else with utility, and so on, with no claim anywhere along the way that anything brought about is properly termed 'valuable.' If something along the way is to be termed 'valuable,' then it must be because it has more than 'utility' going for it and has some relation, extrinsically or in itself, to something which is, in fact, thought to be valuable. And while you can simply decide to call something valuable rather than useful, the former claim demands explanation of a special sort. By 'valuable' you can't simply mean 'useful,' or else it would be enough to strike out the former and stick with the latter. To make a claim that something is valuable is to imply at least that one has a clear and significant meaning in hand which distinguishes this term from possibly related but not synonymous terms such as 'useful,' 'liked,' 'prized,' and so on. To say that something is extrinsically valuable because it leads to something else of extrinsic value is to beg the main question: 'Why are either of them to be considered "valuable" at all?' Because they lead to something else of value? But what does 'value' mean, and how did you get the process of valuation going? Like most matters of importance in philosophy, the debate goes on, and the matter remains unresolved.

7 What I have called 'basic value' refers to non-derivative values. What I now wish to isolate for inquiry is C.I. Lewis' related expression 'immediate value.' Lewis argues that just as there would be no value of

any kind without the immediately given in sense experience to which to refer all judgments, so there would be no value of any kind without the immediately given 'intrinsic value' to which all intelligible value judgments point. He states that 'the only thing intrinsically valuable – valuable for its own sake – is a goodness immediately found or findable and unmistakable when disclosed.'[45] Such value is immediately apprehended, unmistakable when disclosed, and direct. For Lewis, such apprehension is not judgmental and is therefore neither true nor false, although the expression of value findings may be true or false. But as an immediate apprehension, unmediated by either supporting evidence or chains of reasoning, it simply is as it is, that is, as apprehended. Such apprehensions are not to be classed as knowledge, 'because they are not subject to any possible error.'[46] Furthermore, what is directly presented in experience does not require verbalization, and 'knowledge itself might well get on without the formulation of the immediately given.' When we philosophically inquire into the matter, however, we must decide on some way of referring to 'such basic factualities of experience.' Thus, Lewis formulates empirical statements of this class in expressive language. Expressive language is used to express in words what occurs in experience apart from any concern as to whether it is illusory or in any way deceptive. It is difficult, and perhaps impossible, to describe the content of direct experience,[47] yet this difficulty is relatively unimportant since the awareness of what is being described remains firm. To deny the existence of this 'hard kernel in experience' is to deny that experience refers to a given at all. What words do we use to describe this immediately given?

We have already partially covered Lewis' account in our initial discussion of the meaning of 'value.' Immediate goodness is a whole gamut of experience, a general mode of presentation, rather than a single quality without differentiation. No single occasion suffices to delimit its character. 'Good' or 'value' is not simple in Moore's sense. It is, however, a unique gamut of qualities, for Lewis presumably both analysable and definable. Good or value can be analysed by dividing it into its constituent parts or listing its differing modes. We have already glanced at the wide range of immediate values, from the active and self-forgetting to pleasure itself. However varied the kinds and modes of immediate value may be, it is only because of the existence and occurrence of these that anything may properly be termed 'valuable' in any of the various value senses. All senses of value refer either to this realization of the immediately good directly or to their contribution to realizations of such good.[48] Immediate values are the rock-bottom starting points of valuation and those value 'kernels' without which nothing else could be claimed to be genuinely valuable at all. Were there nothing to be found immediately and unmistakably valuable in human experience, there would be little meaning in labelling something as extrinsically valuable. In this sense, an extrinsic value would be productive of something not directly touching human experience in the direct and unmistakable sense of the euphoric and the dysphoric. 'Value' would be another name for 'utility,' and 'utility' has as wide a range of meaning as one wishes to imagine: air is useful for tyres, blood to vampires, refuse for fertilizer, and boats for barnacles, and viruses find living systems indispensable. It is obvious that 'utility' is a term of much wider use than 'value.' Many things may be useful, far fewer valuable, and these only in so far as they relate to findings of immediate value, directly (intrinsically) or indirectly (extrinsically, in at least one of its senses).

8 What I shall call 'generic value,' yet another meaning for 'intrinsic value,' refers to a common core of meaning which all legitimate uses of 'value' or 'good' share. Let me say again that my main point in isolating this and other meanings of 'intrinsic value' is to demonstrate something of the complexity of meanings contained in the term and its uses, and to call attention to the importance of keeping clearly in mind which of the many meanings of the term is, at any given time, under consideration. As 'good' or 'value' is the term upon which 'all Ethics depends,' any systematic inquiry into ethics requires that the meaning of this term be known.[49] For both Moore and Lewis, all uses of 'good' and 'value' refer either to intrinsic value itself or to something which brings about intrinsic value. Since all legitimate uses of the term 'value' refer to value as intrinsic, it is of central importance to state clearly the meaning of this term in all its uses. Major difficulties arise in ethics and value theory when an attempt is made to determine which states of affairs, actions, or things are good, without first knowing or deciding what 'good' means. How can one find an 'x' without knowing what 'x' stands for or describes? This perplexing situation can either lead to the exhilaration born of naïvety and confusion which A.A. Milne describes in *Winnie-the-Pooh* or to Plato's frustration of knowing that no solution will be found since those on the hunt have little or no idea how to distinguish the species sought from some others, or to define the genus, or to discover the differentiate of the species (these quotations appear on page 21 above). Unless 'Woozle' is defined, the chase is blind, as A.A. Milne hints, and any finding is as adequate or inadequate as any other. Take your (blind) choice.

One clarifying result of 'Woozle hunting' and searching in the dark, or as sightless, is that, if nothing more, philosophy is that enterprise, par excellence, which demands that the inquirer be as clear as he or she possibly can be about the meaning, subtleties, and complexities of the key terms and issues of any subject-matter whatsoever. The philosophical educator must always keep front-and-centre this demand for clarity and precision, even at the expense of seeming to 'undermine' the main beliefs and values of his or her students. The goal of such education is not to 'undermine,' however, but to reinforce foundational ideas and concepts through rigorous demands for clarity and precision. To question you about your belief in God is not to get you to abandon this belief but (1) to get it clear and (2) to enable you to construct a case, based on reason and evidence, in favour of it. But before you can move up the ladder of clarity and convincing defence, you must be brought to see the inadequacy and confusion, if not vagueness and vacuousness, of your present understanding and capacity for defence.

This, our eighth meaning of 'intrinsic value,' is itself anything but clear. Moore argues that we must find a clear and unambiguous description of the meaning of 'good,' in its broadest sense – that is, 'value.' But the meanderings of twentieth-century ethics have confirmed the complexity of the issue and have gone no small distance in giving good reasons for abandoning both Moore's tidy solution ('good' is good), and even his tidy question (that is, whether there must be a single and simple property of things to which the term 'good' points). Be that as it may, Robert S. Hartman offers a telling and amusing description of the activities of and difficulties in contemporary value theory and ethics:

It so happens that value knowledge is still in the natural state. Valuing is just going on; there are no experts. There are observers and samplers of 'wild' values and their natural occurrences. There are 'naturalists' who collect values, go out into the woods and gather samples. Much of value theory today is a result of such hiking expeditions into valuation, with values sampled, classified, stuck on needles, dried, pickled and preserved. Treatises on value are the rucksacks full of such samples, reports on the expeditions of collection, the situations of catching, the contexts of trapping, and the like. There are a few who feel that there is a pattern to the whole field and many who feel that its beauty lies in having no pattern.[50]

9 The ninth and final meaning of 'intrinsic value' which I shall consider is provided by Robert S. Hartman, and while his work will constitute the basis of the next chapter, it is well to include his unusual account here, in the interest of thoroughness.

Hartman defines 'value' as a property of concepts which results from a logical operation comparing the properties of the concept of the thing with the idea of the particular thing in question.[51] Thus, a thing is valuable to the degree to which it fulfils its concept, or to the degree to which an actual thing has those properties which one's 'ideal' concept of such a thing has.

Hartman further recognizes three kinds of concepts and, therefore, three possible ways in which a thing can fulfil its concept. The fulfilment of singular concepts yields intrinsic value, and, since the singular thing has no properties in common with any other thing (at least one is not paying attention to such commonness of properties), and since there is no attempt at a selection of properties by focusing on just this or that, the 'thing and observer are one continuous entity; for, if the thing is to be apprehended in its concrete totality ... the thing must be apprehended in toto, in itself, grasped as one in its total *Gestalt*.'[52] Perhaps all this can be simplified, for the moment, by noting that intrinsic valuation is concentration on the person, the thing, or the experience before you, apart from comparison with anything or anybody else, and without concern for later consequences. By being there, totally, without the usual distractions about future consequences, how you look, whether you compare favourably with others, your reputation, or the state of the economy, time stands still and the distinction between yourself and whatever it is that you are concentrating on disappears. Suffice it to say that Hartman's account of 'intrinsic value' results from his own system. He does not attempt to describe common usage or to conclude that everyone who is wise does in fact use the term as he proposes. Rather, he argues that his system of values provides a precise meaning for 'intrinsic value,' whether or not the term has ever been used in precisely this way before. He does not conduct a Gallup poll of ordinary usage but provides another, original meaning for this elusive term.

CONCLUSIONS

Nine meanings attributed to 'intrinsic value' have been discussed: (1) value as it is in itself, somehow part of the nature of that to which it is attributed; (2) objective value; (3) absolute and eternal value; (4) self-justifying value; (5) value as an appropriate end of ethical action; (6) 'basic value'; (7) immediate value; (8) 'generic value'; and (9) the value resulting from the fulfilment of singular concepts (Hartman). A value theorist might well maintain more than one of these meanings within a single theory, and in fact Moore himself uses the term in accordance with meanings (1), (2),

(4), (6), and (8). Discussion of whether or not intrinsic values exist, how they are known, and their significance both to value theory and to ethics depends on a clear and unambiguous indication of the meaning or meanings of the term as it is being used or as it is used in a given value-theory. Alas, most people assume that such terms have fixed meaning, and that any teacher worth his or her salt will make students aware of the meaning of 'value,' 'good,' 'intrinsic,' and other important terms. Would that they could! To pretend that there are such clear meanings, that the case is not only closed but solved, is at best unacceptable laziness and unforgivable lack of professionalism, and at worst an evident and immoral attempt to propagandize, to indoctrinate. Far from being closed, issues of this sort are bubbling with both excitement and confusion, and it is the responsibility of each and every educator to make students (and, ideally, their parents) aware of the contentiousness of the issues and the tremendous amount of work that needs to be done. Even at that, the final aim is not to 'get it right,' to arrive at the correct answer for all times, and then to settle back again into the senility of passivity. No, in those areas which have to do with the most important issues in human living, the 'questions that matter most,' you need not aim to get it right but to get it better – myopia again. It would be odd to ask a sweeper of a kitchen floor to make doubly sure that the floor was perfectly clean, on the assumption that if it was swept perfectly, the floor would never have to be done again. The point is that, however well it is swept, the object of the activity is not to get it clean for ever but to keep at it such that the amount of dirt and dust remains low and the quality of living high. Philosophic issues go on and on, and the important results of inquiry into them concern the cleanliness with which you can then lead your life. Insight, honesty, humility, improvement – these are the characteristics of true philosophic education.

It should not be concluded that we have 'done' value theory. In fact, we have only briefly looked at a central term in value theory, and at that have spent little time looking at the history and wide range of alternative theories generated over the centuries. We have merely scratched the surface. Yet the little that we have done has made evident that even the starting point of value inquiry is in dispute, and I have argued that such disputatiousness is representative of what is to be found with each issue, each concept, each author, and each application. Then, when you turn to ethics proper, the same thing applies all over again. Once you know how you stand on 'value,' you must decide where you stand on deciding what you 'ought to do,' and on how you decide this, and on the relation (or lack of it) between the valued, the valuable, and the morally right. Against this background, what possible meaning can you give to the seemingly obvious request, 'Please just give them the answers?' It is a wrong-headed request based on a view of education in general, and values and moral education in particular, as bucket-filling. Instead, it is the task of the educator to set about emptying the bucket, in order to allow the precious individual first to 'see for himself' and then to 'work it out for himself' now, and then later, and again, and again, and again. Socrates corrupted the youth only from the point of view of those who subscribed to something like the bucket theory of education. They saw his sustained attempt at emptying and cleansing the bucket as purely negative and destructive. He saw their attempt to keep the bucket filled as the chief cause of moral and intellectual paralysis and passivity. Where do you stand?

EDUCATION AS INTRINSICALLY VALUABLE

Before leaving this inquiry into the meaning of 'intrinsic value,' it might prove interesting to attempt to apply it to education itself. Indeed, it is one of the issues with which R.S. Peters has long been concerned, for he observes that education or becoming educated may be conceived of and justified either instrumentally or intrinsically (or non-instrumentally): 'The most all-prevading justification for anything in our type of society is to look for its use either to the community or to the individual; for basically our society is geared to consumption. Even the work of the artist, for instance, is not always valued for the excellences which are intrinsic to it.'[53] But before turning to the examination of Peters' insight that education is all too regularly viewed instrumentally, there is a prior tangle to unravel. For there is a subtle but extremely important distinction to be drawn between the straightforward claim that something is an intrinsic *component* of something I see, and one that further asserts that either or both the intrinsic component and that to which it contributes are of intrinsic value. A house fly is an integral and therefore an intrinsic part of the ecosystem as we know it, but few would also want to claim that the house fly leads directly, and in itself, to experiences of intrinsic value. Glue is an intrinsic part of a bound book, but is not itself of intrinsic value, nor, on most interpretations, is the book. The book may reveal intrinsically valuable experiences, however, or even produce some. Books and works of art require someone to gain experiences of intrinsic value from them, whether the author/painter or some past, present, or future audience. Thus only certain kinds of experiences produced by educational activities are intrinsically valuable; education itself as some sort of ideal, or 'becoming educated' in all of its senses, is not. Something intrinsic to education may itself be without intrinsic value but as an integral part of the whole may be instrumental to one or more experiences which are of intrinsic value in one or more of the senses defined in this chapter.

This clarification now puts us in a position to use the main insights provided by Peters. The instrumental or extrinsic conception of 'education' emphasizes ends extrinsic to the process of education itself. It thus neutralizes the value of education, or even renders it a painful but necessary requirement leading to ends, goals, and jobs extrinsic to education. It is little wonder that Peters objects to questions about the 'aims of education,' for to focus on the aims of education is often to become blind to the aims and values intrinsic to the very process and activities of education *per se*. In Peters' own words, 'People thus think that education must be for the sake of something extrinsic that is worth while, whereas the truth is that being worth while is part of what is meant by calling it "education."'[54] It is educational activities yielding experiences which are 'worthwhile' or intrinsically valuable (that is, 'immediately valuable' or 'basically valuable'; see definitions (6) and (7) above) to the learner and/or the teacher that Peters highlights. Education may be instrumental to job-procurement, a higher salary, a high position, more pleasant work, reputation and social status, and so on, but the process of education that Peters is singling out and that this book has been about is always 'related to some sorts of processes in which a desirable state of mind develops.'[55] Thus, what is most important about education is that it enhances the quality of your living and the value-richness of your experiences and continually adds to your finding of and appreciation of what is worthwhile. In this sense, all non-instrumental education is drenched in values and everywhere permeated by value distinctions and judgments of valuation. More precisely, one should say that what is intrinsic (not intrinsically valuable) to the educational process, when defined as that which brings about a desirable state of mind in those involved, is that it is instrumental to character building, to developing value-sensitivity, to creating new, richer, more appropriate, and more genuinely satisfying wants. What Peters is saying is that what is really worthwhile about education is determined by the degree to which it is instrumental to human values relating to the positive transformation of the person. Education itself is not of 'intrinsic value.' Only experiences had by persons and found good or worthwhile in the living of them can be said to be of intrinsic value (see definition (7) above). And what is intrinsic to education is that it can, right now, excite, engage, sensitize, intellectually and emotionally expand, challenge, frustrate, and creatively confuse an otherwise bored and passive human being. What is intrinsically valuable about education is just this power to transform human beings. Otherwise, education is but another successful or unsuccessful instrument of intrinsic value possibility, or else nothing more than an instrumental expedient to some of the extrinsic things in life. These, of course, are needed, and are values of no small importance. In themselves, however, they are not transformative of the human capacity for understanding, valuing, feeling, and caring. Even extrinsic values are, of course, transformable in their value significance and value quantity for one who is sensitive to intrinsic valuation, as the next chapter will explain. Books, paintings, and on some occasions even house flies can become valuationally enriched if you are able to see things about you in a new way, because of your own transformation. Whatever is experienced (within or without) is significantly worthwhile, and something about which the learner now cares, is involved with, and wishes to know more about.

In part, the view of education which you adopt depends on your understanding of who the human being standing before you is. It has been my contention throughout that the human 'essence' is not fixed or final. As the existentialists have made so clear, a human being *becomes* who he or she is. I have specifically taken this to mean that part of the meaning of being human is that you must take into your own hands the responsibility for evaluating all things 'learned,' for to be 'human' is to be continually growing, expanding, and exploring. To do less than this is to run the risk of sterility and of becoming but a passive shell of apathetic receptivity. What is intrinsic to human nature is growth and exploration, questioning and expanding, appreciating and becoming engaged in an activity for yourself, that is, by making it your own problem or inquiry. Such experiences are themselves worthwhile, that is, of intrinsic value. The value of education must be seen to include this power to transform passivity into active search, appreciation, and decision making. It must lead to experiences of significant worth resulting from the opening of new vistas of understanding and appreciation. At times this will require intermediate states of intellectual ambiguity and the valuational rejection of old ways. Even when the new understanding and values emerge, one knows that this preferable myopia is but a brief place of rest. Transformation and education are always going on in growing people. As I have said, the next chapter will attempt a schema for illuminating the distinctions between intrinsic and extrinsic involvement and appreciation, but here it might be well to conclude with Peters' observations about the importance of being fully engaged in educational activities rather than simply going through the motions as though education is something that happens to you – rather like a bucket theory of education, to parallel the earlier discussion of the bucket theory of mind: 'Perhaps one of the reasons why these economic and sociological descriptions of education can be misleading ... is that they are made from the point of view of a spectator pointing to the "function" or effects of education in a social or economic system. They are not descriptions of it from the point of view of someone engaged in the enterprise.'[56]

5

The value of the person

Education in the West has long emphasized development of the intellect as its primary, sometimes its sole, concern. As a result, 'we deemphasize and even devalue the arational, non-verbal modes of consciousness. Education consists predominantly of "'readin', 'ritin', and 'rithmetic,'" and we are taught precious little about our emotions, our bodies, our intuitive capacities.'[1] Some of the imbalance has been redressed with stress on sex education, outdoor activities and explorations, and various sensitivity and affectivity programs in schools, not to mention religious studies (which continues to be a loaded issue). Still, it remains unclear for many just exactly how this 'ties in' with the intellectual training which continues to be the schools' major concern. it is even more unclear what other 'arational' or non-rational modes of consciousness are being pointed to. What are the various aspects of the person which are to be isolated, encouraged, and then reassembled in the harmonious expression of individuality? The question is ancient as well as modern and concerns teaching the nature of the self. Plato warns in the *Apology* that the unexamined (un-self-criticized) life is not worth living,[2] and his critical examination of the self is made a religious duty as a result of his acceptance of the advice given by the Delphic oracle, 'Know yourself!' In the *Republic* he provides one of his most developed accounts of this 'self' which education is supposed to bring you to know: the self (psyche, or 'soul' in Plato's terms) has three parts; the rational, the spirited or feeling, and the appetitive or passionate.[3] And while this tripartite analysis was probably never meant to be exhaustive of the functions of the self, it is a broad account of its chief functions.[4] Plato continually reminds you that these three parts are not to be groomed in isolation but must be viewed and treated as a unity and harmony of distinctions within the balanced and complex whole of personhood. As educator, then, you are responsible not only for developing the isolatable parts of the self but also for assisting with the harmonious integration of these parts in a balanced personality. No doubt this helps to explain why Plato was so sure that to know the good was to do the good, for this is guaranteed if you assume that your 'real' knowing (as a balanced and integrated individual) includes passionate zeal for putting what you know into action and deep feelings to initiate and maintain that passion. A healthy, 'together' person does not 'know' in the abstract but knows with feeling and will; the healthier the person, the more intense the feeling, the firmer the will. All three dimensions must be alive and well and pulling together in harmonious clarity provided by the leadership of reason.

While my approach in this book has not been to follow Plato's account as the sufficient and last word on the healthy and harmoniously integrated personality, my stress on such health and integration is similar to his. In summary, we have articulated a view of reason which is non-absolutistic in result without being blindly relativistic, have examined the importance of moral education to the curriculum, and in so doing have come to emphasize the importance of habit formation, example, and the environment of the hidden curriculum, the 'sentiment of humanity' or human-hearted concern for others, and the existential emphasis on the subjective factors of willing and choosing as necessary ingredients in human development and education. The activity of human valuation requires more than intellectual clarity. It requires feeling: intense feelings, the passionate commitment of deciding to act, the skills and techniques of putting your decisions into practice with accuracy and effectiveness, with an attitude which grasps existence as worthwhile. It is a mistake to suppose that the job of the educator is to produce healthy intellects or healthy reasoners alone. Such individuals may be unfeeling ivory tower dwellers unable to put what they know into practice, or unskilled practitioners who know, feel, and will with brilliance and intensity but can never pull it off in the world of everyday activity. They are inept implementers. By contrast, the 'well-educated' and 'well-balanced' are those who think critically and clearly, feel intensely, will firmly and with commitment, and have learned to put into practice with finesse the results of these preliminary activities. All these ingredients and activities are part of the background of human valuation. The foreground is the 'way of life' which the background factors come to express. If you do these things well and are in harmony within yourself, you may be said to have a healthy system of values and to be able to express your values effectively in the world. Whether the system and its expression is called religious or philosophical or humanistic is less important than that it expresses a vibrancy of personality which has kept alive the various dimensions, with the resulting tension of the chosen emphasis and correctives being a harmony of differing notes, a continual shifting of notes, intensities, keys, and styles which through it all maintains its integration and steadfastly searches out preferable and worthwhile results. As teacher, you cannot pretend to know what the balance for an individual is to be, but you can make certain that the various parts are alive and well and that the final integration and attitude are never lost sight of. To say more is to assume that we are all alike, that the balance of tension is the same for all 'instruments,' and that the final goal is not only clear and distinct but obviously uniform. It is no small point to note that an orchestra of identical instruments playing the same note in the same way would be both pointless and dull. Chaotic improvisation without concern for the traditions and rules of music would be equally unacceptable.

The harmony and integration of the self are habitually forgotten in modern education because it is seldom emphasized that there are distinct 'parts' requiring differing nurture. Plato speaks of three parts, sometimes of two, and even then makes no claim that the division is either the final one or exhaustive of the richness and diversity of the capacities and functioning of the self.[5] It is perhaps easier here to speak of (1) knowing, (2) feeling, and (3) willing as the chief divisions of consciousness, with (4) the integration and harmony of these constituting the character of the individual. Each of these could be divided yet again, so that will-power, ego-strength, and the capacity to self-start and to persevere might all be included in an analysis of, for example, willing. Additionally, there are the less accepted but quite common claims for additional or altered states and functions of consciousness which might be considered, including meditation, ESP in its various forms, the mystical vision, and the oriental states of enlightenment such as satori or nirvana. Finally, there is the need to take into account the foundational input which comes to you through the senses themselves. Just as you can educate your intellect and stiffen your will, so you can attend to your sense organs in order to refine them and make them more or less sensitive to the stimuli which continually impinge on them. The Scottish philosopher John Macmurray once wrote, 'The education of our emotional life is primarily an education of our sensibility'[6] and added that it is 'an aspect of our experience which is too much overlooked.' He defines 'sensuality' (for him the goal of training in the sense realm) as 'the capacity to enjoy organic experience, to enjoy the satisfaction of the senses.'[7] He is not unaware of the puritanism which, for so much of the modern era, has warned that pleasure or enjoyment is religiously evil and morally bad: 'There lies behind us a long tradition which would persuade us that this capacity is undesirable, and should be eliminated altogether.'[8] We have all too often undertaken through education to suppress our sensuality. On the side of feeling in education, it must be recognized that 'the first stage in any education of the emotional life must be the reversal of this attitude. We have to start by recognizing and insisting that the life of the senses is inherently good.'[9] Indeed, the senses are the 'gateways of our awareness,' and without the input gained through them we would be locked within our own minds. If you are concerned with the fullness and richness of life, then in considerable measure it results from 'the delicacy and quality of our sense-life.'[10] The development of meaning and joy in life appears to rely heavily on our awareness of the world and our capacity to see what we have overlooked before, to see what we have seen before in a new way, and to respond to both with an attitude of being-totally-there in the moment.

THE POINT OF VIEW OF ZEN

On this point we may benefit from an understanding of Zen Buddhism, which recommends that we lose ourselves in the richness of the moment and become the raindrop, or the flower, or the gnarled pine which we see, touch, smell, and even hear before us. The claim that you should 'become' a tree or a flower may appear to be illogical or impossible except as a metaphor of the same intention as comparing your love to a red, red rose. Such comparisons are not to be taken literally, but as a kind of poetic licence which expresses your intensity of feeling. But something very different happens on the Japanese account, and on Macmurray's account as well. First of all, as an artist you may exemplify the sensuality of becoming, for you do not attend to the human body, or the landscape before you, as a means to an end, that is, extrinsically. You attend to it 'for the sake of the awareness itself,'[11] for its own sake, that is, intrinsically. You lose yourself in the richness of the experience of the object which you probably appreciate in a fuller way than most people, or differently. You probably got that way by looking at things for the joy of seeing them, as the musician and the student of bird-song very likely choose their vocation because of their love of music and song. Macmurray is worth quoting at length on this 'intrinsic' sense of sensual awareness:

Sensitive awareness becomes then a life in itself with an intrinsic value of its own which we maintain and develop for its own sake, because it is a way of living, perhaps the very essence of all living. When we use our senses in this way we come alive in them, as it were, and this opens up a whole new world of possibility. We see and hear and feel things that we never noticed before, and find ourselves taking delight in their existence. We find ourselves living in our senses for love's sake, because the essence of love lies in this. When you love anyone you want above all things to be aware of him, more and more completely and delicately. You want to see him and hear him, not because you want to make use of him but simply because that is the natural and only way of taking delight in his existence for his sake. That is the way of love, and it is the only way of being alive. Life, when it is really lived, consists in this glad awareness. Living through the senses is living in love. When you love anything, you want to fill your consciousness with it.[12]

And in filling your whole consciousness with it, there is, at least for the moment, nothing else of which you are aware – not even your own breathing. Your whole consciousness is the tree, your loved one, and the only you that is left is the consciousness of the loved one or the tree. You have become that of which you are aware, by which you are filled. You are totally absorbed in such consciousness, abandoning the standoffish attempt to be 'objective' about what is before you. To make the contrast, Macmurray describes a drawing by George Morrow which has a couple watching a sunset. The woman remarks that the sunset is lovely, but the husband, who is not really absorbed by what is before him, for his mind is elsewhere, adds, 'That reminds me … Do remember to tell our landlady that I like my bacon streaky.'[13]

BECOMING ONE WITH SOMETHING

Whereas we in the West speculate about what might be meant by an artist or anyone else becoming one with his object by the power of absorption and concentration, the East has long practised this capacity and made it an integral part of their cultural training. The Japanese are widely known for their good taste in things aesthetic, and the subtlety of their sensual discernment is often noted. The philosophical underpinning for this cultural capacity is provided by Zen Buddhism. Zen requires that you learn to let go of your ego and then to forget all your assumptions about the object being 'out there' and separate from yourself. Instead, you must make yourself open to the fullness of the experience itself. You must be fully open, that is, lose yourself in the experience such that it is no longer 'your experience,' nor is it an experience of 'that' tree. Instead, all that is left is the experience itself, the givenness of treeness. You lose your ego-boundaries by reaching out and embracing the tree, and then by concentrating your awareness on the tree as embraced, exclusive of all else. Consider the following account:

The painter sits in quite contemplation, intensely concentrating his mind upon the ideal image of the bamboo. He begins to feel in himself the rhythmic pulsebeat of the life energy which keeps the bamboo alive and which makes the bamboo a bamboo, becoming gradually concordant with the pulsebeat of the life-energy which is running through his mind-body complex. And finally there comes a moment of complete unification, at which there remains no distinction whatsover between the life-energy of the painter and the life-energy of the bamboo. Then there is no longer any trace in the consciousness of the painter of himself as an individual self-subsistent person. There is actualized only the Bamboo. Where is it actualized? Internally? Or externally? No one knows. It does not matter. For the word 'becoming' in the particular context here at issue concerns a state of contemplative awareness having in itself no ontological implication.

There is absolutely no 'consciousness of' anything whatsoever. The sole fact is that the Bamboo is there, actualized with an unusual vivacity and freshness, pulsating with a mysterious life-energy pervading the whole universe. At that very moment the painter takes up the brush. The brush moves, as it were, of its own accord, in conformity with the pulsation of the life-rhythm which is actualized in the bamboo.[14]

The same phenomenon of total absorption and complete identification is regularly expressed through the martial arts. You may have read of, and might be able to imagine yourself to be, a samurai swordsman, no longer separated from your sword because you have learned to focus your mind and energy on the circumstances of the encounter. Spontaneously, the sword seems to block a thrust, and without any thinking, your body and the sword together thrust home the decisive blow. You do not think or worry about whether you are as good as your opponent, or about the positioning of your feet, or about your children and wife at home, or about the lessons given by your master. You are totally in the battle, and for the moment this is your whole world. The Japanese samurai is a lethal living weapon precisely because in the moment that is all he is. He is totally there. For purposes of educational theory, it does not matter whether it is morally justified that there be samurai, for the point in question is whether Western culture sufficiently emphasizes the development of the capacity to be completely absorbed in the experiences of living. If you were a samurai, haiku poet, brush painter, potter, musician, or sports figure in Japan, you would be taught from the beginning to apply yourself to the art of single-minded concentration on the experience of the moment. Even now in Japan it would not be an unusual activity for you to sit for an afternoon gazing at a particularly beautiful pine tree. In fact, the sort of concentrated sitting which requires that you become single-minded and eventually 'no-minded'[15] with respect to what is before you, and even yourself, is regularly a part of basic art training. Learning requires that you be still, and stillness includes the capacity to embrace totally whatever is before you in experience.

An important aspect of this capacity for attending to what is given in direct experience is its immediacy. Ordinary cognitive activities are heavily mediated by language, by concepts, by expectations and habits, by stereotypes, and by the imposition of order and regularity so that exceptions are not even seen. Often, when you look at a pine tree, the word 'pine tree' comes to mind at least in the background of consciousness. You are helped to see the tree by being at least half aware of what the concept 'pine tree' stands for and includes. You may only glance quickly at the tree, for you expect that you will see what you have seen so many times before and may even mis-see what is there because you anticipate that it will have the features common to your other encounters with pine trees. To concentrate on your concept of the tree, or to allow your expectations to blind you to what is before you, or simply to glance at it out of lack of interest is to 'mistake the finger for the moon,' as the old Zen story has it. The moon is above you, not nearby, but to point it out to someone you point with your finger. If it is not clear what you are doing, your onlooker may think you are asking him to look at your finger, and so he assumes that the moon you are telling him about is your finger. Similarly, verbal and symbolic expression is but a pointer, a finger pointing at the experiences themselves. To see what you call a pine tree is not to focus attention on the words, the concept, or even the expectations, but rather on the experience before you. Ideally, you still your mind, including your assumptions and expectations, your pigeon-holeing and conceptualization, until you become mirror-like. A mirror is still, like a lake without ripples, better able to reflect what is given without the same degree of distortion. By getting back to the experience itself, you have stilled the mind and made it more capable of seeing or of reflecting what is there in experience. Only the tree remains, with the activities and expectations of the ego stilled and made calm. The tree occupies the entire conscious world of the individual; it is an object of concentration. To this point it is still the consciousness of the tree in your experience. The Zen Buddhist would go still further, to the disappearance of the last trace of your ego-consciousness, so that tree-consciousness alone would exist. For our purposes this is not a necessary step, for what is being emphasized is a state of consciousness which is able to drink afresh and completely from the flowing source of sense-experience. A common saying in Zen is that a true Zen master receives a student each day as though for the first time. He does not assume that this fellow will never learn, or that he will be making progress today because he always has before. A good teacher tries to leave expectations and assumptions about the past nature of a student behind him in order to be open to new and possibly contradictory insights about the student and his or her needs and attributes. Change, not constancy alone, is to be taken as a fundamental characteristic of the world, and of human beings. Fixity is as much a distortion of the ideal as is chaotic flux.

ERNST CASSIRER

Similar ideas are to be found in Western culture, of course, notably in Ernst Cassirer's influential study *Language and Myth*. Cassirer describes what he calls two ways of thinking, or, as I would say here, he contrasts conceptual thinking with concentration on immediate experience:

The aim of theoretical thinking ... is primarily to deliver the contents of sensory or intuitive experience from the isolation in which they originally occur ... it proceeds 'discursively,' in that it treats the immediate content only as a point of departure, from which it can run the whole gamut of impressions in various directions, until these impressions are fitted together into one unified conception, one closed system.

Mythical thinking ... bears no such stamp; in fact, the character of intellectual unity is directly hostile to its spirit. For in this mode, thought does not dispose freely over the data of intuition, in order to relate and compare them to each other, but is captivated and enthralled by the intuition which suddenly confronts it. It comes to rest in the immediate experience; the sensible present is so great that everything else dwindles before it. For a person whose apprehension is under the spell of this mythico-religious attitude, it is as though the whole world were simply annihilated; the immediate content, whatever it be, that commands his religious interest so completely fills his consciousness that nothing else can exist beside and apart from it. The ego is spending all its energy on this single object, lives in it, loses itself in it.[16]

And the pedagogical significance of this twofold account of thinking about and attending to things in experience is not lost on Cassirer. Towards the end of *Language and Myth* he argues that you must maintain a tension between these two ways of thinking, returning to mythical or holistic thinking in order to gain a fresh perspective, or simply in order to drink in another aspect of the richness which you inevitably strip down and filter out in the discursive mode of thinking. Then you return to the discursive mode and reprocess the new manifold, reorganizing it.[17] Returning to the model of chapter 3, the discursive mode is what we there called the nostalgia for unity (the unifying mode), while the mythical mode is the endlessly rich and sometimes chaotic apprehension of experience as disunity. I also argued in that chapter, however, that not all of experience is chaotic, and thus this richness which Cassirer speaks of is both chaotic at times and endlessly rich, and ordered and harmonious at others. Only some of the existentialists seem convinced that it is chaos alone that reigns. Cassirer, mystics of various traditions, artists, scientists, philosophers, and the religious regularly speak of the apprehension of the beneficence, harmony, order, support, and positive wonder of the embracive apprehension of things. Now it is an old chestnut that what you see is extremely dependent on your attitude and expectations. Back in the 1960s, in Boston, experiments were going on with LSD, and people were told to expect wild psychotic experiences. They ingested the drug in antiseptic rooms, with doctors and nurses on hand to help them through their ordeal. Just three miles away, at Harvard, other experimenters were preparing their subjects for 'consciousness-expanding' experiences. They were told to look for growth insights and told of the possible religious and aesthetic flavour of the experiences to come. The environment included music, books, art supplies, rugs on the floor – a cosy set-up in sharp contrast to the stainless steel and white arrangements in Boston. Of course, there were few psychotic experiences at the Harvard site and people claimed great benefit from their experiences. In Boston, few came back for a second try, while at Harvard the lines were always long when a new set of experiments was announced, and some were in line for the fourth and fifth time. Now our interest in drug-taking of this sort has died down, and the lines and the experiments have all but disappeared, but the careful training which both provided support and helped to eliminate fear and other negative emotions also sensitized the subjects to the positive elements of their experience. Many existentialists place one-sided emphasis on the absurd elements in your experience and on your lack of success in finding answers which have a fixed and absolute standing. Cassirer emphasizes the mystery and awe-fulness of the rich and mythically profound world you experience. Macmurray maintains that you must be willing to accept the intrinsic goodness of your sensuality. The Zen Buddhists affirm that you and your experiences are but two sides of the same coin. You are the rest of the universe, and the rest of the universe is you. There is no distinction, no separation. You love nature because nature is a part of the whole of which you also are a part. To say, as the Zen Buddhists do, that all things have buddha-nature is to say that all things are part of the whole and much of their value arises from their interconnectedness. Enlightenment is merely seeing or recognizing what has always been the case – the integration of all things, and the obvious fact that all things are expressions of the 'Crimson Heart of Cosmic Compassion.'[18] The whole universe is an expression of compassion which we can tune in or block out. Similarly, the Judaeo-Christian tradition speaks of the goodness of God's creation. And the attitudinal differences go a long way towards determining what you will or will not be sensitive to in your experience. The rest is often blocked out. Thus, a teacher will want to make certain, if you are an optimist, that you are at least made aware of some of the disunity and disappointments possible over your lifetime, but if you are a pessimist, that you are enabled to turn to and appreciate the order and joy possible in life.

HARTMAN'S ANALYSIS

It will prove useful here to make some new, slightly more technical distinctions in order to help organize what has been assembled thus far as ingredients in an integrated, harmonious, and responsive personality evidencing healthy emotional and sensual development and the capacity to will and enact what is felt and understood. In describing the nature of value experience, Robert S. Hartman isolates three major and distinctive kinds of value and valuation.[19] For my present purpose of applying and benefitting from his general schema, it would be distracting to try here to evaluate the grounds of Hartman's insights or thus confirm or disconfirm his position. It is enough to use his analysis as a 'searchlight' to enable you to peer more deeply into the dark recesses of your own experience and describe in an orderly way how open you are, or may become, to the experiences and valuings of what is around and within you.

In defining 'value,' Hartman first points out that it is a term which refers to the successful result of a logical operation. You have an idea or concept in your mind of what a 'good' or 'valuable' automobile would be like, and you superimpose this expectation on an actual automobile before you. If the automobile lives up to your expectations to a considerable degree, you deem it very valuable, or a 'good automobile.' Otherwise, you judge it fair, or average, or poor. Whether it is a person, a book, or a sunset, even a witch or devil, the same logical operation is performed. Thus, the axiom or basic rule of valuation is that 'a thing is good if it fulfills the intension of its concept.'[20] The term 'intension' needs explanation. The intension of a concept is the meaning or meanings with which you endow it. If you speak of a good automobile, you may mean that it must have doors which shut with a heavy thud and windows that roll down all the way, and that it must operate economically, quietly, and so on. All the properties which go to make up your concept of an automobile constitute the intension or meaning of that concept. Thus, the intension of a concept refers to a set of defining predicates, that is, to those properties or qualities which define that concept. One of the properties of a good chair, for example, is that it be suitable for sitting on. Many things can be sat upon which are not chairs, but a chair which can't be sat upon is not much of a chair, but rather may be a broken chair, a model or miniature chair, or whatever. To quote Hartman: 'Thus, whenever the word "good" is used, there a logical operation is performed. We combine the properties of the concept of the thing with the idea of the particular thing that is called good. When we hear of a good automobile, we combine the predicates of the concept "automobile," which we have in our minds, with the idea of the particular automobile in question.'[21] A thing is 'good' (or 'valuable'), then, to the degree to which it fulfils the intension of your concept of it. Notice that this last formulation makes it clear that you impose your expectations and value-grid on whatever is before you. If you decide that white people are not really people, that is, that they are significantly lacking in humanity because of their pale skin colour, then no white person can be a 'good' person. Or, if you suppose that women are less capable than men, you may say that a particular woman drives 'as well as a man,' indicating that your general view of women is that they are, in this respect, generally inferior to men. Prejudice, racism, and chauvinism are all impositions of fixed and rigid expectational concepts upon the actual people, objects, and experiences before us. Hartman's analysis points out that such rigid imposition of an expectational concept or requirement is but one kind of valuation and is therefore only appropriate in a limited number of instances and circumstances, being inappropriate in a vast number of other instances. There are three sorts of valuational stances possible.

THREE KINDS OF VALUE: SYSTEMIC

Hartman recognizes three kinds of concepts and therefore three resultant ways in which a thing or person can fulfil its concept. There are synthetic (or constructive) concepts, analytic (or abstractive) concepts, and singular concepts (or proper names). Fulfilment of the intension of the first results in systemic value; of the second, extrinsic value; and of the third, intrinsic value.[22] Synthetic concepts are human-made constructions of the mind, and not just abstractions from experience. Examples are the number 7, or the concept of a mathematical point which has no dimensions, or the Latin name of a plant which is so defined as to make it possible and even easy to locate the plant in the wilds. One of Hartman's favourite and most amusing examples of a synthetic concept is *Syringa vulgaris*, the Latin for 'lilac':

In the natural sciences electrons, spaces, waves, and the like are constructs, but also horses, flowers, and all empirical things insofar as they are elements of zoological, botanical, etc. systems. As such they are referred to by Latin names. Lilac, for example, is botanically '*Syringa vulgaris*.' Syringa vulgaris has the minimum attributes which any lilac must have to belong to the botanical class. But 'lilac' has many attributes which *Syringa vulgaris* does not have, all the fragrance and beauty which the poets – but not the botanists – extol. 'Lilac' determines not a logical but an empirical or axiological class. 'When lilacs last in the door-yard bloom'd' is full of everyday meaning. 'When *Syringa vulgaris* last in the door-yard bloom'd' sounds, in comparison, like a joke, and is a joke, for a joke is a transposition of frames of reference. Actually, the transposition means that what the line says is not so or nonsense, and it is; for *Syringa vulgaris* cannot 'bloom.' *Syringa vulgaris* belongs in the botany books and exists only there; and in botany books plants do not 'bloom'; they pullulate. 'Pullulate' connotes the minimum-and-exact-set of attributes which is to 'bloom' as *Syringa vulgaris* is to lilac – and homo sapiens is to man, and homo economicus is to man in a certain setting. All these are the minimum sets of attributes within an everyday concept which make that concept a logical rather than an axiological one, and the thing referred to a member of a logical rather than an axiological class. Such a minimum set of attributes is called a Schema. Logical classes consist of schemata.[23]

Synthetic concepts are constructions of the human mind, are precise, rigorously mean only what they are purposely constructed to mean, and contain no more and no fewer elements than are specifically assigned to them. They may or may not apply to empirical reality. If they do, or are so used, they reduce the richness of reality-as-experienced to the precise and limited requirements of the system of which they are a part. Thus, Galileo was able to represent all motion with his formula for motion relating velocity, distance travelled, and elapsed time, $V = s/t$, only by ignoring everything which was not essential or central to his purposes. The formula will not deal with the seeming speed of something, but only with its measurable speed. It ignores noise, colour, and all the 'inessential' variables. Motion is reduced simply to the factors of the formula and their relations. Synthetic concepts owe their existence to purely human system building. Such concepts have only two possible values – either perfection or non-value: 'There are no good or bad geometric circles.'[24] Perfection is the only positive value within the realm of systemic valuation, and its opposite is non-perfection, or non-value. Geometrically, it makes no sense to talk of an 'almost circle' – an almost circle, for example, might actually be an ellipse, which is a precise concept, and certainly not a 'somewhat circle.' In everyday experience, of course, we speak of an almost circular ellipse, but for the precise geometrician, a circular oval is a contradiction in terms. Other instances of imperfect circularity may be imagined as well, but their irregularity in falling short of the strict norm makes them technically non-circles. Anything not elliptical but still curved and a connected continuous line is either a circle or something else. The valuing which goes with judgments based on systemic concepts and their values is black and white. It is the simplest kind of valuation there is.[25] Because such human-made concepts are stripped-down versions of a richer and diverse body of experience, 'it is obvious that when applied to actual things it "prejudices" them – it is the model of prejudice.'[26] Systemic valuation allows none of the variety of degrees of valuation found in extrinsic or intrinsic valuation. It allows no diversity, no deviation, since things and people either conform to the exact and minimum definition of the synthetic concept or are not members of that class. You encounter such an attitude not uncommonly in the classroom and in life. 'Either you do things my way, or you are no longer welcome.' 'A good student is necessarily one who ...' 'He'll never get anywhere, for he is only interested in art.' 'He learned to read much more slowly than any student I have ever had. He can't be very bright or else he would have been able to follow my lessons the way all the other kids did.' 'What more can you expect of a girl in mathematics, of a black in business, of someone who repeated grade one, of a child from parents like those two, of someone from the south side of town ...?' All geometrical circles, in order to be geometrical circles, must be instances of 'a plane closed curve equidistant from a centre.' It is interesting to note that the absolutist in morality or in epistemology takes the position that moral rules, moral acts, and moral motives, like claims to truth, are either right or wrong – completely correct or totally unacceptable and false. The systemic valuer, the systemic epistemologist, and the moral absolutist all hold to the view that there is either 20/20 vision or there is blindness. They reduce the complexity, richness, diversity, variation, and emergent newness of experience to the single value of perfection or its absence. Galileo was able to achieve precision only because he reduced his interests to a bare minimum and in order to achieve specific results. He did not intend or claim to publish a book on the psychology of the experience of motion or to give an exhaustive account of all the characteristics of things in motion. He merely wanted an absolute standard for measuring the speed at which things travelled. His language and the language of systemic value in general are technical and precise. They are not the language of everyday, nor are synthetic concepts everyday concepts. Systemic value is the value of logical, systematic thought, and in its own sphere, and for its own purposes, it must be just what it is. Systemic concepts and systematic science and language are both indispensible and enormously important human achievements. It is only when they are misapplied that problems arise and distortions occur. This will become clearer, I hope, as we contrast this first kind of valuation with the remaining two which Hartman considers.

THREE KINDS OF VALUE: EXTRINSIC

Everyday things in space and time are known with everyday vagueness and imprecision and are spoken of in everyday empirical language.[27] Everyday language is full of valuational comparison and description – 'Sue is much prettier than her sister,' 'That was the finest car I have ever owned,' 'You wrote a first-rate essay,' and so on. Everyday language relates and/or evaluates things as members of classes. Everyday things are arranged in classes based on common properties, like automobiles, first-class students, boys and girls, all heavy objects, animals, vegetables, and minerals. The concepts determining and defining such classes are analytic and are the result of abstracting. The intensions of analytic concepts are abstractions of properties which two or more things have in common. You 'pull out' or 'pull off' those properties of things which bind them together, making them similar, or related, or identical. When you subsume an empirical thing under an abstracted analytic concept, you admit it to that class as having or possessing more or less of the properties demanded by the concept. Good chairs, good peaches, good teachers, good gardens, and good television sets are subsumed under their appropriate concept in spite of the great variety among them, and in spite of possessing less than all the predicates contained in the concept 'chair' or 'television set.' There are many more attributes in the analytic concept than in the synthetic concept, for they are not precisely made but are made more and more precise through linguistic analysis, careful definition, and lengthy exposition. Analytic concepts, as has been said, are arrived at through abstraction, by 'drawing off' properties in common to two or more things. The 'drawing off' of properties proceeds one-by-one and may continue to more and more specification, without, however, ever reaching the point of complete enumeration of all the properties of the things in question. You can go back to a class of objects, or even to a single object again and again and never see exactly the same limited number of properties in the same way and in the same relation. As we attend more closely, look and listen with attitudes of joy or sorrow, impatience or identification, we see more characteristics of something. The light values change, shadows and reflections alter, the climactic conditions flow on in remarkable variety, and so on. The number of properties of empirical experiences, people and things, is infinite, at least for practical purposes. Cassirer's remarks support this theory: 'The revelation of this inexhaustibility of the aspects of things is one of the great privileges and one of the deepest charms of art.'[28] It is also one of the great joys of life, and as Macmurray has argued, ought to be reason enough for educating the sensual capacity, the sensibilities of our people. It is one of the great points of focus of Japan, where the aesthetic sense is so cultivated as to be virtually identical with religiosity.[29] So important is the aesthetic capacity in Japan that many have claimed it to be the outstanding positive characteristic of that culture. Charles Moore, in representing what he takes to be the learned opinion on this matter, writes:

In comparison with other cultures, the aesthetic has been considered to be the essentially unique expression of spirituality in Japan, as is ethics in China, religion in India, and, possibly, reason in the West. Their love of beauty; their extreme and seemingly universal love of Nature; their attempt to express beauty in all aspects of life (the tea ceremony, flower arrangement, gardens, etc.); the spririt and fact (or, at least, ideal of harmony in philosophy and religion, and in the social and political order) ... these are all well known and accepted as characteristic.[30].

But whether Japanese or American, the artist has long known that 'the aspects of things are innumerable, and they vary from one moment to another.'[31] By contrast, the systemically scientific perspective of synthetic conceptualization of valuation is arrived at by 'impoverishment of reality'[32] by reducing experience to a few characteristics which things have in common. In contrast, the artist looks for things which may not be very common at all or puts the common in a new and different light. Once you come to see the world in a new or different way through the eyes of the painter, actor, musician, or holy person, you are then able to see the world again and again in this light. 'We are convinced that this light is not merely a momentary flash. By virtue of the work of art it has become durable and permanent. Once reality has been disclosed to us in this particular way, we continue to see it in this shape,'[33] at least until we come to see it in yet another light, and then yet another still. As J.Z. Young concluded, a really youthful and interesting brain is one which, some-how, is able to set off on new paths and see things differently, probably because it is continually seeking out new circumstances, new perspec-tives, new ideas, new critiques (see page 36 above). Senility, you will recall, is the absence of such change, such newness, such challenges and threats to the way in which you have viewed and valued our world and yourself.

In practice, the analytic concepts which we form are often remarkably rich in the numbers of predicates in their intensions. Hartman uses the example of the expert wine taster who admits to being able to identify 158 properties belonging to good wine.[34] Few people are that adept at distinguishing wines, or in choosing automobiles. But the more you know about a thing, the more properties there are in your concept of that thing. An automotive engineer knows the properties of as many as fifteen thousand parts and, when choosing his own car, will probably concern himself not with the sound of the car door shutting but with the specifications of certain strategic parts about which the average buyer knows little or nothing. Whether you are a mechanic or an average buyer, the activity of extrinsic valuation is the logical operation whereby the intension of the concept of a 'good auto' in your mind is compared with an actual auto in the everyday space-time world, in other words, in the showroom. Unlike systemic value, extrinsic value admits of infinite degrees of value. Something may have between one and ten of the ten properties contained in its intension, and still be that kind of thing. It may more or less fulfil the intention of its concept in any of 2 to the tenth minus 1 ways (which formula refers to the number of possible combinations of properties within the set of ten properties), or in 1023 different ways. Is it any wonder that you experience seemingly unending variations in the extrinsic value of things? Thus, extrinsically speaking, Hartman calls something 'good' in its class if it has all, or almost all, of the ten properties, 'fair' if it has more than half but less than most, 'so-so' if it has half of them, and 'bad' if it has less than half but at least one of them. If you could be precise about your norm concept, indicating just how many properties you wished to attend to, then you could be precise in determining just to what extent something in the space-time world measured up to the norm. Of course, the empirical world is 'inexhaustible,' and so you never do have abstract concepts as fixed as that, although you may have rules of thumb which apply with seeming precision for practical purposes.

The value resulting from the application of analytic concepts is termed 'extrinsic' because the standard of value used is not simply the experience, object, or person under scrutiny but its, his, or her membership in the class. The class concept is the norm, and the thing is valuable extrinsically to the degree to which it measures up to the full value of its class concept, and not to the degree to which it is valuable in itself. Flowers, plumbers, and chairs are valued extrinsically to the degree that they fulfil the concepts of 'flower,' 'plumber,' and 'chair' in general. Teachers and students will be familiar with the way in which your standing in the class or grade on a paper is always comparative. A good teacher will note that a mark of 26 is considerably better than a mark of 0 and shows marked improvement, but the comparative result is still a 'failure,' for it is below the acceptable comparative standard which exists outside the individual student, improvement notwithstanding. And the point here is not to criticize that recognition, for, as with systemic valuation, extrinsic valuation is an indispensable part of human judgment and decision making. We must classify, compare, rank, judge relative merit and defect, and recommend on the basis of external criteria and established (external) standards. The only point to remember is that this is but one of three ways of valuing things and people. It is not the only way of evaluating, for it is but one third of the whole story.

If the intension of a concept is that defining set of properties or predicates which serve to identify and distinguish that thing, then the extension of a concept is that set of entities to which the concept actually (and potentially) applies. The extension of the concept 'good auto' consists of all actual autos which live up to or fulfil the intension of that concept. In general, the more specific you become in your description of something by including many properties in its intension, the smaller will be the range of the extension of the concept. If you simply require that something 'exist,' then almost nothing is eliminated from your net, except those things which do not exist, like unicorns and people long since dead. On the other hand, if you speak of 'existing, red, small, fast moving, intelligent, two-legged, vegetarian animals,' the class of things having all of those properties is either very small or non-existent, that is, without an extension. You know what the class is or would be, but the class has few or no members. You have become so specific as to narrow the field down to such an extent that almost nothing qualifies. At least with respect to analytic concepts, the fewer the properties, the more general the concept, and the more general the concept, the greater its extension. Extension and intension vary in inverse proportion. Abstract concepts with the widest extension, like 'being,' are the least rich intensionally. At the lower levels of abstraction, you may draw off properties which several things have in common, but generally the more properties, the fewer things will be found which have these properties. The least specific concept is a definition which, at minimum, must contain two attributes, a genus and a differentia. The most specific concept possible is the singular concept, or proper name. Analytic concepts, then, occupy the intervening area between a definition and a singular concept. The limit of analytic concepts on the one side is the synthetic concept, that is, its determination in a minimum of terms. The limit of analytic concepts on the other side is the singular concept, that is, the analytic concept determined in a maximum of terms.

THREE KINDS OF VALUE: INTRINSIC

The singular concept or proper name (Hartman's 'unicept') has the richest intension of all concepts and, correspondingly, the most limited extension. A singular concept, or proper name, refers to one thing and one thing only. Its extension is of the barest minimum, and its intension, neither selective nor abstractive, includes the infinity of properties which any singular thing appears to have or does in fact possess. Singular things are apprehended as unique existents. Singular concepts and the persons or things corresponding to them are unique, one of a kind: 'To extensional singularity belongs intensional uniqueness.'[35] Singular things are apprehended in their full concreteness. There is no selection of properties, no separation of thing and concept, at least not during the act of apprehension: 'Thing and observer are one continuous entity; for, if the thing is to be apprehended in its concrete totality ... the thing must be apprehended in toto, in itself, grasped as one in its total *Gestalt*.'[36] The singular thing is apprehended through involvement of the subject in the object, by identification or compenetration,[37] or by interpenetration.[38] Involvement varies from occasion to occasion and person to person, but the singular thing 'in itself is the totality of all these aspects.'[39]

The language of singular concepts is the language of metaphor and poetry.[40] A metaphor, for Hartman, is a word used to mean any other word, or combination of words, in your own or any other language or group of languages. A metaphor is a 'set of predicates used as a variable.'[41] Examples of words used metaphorically, whether in metaphors or similes, are not difficult to find: 'She is a peach,' 'My love is like a red, red rose,' 'He grew tree-straight,' 'poems are like glass,'[42] and 'Babies are sweet.' Metaphorical language is the 'language of lovers and artists, mystics and prophets.'[43] It is the language of those who become totally involved in what they are apprehending, who identify with their object, and for whom the Gestalt of experience occupies all their consciousness, becomes their whole world.[44] The experience is attended to in itself, and for its own sake alone, and thus is what it is intrinsically, and not for anything else, nor is it comparable to anything else, except metaphorically.

Intrinsic value is the fulfilment of the singular concept. It is called intrinsic value or intrinsic goodness because the value inheres in the thing itself, not in its membership in a class, or comparatively (as with extrinsic value). Something of intrinsic value is in a class by itself because it completely fulfils the intension of its own concept. That concept is singular and unique. Only as a person do you have within yourself your own concept of yourself and therefore the standard or normative concept of yourself. Someone else can't have it for you. Someone may influence or contribute to a change in your self-concept, but the concept must itself be within your own consciousness. You are intrinsically valuable to yourself if you fulfil your own concepts or yourself, that is, if you are in accordance with your conscience or self-image, or are what you feel you ought to be. The concept in question is 'me'/'myself'/'I' in each case. If you fulfil or actualize yourself, then you are in accord with your own self-concept, true to yourself, or authentic/real/genuine/sincere/integral/harmonious.[45] If you are a non-person, you have no concept of yourself within yourself, and you become of intrinsic value only when a person identifies with you and views you in your uniqueness and concreteness. Ideally, someone loves you because you are the way you are. I shouldn't love you simply because you grow in my image, or as I might prefer. Rather, I must experience you as what I respect and value in your own right. Mayeroff says this with precision and with feeling in his *On Caring*:

Instead of trying to dominate and possess the other, I want it to grow in its own right, or, as we sometimes say, 'to be itself,' and I feel the other's growth as bound up with my own sense of well-being. The worth I experience in the other is something over and above any value it may have for me because of its ability to satisfy my own needs. For a caring parent, the child is felt to have a worth of his own apart from his power to satisfy the parent's needs; for the caring musician, the music is felt to have a worth of its own apart from what it is able to do for him. In other words, I experience what I care for as having worth in its own right.[46]

You know and love a beautiful flower just the way it is, not because of what it will lead to or help produce, or because it is a 'grade-A' prize winner. As the Little Prince came to discover, his own humble rose was for him the whole world, not because it was the equal of all other roses but simply because it was this rose – his beloved rose.[47] D.T. Suzuki makes the same point in contrasting the Japanese and Anglo-Saxon attempts at gaining knowledge of a single flower.[48] The contrast verges on becoming more caricature than studied report, but the bold strokes only make the point easier to grasp. Alfred Lord Tennyson becomes Suzuki's foil, and his famous 'flower in a crannied wall' serves as the model of much Western analysis. Tennyson is not content simply to observe the flower, for that leaves him separate from it and mystified by it. He suggests that if he could pluck it out of the wall, and (Suzuki adds) dissect it and run tests on it in the laboratory, he might discover what it is and what man is, and even unlock the secrets of the universe. The Japanese poet Basho, however, is content to contemplate the flower growing by the hedge, and he does so until the distinction between himself and the flower recedes, and, in an act of identification or empathetic compenetration, there is only consciousness of the flower. To pluck it would be to kill it, and that would be unthinkable for any true lover. You protect, nourish, and support what you love. Only the ability to make the flower your whole world, to mirror without a ripple this exquisite beauty, can bring you closer to it. It is your whole world in intrinsic valuation. Similarly, as a nature mystic, you feel oneness with the universe because it is the sort of universe it is –

because you see that it is good, worthwhile in itself, intrinsically valuable. As a religious mystic, you identify or gain union in some sense with the wondrous nature which is God Almighty.

INTRINSIC GOODNESS AND BADNESS

The opposite of such total involvement is indifference, and being indifferent to the uniqueness of things is one form of intrinsic badness.[49] Those who shot Indians for sport or gain on the frontier were said to feel justified in doing so because the Indians were not really human beings. They were hardened to the suffering, the agony, the horror of a woman being raped – she was only a squaw – or her family being slaughtered – they were only savages. You may find it hard to identify with animals, to wonder at their uniqueness and right to exist, quite apart from whether or not they are capable of feeling pain in the same way that you do. If there is a case for the claim that your greatness of character is measured by the extent of your concern or caring for another, that is, of your capacity for empathetic identification,[50] then if you can take only what you need, destroy only what you must, and leave this world with little more than your footprints left behind, you are the saint and the moral individual. But this kind of attitude of respect and concern for all that exists, animate and inanimate, seems analogous to what Lawrence Kohlberg argues for in his projected Stage Seven. On such grounds a major aim of education is the expansion of your capacity for caring, for love, for identification, with personal growth beginning with early egoism and expanding to concern for a few others, to concern for many others, to concern for all equally, to concern for animals and all other life forms, and finally to the point where you show concern for all things that exist – a kind of 'cosmic enthusiasm.'[51] The moral journey for Kohlberg might be schematized as the stage-by-stage enlargement of what is to be included in your ethical deliberations, and for Hartman as the increasing capacity for intrinsic valuation, as the development of the ability to identify with and to compenetrate through empathetic openness, that is, the capacity for caring.

THE WHOLE PERSON

It must be stressed that an act of caring-as-identification involves the whole of your person, not just a part of you – and it involves all of you intensely. This is no small point, and it actually helps to explain why a

Kohlberg assumes that one who is capable of widely embracive judgment will be a loving person. He is loving because he is totally involved, emotionally as well as intellectually, and with his will fully engaged. Perhaps this point can be more fully grasped if we return to José Ortega y Gasset's imaginary deathbed scene, as briefly discussed in an earlier chapter.[52] A single happening is viewed from four different perspectives, that of a painter, a reporter, a doctor, and the dying man's wife. All are actively involved in the incident, but the degree of, and for Hartman the nature of, emotional involvement is different. The painter is interested only in a constellation of spatial and optical elements, of light and shadow. He is viewing the scene systemically, and the resultant values are systemic values. The reporter concentrates on the facts of the everyday event, and so his value experiences are extrinsic, and possibly systemic as well. The doctor views the event of the dying 'patient' professionally, and thus probably concerns himself with the systemically scientific technicalities of his profession, after attending to the empirical facts of the patient's condition and difficulty. Finally, the wife values intrinsically the life of her dying husband, himself of intrinsic worth. She is completely involved in and identified with her beloved husband. For her, 'the distance shrinks to almost nothing.'[53] Ortega himself measures these four perspectives by 'the emotional distance between each person and the event they all witness.'[54] The other participants are more or less removed, and emotional identification, if anything, is likely to get in the way. For the wife, there is great intensity of feeling. Intrinsic valuation is an act of identification involving the whole person, not just a part of him. It is an emotionally intense identification and interaction with that about which one cares. And this capacity to care intensely about the nature and worth of something other than yourself is termed by Hartman 'transparency,' that is, transparency of character. Such transparency, as Hartman makes abundantly clear, is the result of an attitude of openness involving the capacity of your whole person to reach out and embrace, without smothering the embraced or clutching so firmly as to leave traces of your own strength on the now somewhat deformed-in-your-own-image other person.

The kind of knowledge relevant to intrinsic valuation is exceedingly rare. It is the capacity of complete concentration on a thing or person, the personal involvement of the artist, the inventor, the teacher: the capacity of empathy and sympathy. It is the kind of knowledge possessed in the highest degree by the creative genius. It is possible only in a person who is himself fully integrated and has all his powers available for outgoing and meeting persons or things. This is not the 'outgoing' of the extrovert or the back-slapper, who meets persons extrinsically. It is the projecting of the whole person into others ... This kind of knowledge is direct, immediate, 'intuitional,' it is that of the complete person encompassing the world. It is not a matter of the intellect but of character.[55]

Reflecting back for a moment to the precise and formal nature of Hartman's three kinds of concepts, to his axiom of formal valuation (a thing is good or valuable to the degree to which it fulfils the intension of its concept), you may find it a bit surprising at first glance that he places emphasis on the whole personality in valuation and de-emphasizes the role of the intellect. Yet the surprise will quickly fade when you recall that the philosophical formality of Axiology is an intellectual, conceptual activity, but that valuation itself is much more than its measure, as the weather outside is much more than the thermometer on the wall. In intrinsic valuation, what is being measured is a particular state of consciousness, an approach to experience which is unique and distinctive. For something to be valued intrinsically is for it to be attended to with an intensity which shuts out all else, and which concerns itself not at all with further consequences or other pragmatic issues. It is, if only for a moment, the only thing in your world of momentary consciousness. It is your 'whole world,' in a moment which is indistinguishable from an eternity.[56] By contrast, the most common sort of value blindness results from the inability to embrace or to incorporate a particular thing into yourself and from identifying yourself instead with a thing, a class, a function, a system or institution, or an ideology. All of these are extrinsic or systemic concepts, and none look at you as you are by yourself. Extrinsically, you can think of yourself as a businessman, a teacher, a housewife, a writer. If the business collapses, or your teaching is predictably awful, or you are divorced, you are totally shattered, for there is nothing left of yourself. If anything is left, it may be just as extrinsic and precarious: your spouse or children, whose success (excellence in a class) you share vicariously, or your expectation that the Marxist state will soon overcome. To identify yourself with the extrinsic and systemic alone is to deny your intrinsicness, your exclusive and unique worth as a person. You have lost the entire inner world of self, your interiority, and have exchanged it for a mess of functional or objective pottage, of associations and 'awards.'

INTERIORITY

A 'self' with an interior has consciousness which is self-conscious, and which constantly strives to distinguish external appraisal from internal, membership in a group from the totality of characteristics which constitute the person, and the externally accepted view from the internally acceptable view. Indeed, the procedure for developing this capacity for intrinsic valuation is the enriching of your awareness of your own interiority, that is, of your own self-consciousness. And it is no small irony that concentrating thus on the study of the self results in the ability to begin to lose it. 'To study the self is to forget the self,' advised the Zen master Dōgen, nearly a thousand years ago. To become conscious of yourself, you can choose and define your own ends, purposes, goals, and essential character. You can thus become increasingly aware of the extent to which these ends and your choice of character are suitable, acceptable, and sufficient. You may also decide the extent to which you actually live up to or embody these aims and ideals. Neurosis is often the repressing of the fact that your actual and ideal goals are 'out of sync.' Such a neurosis is a healthy sign, valuationally, for it makes it obvious that you are at least sensitive to higher things. The problem may in fact result from your being far more sensitive than most but unable to allow time for growth or make allowances for human finitude. Insensitivity to intrinsic value may be seen in your identifying with the goals of others in a passive and unthinking way, or with the charter or creed of an institution or nation, or in your otherwise living by 'remote control'/habit/rote/laws and rules uncritically parroted/peer pressure/pursuit of the rewards of society as though they contained any of the seeds of interior growth. None of this is to say that if you follow rules, obey the laws of the land, or wish to be recognized by your society as a major contributor, you are thereby not intrinsic. It all depends, as the existentialists have stressed from their beginning, on how you come to act in any of these ways. If you choose self-consciously to abide by the laws of the land and identify with the aims and objectives for which they were instituted, then you are authentic and possess a high degree of interiority. It is not that non-intrinsic valuers squint at the interior self but do not see it clearly, but that they are looking in the wrong direction altogether. In a word, they have not yet discovered their own interior, or they repress what knowledge of the self they do have because of the cognitive and emotional dissonance created by the discrepancy between who they ought to be and who they actually are, between what their country is doing and what they claim or wish it was doing, between what their reputation or position seems to say about them and what they really see themselves as being like. The interior is sacrificed in order to preserve the external semblance, supposedly a reflection of their true inner being.

This interiority of self-consciousness, of existential subjectivity, is more a way of being-in-the-world than the growth of a faculty of a new organ. To try to objectify it or even to freeze it conceptually or descriptively is already to lose it, is to be looking in the wrong direction. Hence, what is caught is never what did the catching, and what does the catching is what you wanted to catch and missed, not what you actually caught. All attempts to ensnare it fail, for the very reason that all such attempts are made by the very thing to be ensnared. If you would concentrate on the power and process of ensnarement itself, then you would be as close to it as you can come objectively. You already have it subjectively, of course, if you but look within. The interiority of self-consciousness is the self, and while you can never objectify it, you can become aware of your interiority continually through your own activity of reflection. It is that which cannot itself be seen by itself, and yet which does all seeing, and makes all seeing possible. It is like your own eye, which (except in a mirror) can see everything but itself. It is beyond all description and objectification, and yet makes all describing and objectifying possible. It is not a measurable, objectifiable self, but not because it does not exist, or, like claims of fairies and unicorns, must simply be believed in. It is the most 'empirical' of facts, if you allow direct experience to count as empirical. Can you catch your self trying to catch yourself, trying to catch your self, trying to catch your self ...? All of this takes place in direct self-consciousness, in direct experience. It is not a mere belief. And this power of reflexivity, that is, of casting your attention back on what you are conscious of and on your means of consciousness, is also the power of critical reflection and self appraisal and awareness. Your habits, prejudices, beliefs, hopes, projects, loves, sexual fantasies, human heartedness, fears, discomforts, and pains and pleasures may all be looked at directly by focussing within.

TRANSPARENCY AND OPAQUENESS

Hartman terms this reflexive capacity the 'transcendental Self':[57]

Now everybody has a Self, but not in the same degree. In other words, the awareness of self force can be very opaque, and that is the case when the empirical self is confused with the transcendental Self. And this is what the positivists do.

They are very opaque selves. And the Self can develop, differentiate itself, articulate itself to complete transparency. If one has a very transparent self, then one has peculiar experiences such as what people call telepathy. But it is not really telepathy, because you are not away from anything; that is really closeupathy, you see. You are really close up to everything. And to others – you have immediate 'intuition,' you have great sensitivity, and so on.[58]

To be unaware of a value dimension is to be 'opaque,' in this respect. The more aware you become, the less opaque and the more transparent you are. Hence, the measure of your capacity to value intrinsically is your degree of opacity, or transparency of self, by means of which you are enabled to empathise or interpenetrate with all that comes to you, including your awareness of the nature of your own way of life, character, and fulfilment of chosen projects. If you are intrinsically aware, you are as large as the whole universe. 'Man is as large as the whole universe, because he is defined by the range of his consciousness.'[59] And in so far as you continue to transcend all previous views, even of yourself, you continue to transcend your 'range of consciousness.' 'In other words, even the most transparent consciousness still has infinite depth, or further transparency. That is the measure.'[60] The transcendental self is the capacity for reaching out to embrace, and for taking into itself what it is aware of. This capacity to embrace, to empathize, to love is measured by the degree of transparency achieved. Transparency is the awareness of your own conscious self in terms of its reflective capacity to evaluate itself, and to determine itself, thereby allowing it to become free from its own determinations in order to be able to reach out and embrace another in total concentration and caring for that something as it is in itself, and apart from all other considerations. Greatness of character is measured by the extent and by the nature of your concern.

Transparency begins with the pure awareness that you are,[61] and is typified by the capacity for the total abandoning of self and all other extrinsic considerations, in the act of intrinsic valuation. To focus on a raindrop on an autumn leaf is to allow that raindrop to fill your full field of consciousness. You don't ask questions about what raindrops are made of, or about why a raindrop is a raindrop.[62] You see as though for the first time, and with the same concentration and appreciation of mystery which occasions any engrossing and remarkable first-time experience. As a result of this 'whole world' concentration (at its height both totally selfless and objectless in that only the experience itself is attended to) you are wide open to the fullness of experiential immediacy given in the now. You approach this whenever you can concentrate on a task, a person, or an object. The immediacy and total filling of consciousness by whatever is there in front 'makes a person feel very deeply.'[63] There are no distractions, no negative emotions to cloud your transparency, no fears or bad memories, ambitions, hopes – there is just being-here-now. It is the freedom to be able to put your self totally into anything, to take anything into your self as ultimately concerning, to become a tree, a raindrop, or another person (in another's shoes).

COMPASSION

Hartman contends that 'compassion is one of the properties'[64] of a transparent person, for if you are transparent, you live with, indeed you live or exist as, every other thing, living or non-living. You are St Francis' 'Brother Fire,' Schweitzer's 'Brother Africans,' the 'living rocks' of a Zen stone garden, and the universe or 'Living God' of the mystics. Universality of empathy, or affinity, or concern is a characteristic of the transparent you. 'You can actually gauge a person's transparency of consciousness by his compassion.'[65]

If you are not particularly sensitive to intrinsic values, that is, are opaque, then you need crude, or blunted, or extreme stimulation in order to feel anything at all.[66] You would be aware enough of interiority to know that you craved such experiences involving the entire self but would be nearly intrinsic-value blind, and so would have to be drenched before sensing rain. As an opaque character, you often identify with disorder, distortion, and destruction simply because only by the extremes which these terms imply can an intrinsic (dis)value experience be bold and powerful enough to get through. You can identify with intrinsic disvalue in just the same intense ways that you identify with intrinsic value. Hartman's heart-rending example of the Nazi Irma Greese, who tied the legs of women in labour together, is a poignant example of such intrinsic disvaluation. Irma Greese used life to kill life, and we are told of the sadistic pleasure she took in the screams of agony which served as indicators that what she wished to achieve was occurring. She was perhaps unable to identify with another human being deeply enough to give her moments of transparency and total concentration. She may never have thought twice about a raindrop, completely insensitive to its uniqueness and mystery. But she could presumably 'get high' on the agony of others, particularly other women with whom she could identify, but only in the act of torture and murder. It is likely that she knew the characteristics of the sort of experience she craved, but could only find them in acts of extraordinary cruelty and savagery. It is not clear that early training in sensuality, à la John Macmurray, or in Kohlberg's putting yourself in another's shoes through imaginary situations would ever turn an Irma Greese into a normal person able to gain satisfaction from non-destructive and appreciative acts. It is less doubtful, however, that part of the task of civilizing and educating is to assist the young in being able to appreciate and become increasingly sensitive to the people around them, the world around them, and their own intrinsic goodness or unique positive capabilities. The opaque character is like a blind person who wants to see something, but to whom nothing gets through. 'So, you give him the greatest nuclear explosion possible, and maybe he sees something then.'[67] If you were a valuational dullard, particularly at the level of intrinsic value, you would be nearly totally insensitive, living only for yourself, lacking badly in compassion, and requiring heavy, chaotic, and loud stimulation.[68] You would be 'turned on' by rape, and yet remain unsatisfied. You would become a success at all costs, but still remain unsatisfied. You could enjoy a film in which thousands of people are killed, or burnt, for fewer killings would leave you bored and unmoved. Perhaps you might eventually shoot a famous figure, but still you would be nobody. But the little Zen master is what he is. He accepts that, cherishes that, then gives up even the cherishing, and just fully engages in the experiences of life. He is stimulated to ecstasy by a single drop of dew, or a reflection of the moon in a puddle, or by a cricket in the night. 'The more transparency, the more intensity of experience' is possible.[69] This is axiomatic, for it is your whole world, and one which fully engages your whole being, physically, emotionally, intellectually, volitionally. An aim of education is the development of the capacity for intrinsic valuation, the attempt to create an intrinsically responsive human instrument. And whereas the opaque consciousness implodes, withers, and shrinks until the ego becomes the whole world, and nothing else is of interest in itself except in so far as it stimulates your ego pleasures and satisfies your ego needs, the transparent consciousness explodes, until the ego embraces the universe, then loses itself and finds that even little things afford one the possibility of infinite appreciation. Everything becomes aesthetically sacred and religiously worthwhile for its own sake, as a centre of intrinsic value. Even the tiniest experience may be the trigger for a giant explosion in the self – and thus in one's cosmos. The intentional crushing of an ant may reveal as much insensitivity as the beating of a child, and may occasion intense sorrow if you observe it. Perhaps it is because you have become such an intense instrument of sensitivity and identification with people, growing things, and things, that you may become a defender of morality, human worth, and the right of all things to be left alone unless there is an overwhelming reason to the contrary.

TRANSPOSITIONS

A great deal of difficulty arises in valuation because of the confusion of, or insensitivity to, the three distinctive value realms. A disvalue may be analysed as a transposition, an inappropriate association of a subject from one value realm with a predicate from another. Food is a positive value when being chewed and enjoyed, but a disvalue when stuck in the throat. A bad accident is a disvalue for those involved, but a positive value for the junk yard or repair shop, or for anyone who learns from its warning. 'Thus, any good thing can be converted into something bad, that is, into a compound which is not a composition but a transposition, when it breaks into pieces, gets distorted, gets mixed up with something that is not in accord with its meaning, as honey with barbed wire, a bone in the throat, an inkblot on a print.'[70]

To view you as nothing more than a means to an end (extrinsic value), or purely vocationally as a good teacher (good as a member of the class to which you belong), or as a part of a vast machine or system (soldier number 76511a, social insurance number ...), may stand as an example of the disvaluation of people, if you are not concurrently aware that you are more than extrinsically and/or systemically valuable. You are a unique, intrinsically worthwhile centre of value. To be blind to this dimension and to value yourself or another only in one of the three possible ways is to be both a valuational dullard and guilty of disvaluation to the extent to which you claim that the type of valuation that you do understand is the total value there is. It is not that you are never to be viewed extrinsically and systemically, but that you are, at the same time, always to be viewed at the highest valuational level. If you are treated as a member of the administrative team, you must be fully aware that you are much, much more than that. You are to be treated in ways appropriate to a being of intrinsic value as a general rule. You must be able to identify with yourself, see things from your own perspective, be transparent enough yourself to grasp the implications of the administrative decision on you, and so on. You will still have to act with extrinsic and systemic integrity as well, but not by blocking out the intrinsic dimension. The doctor or nurse who becomes insensitive to the suffering of patients and the teacher who simply assigns the grades earned without considering how to turn the news of failure into a growth experience are examples of people who cope with intrinsic value by blocking it out. Consider the following example:

In the reality of our lives, the four [intrinsic, extrinsic, systemic, transpositional] valuational dimensions are intermingled. Thus, a policeman does not necessarily look at criminals only systemically; quite the contrary, he may come to see them with so much understanding that he finds the task of fulfilling his professional obligations difficult. The same may happen in the directly opposite case; someone close to the person responsible for the accident – perhaps the father or son – even though he might intrinsically value the situation, does not therefore cease to be aware of the disorder and chaos which the collision represents; on the contrary, he may feel it more profoundly. He may be aware of its simple layers, the systemic and extrinsic, the logical and the social, and the need to prevent or avoid it systemically. Thus, there appear conflicts of value; he may wish to have the son or father set free, and on the other hand cannot help agreeing with the police.[71]

This narrative demonstrates Hartman's thesis that (1) the categories of axiology, the 'study of value,' can be applied to anything, and (2) that anything whatever can be valued in all four ways.[72] There is nothing wrong in itself with treating a person as a cog in an administrative machine, or as a living biological system to be treated by the system known as medicine. Indeed, scientific, organizational, societal, and even educational systems must be (systemically) ordered if they are to function either efficiently or at all. You start the school day at nine o'clock rather than leaving it up to the whims of each individual student or teacher. Otherwise there would be chaos without learning. But the teacher who decides that the smooth functioning of the school system is the highest value has probably forgotten the realities of the extrinsic and the complexities of the intrinsic dimensions. The systemic approach is 'necessary in all situations that demand discipline.'[73] Such systemic valuation is necessary in all life and death situations, like stopping at stoplights and at railway crossings. 'Discipline may, in this sense, be defined as voluntary emergency. Until a child develops this kind of self-emergency, education must provide it, and it can only do so by force – this is the very nature of emergency. It is here where progressive education is axiologically deficient.'[74] Early habit training is essential to the development of an individual with the qualities of autonomy and interiority. But Hartman is firm in warning that, 'in most life situations ... systemic valuation is out of place.'[75] Thus, while it is of extreme importance to make certain that you have an identification tag on your arm as a patient in a hospital, to ensure that proper attention will be given should you be mistaken for someone else while unconscious, it would be a disvaluation to reduce you to the status of a 'case.' You are much more than a case, and it is not insignificant to observe that the great crimes against humanity in this century have occurred when people were reduced to numbers: in concentration camps, as 'subjects' in experiments, as 'statistics' in war, world wide or 'limited.' The disvaluation occurs when a human being is reduced to the lower value categories. Normally, we ought to value a person in all three ways. As a student, you are responsible for following rules and doing what is required. You are also ranked as a member of a class and pressured by them as well as by the teacher to conform to some norms or other. You are furthermore a unique constellation of characteristics, unlike anyone else, and should be encouraged to grow and emerge in your own way so long as you are sensitive to the values of others. In so far as Hartman maintains that the richer the concept in terms of properties, the higher the resultant values, the intrinsic dimension is the highest and most valuable, never to be reduced to anything less. Thus, it is worse to value a person systemically but not intrinsically, than intrinsically but not systemically. But it is better to value a person in both these ways, and extrinsically as well. Full value sensitivity requires it. And the teacher, therefore, is charged with being the valuationally sensitive guide who keeps alive the tension amongst all the value dimensions, while stressing the highest or intrinsic realm as the most valuable and the less commonly achieved.

INTRINSICALLY VALUABLE THINGS

The value of a person remains the normative standard for intrinsic valuation, and indeed its ultimate cause. But anything may be intrinsically valued. Hartman provides the unexpected and humorous example of the valuing of a button. You can value a button systemically, as in the case of the symmetrical array of buttons on a coat. If one is missing, even though it is never used but is present for decorative reasons only, you want it replaced in order to restore the original pattern or system. Or again, still systemically, any given button must be either there or not there, and thus you 'cannot stand it when it is half there and half not, hanging on one thread.'[76] Extrinsically, the button may be valued as an unusually fine kind of silver button, made of real silver, and hand engraved. You are willing to pay more for it because it is an outstanding example of its kind.

Intrinsically, you may value the button as a work of art which is so remarkable that you are aesthetically thrilled by its beauty and are lost in it. This is unlikely, of course, for buttons seldom reach such aesthetic heights and are primarily instances of systemic and extrinsic valuation. Transpositionally, a button may become an object of intrinsic valuation if you are a button fetishist. Hartman recalls that he 'knew a fetishist of this kind who had a button sewed to his navel, and this was the dearest thing he had.'[77] Buttons became more important and more valuable than persons to this man, and so he transposed frames of reference, by responding intrinsically to something whose value was normally recognized as extrinsic or systemic. He was obsessed by the need to 'have' buttons, or to make a button a part of himself. He could have become one by simply identifying with it, as with a raindrop, but to make one part of his physical 'system' is to confuse intrinsic empathy with systemic surgery. That is the transposition.

VALUES AND EDUCATION

The aims of education include value sensitization at all three levels, and the capacity for keeping the frames of reference appropriate and distinct in order to avoid transposition. None of this is either obvious or easy. It is, on the contrary, easy to dislike a person for being systemically disorganized or unruly. The 'person,' however, is to be found at the intrinsic level, and only the 'student' or 'class member' at the systemic and extrinsic levels. Or a student may 'always' hand in poor work, and so you come to expect this to continue. Intrinsically, you should greet the child each time as though it were for the first time, for the possibility of a 'breakthrough' is ever-present, even though it may never come. It may never come because you give up, and so the prophecy which has become your habit is a self-fulfilling one. Or you may find the student a source of irritation systemically, owing to disruptive behaviour in the classroom, and a disaster extrinsically, as a failing student. You may transfer these incapacities to the intrinsic level and come to dislike the child generally, blocking out what may be apparent at the intrinsic level if you would only keep yourself open to the child as person. I am tempted to give examples of people who later became great extrinsically and systemically but who were given up for lost because they didn't measure up to the expected extrinsic and systemic standards initially. What is found in such cases is that they were remarkable people intrinsically, who just didn't get it together early on. Winston Churchill is often cited as a late starter, and it is evident that he didn't quite fit into the system. The very uniqueness that caused him grief at the beginning led to an immense social contribution at maturity. Only the teacher who is open to the infinite growth potential of a person at the intrinsic level will be able to do anything positive about the blockages at the systemic and extrinsic levels. If you are to give up on or even dislike a person, let it be for intrinsic reasons, and for nothing less. An Irma Greese was a destroyer of intrinsic values, and so was a person to be feared and controlled, even despised. A messy child is out of order only at the lowest valuational level, not the highest.

VALUES AND ETHICS

Hartman defines ethics as intrinsic valuation applied to persons.[78] It is the complete involvement of one person with another, and the persons are empathetically related so as to form one unit, one *Gestalt*-in-experience: 'We may call this relationship between persons Community.'[79] The application of extrinsic valuation to persons is functional, as relating members of the same class, and the resultant relationship is not community but 'collectivity.' The application of systemic valuation to persons yields conformity or the application of one concept on all members of the group, making them all appear alike. Individuals are not thought of as persons, or even as functions, but merely as elements of a system of social organization.

Intrinsically, individuals are instances of different, unique concepts. That is, when you are related to another person, the other person treats you as a class by yourself. Such mutual self-involvement produces yet another class of which their own separate classes are intrinsic parts: 'Here we have the phenomenon of co-operation.'[80] Since they are both part of a common and shared whole there is no opposition between them. The achieved unity is the result of the full involvement of the persons interacting, and the reward is joy arising out of that holistic interaction.

Extrinsically, individuals are instances of the same concept, but to varying degrees. Two people may interact as lawyers, and this professional link is extrinsic and not intrinsic to the individuals as persons. Whereas co-operation is the norm of intrinsic involvement, competition is the norm of extrinsic comparative valuation. If the lawyer with whom you interact is shown to be less capable, you will look that much better. The nature of competitive interaction is comparitive. At the intrinsic level, for another to become worse is to make the whole of which you are a part worse, and thus you are worse because of a friend's hardship. At the extrinsic level, you may become better if another is worse, for the concept to which your betterness and worseness is compared is functionally external to our persons.

Systemically, individuals are instances of the same concept, and to the same degree. All interaction must be seen as conformity or disconformity. Indeed, people are not to be thought of as individuals, and certainly not as persons, but as elements in a system. The principles of conformity are to be applied absolutely and in an authoritarian manner, for there are no shades or exceptions. To be a proper part of a system you either completely conform or must be treated as a non-conformist or traitor. In a system, what counts is the system and its procedures. 'This goes not only for the system's victims but also for its agents. They act as elements of the system and as nothing else.'[81] Those who argue that they 'had to do it,' or were 'simply obeying orders' are placing the system first. It is little surprise, therefore, that 'the world of systemic value is the haven of those who lack self,' that is, who lack fully differentiated intrinsic value sensitivity. Systemic value which dominates and squeezes dry the intrinsic value sense is hell for those who consciously live their own inner intrinsic self. 'Hence the tragedies when the two dimensions of value collide, from *Antigone* to *Dr Zhivago*.'[82] It is also the curse of any parent or teacher convinced that nothing is more important than order and discipline. At least two things are more important. The comparative growth of your human capacity at the extrinsic level, and your intrinsic interaction with the teacher who, together with you, constitutes the *Gestalt* of a happy and humane learning environment. There is little doubt in my mind that the intrinsic or personal or empathetic dimension is the most underemphasized and least apparent aspect of North American education.

Conclusion

At the end of the chapter on moral education (chapter 2) I maintained that Kohlberg's Stage Seven reasoning was not a separate stage of reasoning at all, but a refined and articulate system of reasoning which, in less articulate and quite different forms, is present at other stages as well, and very likely at all stages. Stage Seven describes a metaphysics, a religion, a way of life, or simply a philosophy (in the comprehensive sense of a context for whatever one holds, values, believes, perceives, or does). Most of us are considerably less consistent or comprehensive than Spinoza, Plato, St Augustine, Confucius, or even Schweitzer or Teilhard de Chardin. To the extent to which all education ought to be philosophically adept and penetrating, however, all education includes the continuing attempt to make your reasoning, valuing, and perceiving as consistent as possible. This requires relational as well as internal consistency amongst various ingredients and arguments. Consistency itself demands a concern for the coherence of your positions by themselves and as interrelated and integrated. As a serious student (teacher, citizen, religionist, and so on), you talk in terms of your 'philosophy,' that is, the integration of a web of meaning and understanding which is increasingly coherent and which appears to respond to the so-called facts as they have come to be accepted. An egoist presents a philosophy of life, even though it may seem difficult consistently to argue the position that everyone's private interest is in the 'highest court of appeal' while admitting that there are as many billions of high courts as there are people in the world. A view is no less an attempt at systematic organization for not succeeding. In any case, there are too many powerful insights coming from serious egoism merely to dismiss the position as internally inconsistent. What is important for our purposes, however, is the claim that all 'facts,' 'values,' 'rules and principles,' 'political ideals,' and so on rest on and are interrelated in a more systematic view of the whole which, in our culture and others, has often been termed one's religion. Those who have argued that what is most wrong with our schools and with the various attempts to teach morality in them is the teaching of rules and principles without a holistic perspective which embraces, nourishes, and grounds these ingredients may also have been correct. This, no doubt, is what makes the teaching of morals in the schools such a contentious issue. You cannot just teach the ingredients or parts of morality without giving expression to the whole, that is, to your own philosophy of existence, or to some of the philosophies of the whole which serve to make sense of and justify the specific rules and principles. Yet, if you enter into the consideration of the whole, you leave what Kohlberg identifies as 'morality' and enter the sphere of ethics or religion. The result may be unconstitutional in some nations, or unwise, or both. You are likely to be branded as a Humanist, a Christian, or a Jew, or even as a 'foreigner' with 'inferior and dangerous' views. The only escape seems to be to keep away from ethical matters, or to stop short of speaking of the more comprehensive basis for your perspective on the world. Such impoverished teaching is both regrettable and understandable. But it results from a misunderstanding of the aims and purposes of education in the first place. This misunderstanding appears to be firmly entrenched within the teaching profession, as well as outside it, and may be characterized as the belief that the aims of education consist in providing the 'facts' of the various matters studied. If 'facts' are merely conventions or indicators, and are the hard-won but not absolute wisdom of the race, then the job of the teacher merely begins with the rehearsal of the state of the various arts. Then begins the hard work of coming to see for yourself that the wisdom is correctly labelled 'wisdom' because of the answers provided. This hard work is followed by attempts to stuff more of the tube into the established tyre by critically re-evaluating the view and by considering the alternative positions, also called 'wisdom,' which approach the issues and provide answers in ways different from the established way. If it could be shown both inside and outside the teaching profession that the charge of 'heresy' may actually reveal in the accusers a tendency towards blind acceptance – that is, a tendency to teach as though the authority of final truth were in your professional kit – and the willingness to pack facts into otherwise inactive heads, there would be little difficulty in enlisting the aid of parents, orthodox and unorthodox, religious and non-religious, political and apolitical, in exploration into the questions and answers which have mattered most to those who have cared, thought, and acted with commitment and integrity, and continue to do so.

In the meantime, Stage Seven thinking found in the 'natural mysticism' of Kohlberg, the philosophy of Spinoza, the Christian, Jewish, Confucian, Zen Buddhist, Buddhist, Taoist, Islamic, Humanistic, Hindu, and any other systematic and comprehensive outlook on the world develops into its mature philosophical form only later on in the life of an individual. Therefore it is important to ensure that you 'bed down' in the best wisdom you can get your hands on, and at the earliest stages of your development. At the same time, to 'bed down' is not to require an uncritical teaching and learning stance or the blind and passive recitation of material (or simply to 'retire' intellectually). It is necessary to give the young and the not-so-developed a place to stand from which to act and respond as moral citizens and secure persons. Nevertheless, it is not necessary to hide from them that intellectual integrity which continues to search out, qualify, prune, and polish any positions before them. To be less than absolutely certain is not to be blind, nor is it to be wishy-washy or bland. To confess all your perplexity to someone who would not be able to follow your meanderings would be no better, nor is it necessary in the earlier-stage development of moral and value-sensitive human beings. You can learn to care without being able to understand Spinoza, and can learn to treat a person or a flower as an end in itself without understanding the complexities of Hartman's account of intrinsic value. To be open to another, and to the world, and to be both gentle and enthusiastic is possible from early childhood, and long before the complexities of reasoning are generated. Camus may serve as a guide for those of us in communities, in societies, in schools, and in our own homes, who must decide how we want to live together by coming to agreement about what we value in behaviour and attitudes, and what we will allow of citizens in support and defence of such behavioural attitudes. This in itself does not provide an ethical system to purvey and enforce. It does suggest, however, how you go about establishing one, and how you keep alive the ideals of improving it, each other, and yourself, as well. Ethics is a process, and it involves every part of yourself and of others in interrelation with you as well as your attitudes and understanding of the worth of the cosmos and of your place in it. All moral thinking and acting will, if seriously and exhaustively reflected upon, lead you to Stage Seven questions and responses. Stage Seven perspectives are those without which there would not be any 'facts' or 'principles and rules' or values whatsoever. Thus the question 'Why should I be moral?' is but the tip of the iceberg, for there are other higher-stage questions floating below water level. 'What is worthwhile?' and 'What can I discover?' and 'How can I come to feel at home in the cosmos?' are but a few of the additional questions which you may come to ask and find various kinds of answers to. At its extreme end, moral education is the ongoing development of a way of being in the world, a way of life which traditionally has been named 'wisdom.' It is just that so few reach beyond the beginning and the middle to the more developed end, which itself continues to expand, enlarge, and deepen. Wisdom, too, is a process without termination.

In applying the various dimensions of moral education to the practice of education itself, is it too much to ask that education aim at the continuing expansion of your potential for gaining intellectual understanding, deepening your capacities to feel and care, and cracking brittle and narrow ego-boundaries by embracing what is other than yourself? The range of your intellect, the extent of your sympathy or empathy, and the sensitivity of your capacity to value the other being as it is in itself could, when taken together as a program of study, serve well as a basis for modern educational practice.

Lawrence Kohlberg's six stages of moral judgment

There are numerous versions of the six stages, but the following is taken from Kohlberg's recent book The Philosophy of Moral Development, *volume 1 of* Essays on Moral Development *(San Francisco: Harper & Row 1981), 409–12.*

LEVEL A. PRECONVENTIONAL LEVEL

Stage 1. The stage of punishment and obedience

Content: Right is literal obedience to rules and authority, avoiding punishment, and not doing physical harm. 1 / What is right is to avoid breaking rules, to obey for obedience' sake, and to avoid doing physical damage to people and property. 2 / The reasons for doing right are avoidance of punishment and the superior power of authorities.
Social perspective: This stage takes an egocentric point of view. A person at this stage doesn't consider the interests of others or recognize they differ from actor's, and doesn't relate two points of view. Actions are judged in terms of physical consequences rather than in terms of psychological interests of others. Authority's perspective is confused with one's own.

Stage 2. The stage of individual instrumental purpose and exchange

Content: Right is serving one's own or other's needs and making fair deals in terms of concrete exchange. 1 / What is right is following rules when it is to someone's immediate interest. Right is acting to meet one's own interests and needs and letting others do the same. Right is also what is fair, that is, what is an equal exchange, a deal, an agreement. 2 / The reason for doing right is to serve one's own needs or interests in a world where one must recognize that other people have their interests, too.

Social perspective: This stage takes a concrete individualistic perspective. A person at this stage separates [his] own interests and points of view from those of authorities and others. He or she is aware everybody has individual interests to pursue and these conflict, so that right is relative (in the concrete individualistic sense). The person integrates or relates conflicting individual interests to one another through instrumental exchange of services, through instrumental need for the other and the other's goodwill, or through fairness giving each person the same amount.

LEVEL B. CONVENTIONAL LEVEL

Stage 3. The stage of mutual interpersonal expectations, relationships, and conformity

Content: The right is playing a good (nice) role, being concerned about the other people and their feelings, keeping loyalty and trust with partners, and being motivated to follow rules and expectations. 1 / What is right is living up to what is expected by people close to one or what people generally expect of people in one's role as son, sister, friend, and so on. 'Being good' is important and means having good motives, showing concern about others. It also means keeping mutual relationships, maintaining trust, loyalty, respect, and gratitude. 2 / Reasons for doing right are needing to be good in one's own eyes and those of others, caring for others, and because if one puts oneself in the other person's place one would want good behaviour from the self (Golden Rule).

Social perspective: This stage takes the perspective of the individual in relationship to other individuals. A person at this stage is aware of shared feelings, agreements, and expectations, which take primacy over individual interests. The person relates points of view through the 'concrete Golden Rule,' putting oneself in the other person's shoes. He or she does not consider generalized 'system' perspective.

Stage 4. The stage of social system and conscience maintenance

Content: The right is doing one's duty in society, upholding the social order, and maintaining the welfare of society or the group. 1 / What is right is fulfilling the actual duties to which one has agreed. Laws are to be upheld except in extreme cases where they conflict with other fixed social duties and rights. Right is also contributing to society, the group, or institution. 2 / The reasons for doing right are to keep the institution going as a whole, self-respect or conscience as meeting one's defined obligations, or the consequences: 'What if everyone did it?'

Social perspective: This stage differentiates societal point of view from interpersonal agreement or motives. A person at this stage takes the viewpoint of the system, which defines roles and rules. He or she considers individual relations in terms of place in the system.

LEVEL B/C. TRANSITIONAL LEVEL

This level is postconventional but not yet principled.
Content of transition: At Stage $4\frac{1}{2}$, choice is personal and subjective. It is based on emotions, conscience is seen as arbitrary and relative, as are ideas such as 'duty' and 'morally right.'
Transitional social perspective: At this stage, the perspective is that of an individual standing outside of his own society and considering himself as an individual making decisions without a generalized commitment or contract with society. One can pick and choose obligations, which are defined by particular societies, but one has no principles for such choice.

LEVEL C. POSTCONVENTIONAL AND PRINCIPLED LEVEL

Moral decisions are generated from rights, values, or principles that are (or could be) agreeable to all individuals composing or creating a society designed to have fair and beneficial practices.

Stage 5. The stage of prior rights and social contract or utility

Content: The right is upholding the basic rights, values, and legal contracts of a society, even when they conflict with the concrete rules and laws of the groups. 1 / What is right is being aware of the fact that people hold a variety of values and opinions, that most values and rules are relative to one's group. These 'relative' rules should usually be upheld, however, in the interests of impartiality and because they are the social contract. Some nonrelative values and rights such as life, and liberty, however, must be upheld in any society and regardless of majority opinion. 2 / Reasons for doing right are, in general, feeling obligated to obey the law because one has made a social contract to make and abide by laws for the good of all and to protect their own rights and the rights of others. Family, friendship, trust, and work obligations are also commitments or contracts freely entered into and entail respect for the rights of others. One is concerned that laws and duties be based on rational calculation of overall utility: 'the greatest good for the greatest number.'
Social perspective: This stage takes a prior-to-society perspective – that of a rational individual aware of values and rights prior to social attachments and contracts.

The person integrates perspectives by formal mechanisms of agreement, contract, objective impartiality, and due process. He or she considers the moral point of view and the legal point of view, recognizes they conflict, and finds it difficult to integrate them.

Stage 6. The stage of universal ethical principles

Content: This stage assumes guidance by universal ethical principles that all humanity should follow. 1 / Regarding what is right, Stage 6 is guided by universal ethical principles. Particular laws or social agreements are usually valid because they rest on such principles. When laws violate these principles, one acts in accordance with the principle. Principles are universal principles of justice: the equality of human rights and respect for dignity of human beings as individuals. These are not merely values that are recognized, but are also principles used to generate particular decisions. 2 / The reason for doing right is that, as a rational person, one has seen the validity of principles and has become committed to them. *Social perspective:* This stage takes the perspective of a moral point of view from which social arrangements derive or on which they are grounded. The perspective is that of any rational individual recognizing the nature of morality or the basic moral premise of respect for other persons as ends, not means.

Notes

INTRODUCTION

1 Plato *Apology* 18b–c, 26b–c. Unless otherwise specified, all quotations from Plato are taken from Edith Hamilton and Huntington Cairns (eds) *The Collected Dialogues of Plato* (New York: Bollingen Foundation 1964).
2 Plato *Republic* 533b–c
3 Geoffrey Payzant *Glenn Gould: Music and Mind* (Toronto: Van Nostrand Reinhold Ltd 1978) 49–50, 67. Payzant quotes a telling passage from Paul Myers ('Glenn Gould' *Gramophone* 50, no 597 [February 1973] 1478) on page 50: 'He is never concerned with traditional views of interpretation, nor with the already recorded versions of a work which are regarded as the yardsticks of performance. Instead, he prefers to perform a piece almost as though it were newly composed, awaiting its first interpretation. When he is in the studio, he likes to play as many as ten or fifteen interpretations of the same piece – each of them quite different, many of them valid – as though examining the music from every angle before deciding upon a final performance ... I have also found the greatest enjoyment from listening to a Gould performance of a work I believe I already "know" for, as he pulls it apart and reconstructs it in this unique manner, he reveals new facets of the music which I, for one, may never have considered.'
  Payzant adds that Gould holds 'that each separate performance of a piece should be unique in the history of that piece, and in the personal history of the performer' (page 67). By contrast, the opposite but commonly held view is 'that for any particular piece of music there must be one correct way of performing it, an abstract paradigm performance of it' (page 67).
4 Plato's 'later' dialogues such as the *Parmenides*, *Cratylus*, and *Sophist* include Plato's own critiques of his position, and the *Seventh Letter* speaks of the 'inadequacy of language' to express the highest insights of philosophy and

retreats to an ecstatic intuition which comes 'in a flash understanding' (344b), quite beyond words and symbols.

5 Alfred North Whithead *The Aims of Education And Other Essays* (New York: New American Library of World Literature 1963) 13: 'In training a child to activity of thought, above all things we must beware of what I will call "inert ideas" – that is to say, ideas that are merely received into the mind without being utilized, or tested, or thrown into fresh combinations.'

6 Rollo May *The Courage to Create* (New York: W.W. Norton & Co 1975) 95

7 Paulo Freire *Education for Critical Consciousness* (New York: Seabury Press 1974) passim. Writing of Brazil's emergence into more democratic modes of citizenship, Freire observes that what was needed were '*solutions with the people* and *never for them or imposed upon them*. What was needed was to go to the people and help them to enter the historical process critically. The prerequisite for this task was a form of education enabling the people to reflect on themselves, their responsibilities, and their role in the new cultural climate – indeed to reflect on their very *power* of reflection' (page 16).

8 Plato *Republic* 514a–521b

CHAPTER 1

1 Plato *Symposium* 202–4. The claim that the 'lover of wisdom' stands 'midway between knowledge and ignorance' is retold by Socrates but attributed to the priestess Diotima, in keeping with the various intoxications of the evening's symposium and banquet. What human beings have is 'correct opinion,' which is superior to ignorance, and in several of the later dialogues Plato tries to show that something more than correct opinion is possible, and the theory of forms and the account of dialectic are employed towards this end. Whether Plato succeeded, thought he had succeeded, or even expected to succeed in gaining more than correct opinion is itself a matter of philosophic interpretation. What is certain is that he intended that every serious reader of his works struggle to decide that question for himself or herself.

2 Ibid 200b

3 Plato *Apology* 30e–31a. 'I suspect, however, that before long you will awake from your drowsing, and in your annoyance ... finish me off with a single slap, and then you will go on sleeping till the end of your days, unless God in his care for you sends someone to take my place' (31a). The teacher is to awaken the listener from his passive slumber – that is the primary requirement of education, and the most dangerous.

4 Plato *Meno* 71e

5 Plato *Meno* 80a–b

6 Plato *Apology* 24b–c

7 William James *Some Problems of Philosophy* (New York: Longmans, Green & Co 1948) 50. James goes on to say that 'out of this aboriginal sensible much-ness attention carves out objects, which conception then names and identifies forever – in the sky "constellations," on the earth "beach," "sea," "cliff," "bushes," "grass." Out of time we cut "days" and "nights," "summers" and "winters"' (page 50).

8 Cf R.H.S. Crossman *Plato Today* (London: George Allen & Unwin 1959); Karl R. Popper *The Open Society and Its Enemies* (Princeton: Princeton University Press 1950). Selections from these and other writings on Plato's political stance may be read in T.L. Thorson *Plato: Totalitarian or Democrat?* (Englewood Cliffs, NJ: Prentice-Hall 1963).

9 Cf John Wild *Plato's Modern Enemies and the Theory of Natural Law* (Chicago: University of Chicago Press 1953); John H. Hallowell *The Moral Foundation of Democracy* (Chicago: University of Chicago Press 1954). Again, as in the previous footnote, Thorson's book is highly recommended here.

10 Popper *The Open Society* chapters 6, 7, and 8

11 Norman Gulley *The Philosophy of Socrates* (London: Macmillan & Co 1968) 72–4; 'It seems obviously unlikely that a lively and original mind such as Plato's would be content simply to present Socrates' thought and method without introducing at all his own refinements and evaluations' (page 72).

12 Plato *Meno* 80d

13 A.A. Milne *Winnie-the-Pooh* (Toronto: McClelland & Stewart 1925) 34–6.

14 Émile Bréhier *The Hellenic Age* tr Joseph Thomas (Chicago: University of Chicago Press, Phoenix Books 1963) 53. Cratylus, allegedly one of Plato's early teachers, and a proponent of an extreme or radical flux doctrine, denied that there was anything stable in the world and ceased to speak so as not to give credence to the assumption that anything persisted or existed, even for a moment. Whereas Heraclitus had taught previously that one cannot step into the same river twice, for fresh water changes the river continually, Cratylus concluded that you can't step into the same river even once, for to speak of change requires the assumption that something first recognizably existed as such and such and then changed. Cratylus serves well as the symbol of the hopelessness and futility of total scepticism.

15 Ralph Barton Perry *Realms of Value: A Critique of Human Civilization* (Cambridge: Harvard University Press 1954) 426.

16 Eric Havelock *Preface to Plato* (Oxford: Basil Blackwell 1963) 190

17 Ibid 134–42, 165

18 Ibid 43

19 Ibid 47

20 Ibid 159

21 Ibid 209

22 Ibid 158–9, 209
23 Plato *Meno* 81a–b (B. Jowett [tr] *The Dialogues of Plato* [New York: Random House 1937])
24 Ibid 86c. Not all translations express this doubt as openly as the Jowett translation. The general caution about a story heard from priests and priestesses stands, in any case.
25 Ibid 81d–e
26 Cf *Parmenides, Theaetetus, Sophist, Philebus, Politicus,* and *Cratylus.* While Plato appears to have maintained his 'theory of forms' to the end, his variations on and criticisms of that central doctrine remarkably altered his earlier position, allowing him to say 'new and interesting things which are still relevant to philosophy as we now understand it' (W.G. Runciman *Plato's Later Epistemology* [Cambridge: Cambridge University Press 1962] 133).
27 Karl R. Popper *Objective Knowledge: An Evolutionary Approach* (Oxford: Oxford University Press 1972) 361
28 Ibid 360
29 Bryan Magee *Popper* (Glasgow: Fontana/Collins 1975) 68
30 Ibid 60
31 Karl R. Popper *Unended Quest* (Glasgow: Fontana/Collins 1978) 52
32 Whitehead *The Aims of Education and Other Essays* (New York: New American Library of World Literature 1963) 13–26. 'Every intellectual revolution which has ever stirred humanity into greatness has been a passionate protest against inert ideas. Then, alas, with pathetic ignorance of human psychology, it has proceeded by some educational scheme to bind humanity afresh with inert ideas of its own fashioning' (page 14).
33 Popper *Objective Knowledge* 342
34 Francis Bacon *The New Organon and Related Writings* ed Fulton H. Anderson (New York: Liberal Arts Press 1960) 93 no xcv
35 R.M. Hare 'Religion and Morals' in Basil Mitchell (ed) *Faith and Logic: Oxford Essays in Philosophical Theology* (Boston: Beacon Press 1957) 192. The principles in the mind which govern cognition 'are part-determinants of what we experience.'
36 Neil Postman and Charles Weingartner *Teaching as a Subversive Activity* (New York: Dell Publishing, Delta paperback 1969) 1–15
37 J.Z. Young *Doubt and Certainty in Science: A Biologist's Reflections on the Brain* (Oxford: Oxford University Press, Galaxy 1960) 70
38 Robert Hogan and David Schroeder 'Seven Biases in Psychology' *Psychology Today* 15, no 7 (July 1981) 14
39 Young *Doubt and Certainty* 106
40 John Anderson *Education and Inquiry*, ed D.Z. Phillips (Oxford: Basil Blackwell 1980), 166

41 I.A. Snook *Indoctrination and Education* (London: Routledge & Kegan Paul 1975) 60

42 Ibid 55–6

43 Freire *Education for Critical Consciousness* (New York: Seabury Press 1974) 45

44 Ibid 46

45 That the teacher or discussion leader may both know and not know where the class lesson or conversation is going is not always recognized. Richard Robinson, in his *Plato's Earlier Dialectic* (Oxford: Oxford University Press, 2nd ed 1953), complains that the 'Socratic slyness or irony' is insincere (page 8). Socrates' 'language implies that he himself did not foresee the course the argument has taken, but was led along by it blindfold; and that for all he knew the argument might have turned out a proof instead of a disproof of the original thesis' (page 8). But Socrates intended from the beginning 'the refutation of the primary answer' (page 9).

Robinson's error lies in forgetting that Plato had to write down the dialogues as finished literary pieces and thus knew how they were to come out. What he attempts to portray, however, is a genuine and sincere interchange between participants, one of whom may be wiser and more experienced than the other but destroys only those arguments which are the weaker and is continually in search of stronger ones. Portrayal is incomplete and ongoing. What Socrates claims about knowing only that he doesn't know may remain a sincere confession, while it is at the same time balanced against the recognition of inferior answers and the unjustifiable claims of dogmatic certainty. Socrates and Plato as author learn as they go along, but Plato has to state what is learned as though it were more fixed and final than it is, for the dialogues must include refutations and tentative conclusions in order to be written down at all. Plato's warnings about the inadequacy of the written word in the *Seventh Letter* should be taken very seriously indeed (*Seventh Letter* 340d–345a).

46 Freire *Education* 58

47 Anderson *Education and Inquiry* 128

CHAPTER 2

1 William K. Frankena *Ethics* (Englewood Cliffs, NJ: Prentice-Hall 1963) 3–4

2 Ibid 12

3 David Purpel and Kevin Ryan (eds) *Moral Education ... It Comes With The Territory* (Berkeley: McCutchan Publishing Corporation, Phi Delta Kappa Publication 1976) 9

4 Aristotle *Nichomachean Ethics* 2.9. 1109a, 23–8: 'For in everything it is no easy task to find the middle, e.g. to find the middle of a circle is not for every one

but for him who knows; so, too, any one can get angry – that is easy – or give or spend money; but to do this to the right person, to the right extent, at the right time, with the right motive, and in the right way, *that* is not for every one, nor is it easy; wherefore goodness is both rare and laudable and noble' (R. McKeon translation, *Introduction to Aristotle* [New York: Random House, Modern Library 1947] 346).

5 Barbara Amiel 'A Lesson in Oversimplification' *Maclean's* 94, no 24 (15 June 1981) 61

6 Purpel and Ryan *Moral Education* 73

7 Kathleen M. Gow *Yes Virginia, There is Right and Wrong!* (Toronto: John Wiley & Sons Canada 1980) 3

8 While various texts could be cited here, one of the best and most helpful examples is found in Lucius Garvin *A Modern Introduction to Ethics* (Boston: Houghton Mifflin 1953) 442–6. The example and an imaginary 'Student Forum' are followed by a lengthy chapter on social justice, to which they serve as 'prologue.'

9 John S. Stewart 'Problems and Contradictions of Values Clarification' in Purpel and Ryan *Moral Education* 136.

10 Ibid 137

11 Ibid

12 Jack R. Fraenkel 'The Kohlberg Bandwagon: Some Reservations' in Purpel and Ryan *Moral Education* 291–307

13 Peter Scharf (ed) *Readings in Moral Education* (Minneapolis: Winston Press 1978) 294

14 Lawrence Kohlberg *The Philosophy of Moral Development* vol 1 of *Essays on Moral Development* (San Francisco: Harper & Row 1981) 98

15 Lawrence Kohlberg 'Stages of Moral Development as a Basis for Moral Education' *Moral Education: Interdisciplinary Approaches* ed Clive Beck et al (Toronto: University of Toronto Press 1971) 71

16 Ibid

17 Mary Warnock *Education: A Way Ahead* (Oxford: Basil Blackwell 1979) 81

18 Although Kohlberg's six stages are well known, it still proves helpful to refer back to the definitional table from time to time; a recent version is therefore provided as an appendix to this volume. In this version Kohlberg mentions the controversial Stage Four-and-a-half, which is important enough to require some explanation.

Stage Four-and-a-half or 4A is a hypothesis devised to explain why individuals who were previously operating at Stage Four could shortly afterwards be scored as Stage Three or even Stage Two moral reasoners. The explanation earlier given by Kohlberg and his researchers is that the regression is actually but the beginning of a transitional process whereby individuals gradually left the comforts of conventional Stage Four thinking and moved into the more advanced post-conventional thinking of Stage Five. It was noted that the phenomenon occurred mainly among second-year college and university students who were very likely to be questioning most of their more customary beliefs in the light of the challenges of higher education. At all events, Stage Four-and-a-half is not an actual regression, but a progression to post-conventional thinking which begins with a sweeping rejection of much of the thinking and many of the conclusions of the earlier stages. It is, thus, not itself a genuine stage at all, but a transitional state.

19 Cf J. Nicolayev and D.C. Phillips 'On Assessing Kohlberg's Stage Theory of Moral Development' in D.B. Cochrane, C.W. Hamm, and A.C. Kazepides (eds) *The Domain of Moral Education* (New York: Paulist Press 1979) 251–66; W. Kurtines and E.B. Greif, 'The Development of Moral Thought: Review and Evaluation of Kohlberg's Approach' *Psychological Bulletin* 81, no 8 (August 1974) 153–70

20 Lawrence Kohlberg 'Indoctrination Versus Relativity in Value Education' *Zygon* 6, no 4 (Dec. 1971) 295

21 Scharf *Readings* 37

22 Ibid

23 Lawrence Kohlberg 'The Concepts of Developmental Psychology as the Central Guide to Education: Examples from Cognitive, Moral, and Psychological Education' in M.C. Reynolds (ed) *Proceedings of the Conference on Psychology and the Process of Schooling in the Next Decade: Alternative Conceptions* (a publication of the Leadership Training Institute/Special Education, sponsored by the Bureau for Educational Personnel Development, u.s. Office of Education, n d) 4

24 Richard S. Peters *Reason and Compassion* (London: Routledge & Kegan Paul 1973) 24

25 This is substantiated in many places in Kohlberg's writings, for example in *Philosophy of Moral Development* 97–147.

26 Lawrence Kohlberg and Elliot Turiel 'Moral Development and Moral Education' in G. Lesser (ed) *Psychology and Educational Practice* (Chicago: Scott Foresman 1971), 134

27 Ibid 439

28 Ibid 452

29 Ibid 454

30 Lawrence Kohlberg et al *Assessing Moral Stages: A Manual* (preliminary ed, Harvard University, Center for Moral Development 1977) part I, 5

31 Kohlberg *Philosophy of Moral Development* 123. An elaboration of the stages

and religious faith is to be found in James W. Fowler *Stages of Faith* (San Francisco: Harper & Row 1981).

32 Ibid 137
33 Ibid 178
34 Ibid 180
35 Ibid 170
36 Ibid 178
37 G.E. Moore *Principia Ethica* reprint (Cambridge: Cambridge University Press 1959) 6
38 Kohlberg *Philosophy of Moral Development* 172
39 Lawrence Kohlberg 'The Claim to Moral Adequacy of a Highest Stage of Moral Judgement' (unpublished manuscript 1977) 38. I shall hereafter refer to this paper as '"The Claim to Moral Adequacy," (1977)' in order to distinguish it from the 1973 paper with the same title in the *Journal of Philosophy* 70, no 18 (25 October 1973) 630–46. An edited third version of this article appears in Kohlberg's *Philosophy of Moral Development* 191–226, with the quoted passage appearing on page 214.
40 Kohlberg *Philosophy of Moral Development* 214
41 Ibid
42 Kurt Baier *The Moral Point of View* (Ithaca: Cornell University Press 1958) 202–3
43 Kohlberg *Philosophy of Moral Development* 214
44 Ibid 171
45 R.M. Hare *Freedom and Reason* (Oxford: Oxford University Press 1963) 4. See also Hare's *The Language of Morals* (Oxford: Oxford University Press 1952) 175–9.
46 Hare *Language of Morals* 171
47 Hare *Freedom and Reason* 51
48 Ibid
49 Kohlberg *Philosophy of Moral Development* 171
50 Ibid
51 Baier *Moral Point of View* 310
52 Kohlberg 'Claim to Moral Adequacy' (1973) 642
53 Baier *Moral Point of View* 202
54 Ibid. See note 42 above.
55 Jan Narveson *Mortality and Utility* (Baltimore: Johns Hopkins Press 1967) 283
56 Hare *Freedom and Reason* 51
57 Kohlberg 'Claim to Moral Adequacy' (1973) 638; *Philosophy of Moral Development* 217
58 Kohlberg *Philosophy of Moral Development* 12

59 Kohlberg 'Claim to Moral Adequacy' (1973) 638; *Philosophy of Moral Development* 217
60 'Claim to Moral Adequacy' (1973) 639; *Philosophy of Moral Development* 217
61 'Claim to Moral Adequacy' (1973) 639; *Philosophy of Moral Development* 218
62 Kai Nielsen 'Ethics, Problems of' in Paul Edwards (ed) *The Encyclopedia of Philosophy* (New York: Macmillan Publishing Co and The Free Press 1967) III 131
63 Ibid 132
64 Ibid 131–2
65 Eg, Kohlberg, 'Stages of Moral Development as a Basis for Moral Education' 46. The term 'formalist' is used equivocally in the current philosophical environment. It may mean, as in Hare's case, one who analyses moral concepts, or it may refer to the deontologists. Hare is amongst the most active in challenging the claims of the deontologists, and in attempting to establish a way between the contemporary debates, towards a new synthesis of the utilitarian and formalist/deontological perspectives (see his most recent book, *Moral Thinking: Its Levels, Method, and Point* (Oxford: Oxford University Press 1981).
66 R.M. Hare 'Ethical Theory and Utilitarianism' in H.D. Lewis (ed) *Contemporary British Philosophy* (New York: Humanities Press 1977) IV 115–18, reprinted in Amartya Sen and Bernard Williams (eds) *Utilitarianism and Beyond* (Cambridge: Cambridge University Press 1982) 24–7 (subsequent page references are to the former edition). An even stronger claim is made by Jan Narveson in his essay 'Rawls and Utilitarianism' in Harlan B. Miller and William H. Williams (eds) *The Limits of Utilitarianism* (Minneapolis: University of Minnesota Press 1982), 141–2: 'If I am right ... then whatever Rawls has done, he most certainly has not constructed an "alternative" to utilitarianism, and only confusion could make us think so ... Rawls may not be a utilitarian: But the theory of *A Theory of Justice* is."
67 Kohlberg 'Claim to Moral Adequacy' (1973) 635
68 Baier *Moral Point of View* 190
69 Ibid 191
70 Ibid 57
71 Taken from various places in Kohlberg's writings. You the reader may wish to check out the general claim that Kohlberg's stage definitions are conceptually loose by referring to note 18 above.
72 David Lyons 'Human Rights and the General Welfare' in *Philosophy and Public Affairs* 6, no 2 (1977) 113
73 Frankena *Ethics* 44
74 See notes 71 and 18 above.

216 Notes to pages 74–6

75 Eg, see Kohlberg, 'Claim to Moral Adequacy' (1973) 17: Kohlberg *Philosophy of Moral Development* 200: 'In the Heintz dilemma, let us imagine someone making the decision under the veil of ignorance, ie, not knowing whether he is to be assigned the role of husband, wife or druggist. Clearly, the rational solution is to steal the drug; ie, this leads to the least loss (or the most gain) to an individual who could be in any role. This corresponds to our intuition of the primacy of the woman's right to life over the druggist's right to property and makes it a duty to act in terms of those rights.'

The point could be made differently, by noting how hard it is for Kohlberg to keep utilitarian considerations within the confines of Stage Five characterization: sometimes the utilitarian is forced to accept crude aggregationism, leaving aside possible and actual circumstantial, personal, social, or other elements ('Justice as reversible role-taking agrees with utility in denying an absolutionist concept of the right to life which would allow all to die in order to avoid coercion. It disagrees with utility in what it means to count each person's life as one. This cannot be arrived at by aggregating lives to find a solution, but requires taking the point of view of each individual claiming his right to life as equal to that of others' [page 29]), while good-naturedly admitting that the Stage Six formalist can claim the 'right to life' principle to operate so that nothing of personal significance is left out, or ignored, or under- or over-played; at other times he is unable to cope with situations which the formalist can handle with ease. ('The whole use of utilitarian thinking is far fetched because intuitively we would decide through "moral musical chairs" and test our imaginative role-taking with reality. If the prior date were made with the new friend Tina, and the old friend, Joanne, had the urgent need, we would call up the new friend and explain. We would expect her to trade places with Joanne, the old friend, and since her need was not as great, release her from the promise' [page 31]). In fact, if this last conclusion is not as good or indeed a better utilitarian solution to the problem, precisely as it is articulated by Kohlberg, then I fail to understand why not.

76 R.M. Hare 'Ethical Theory and Utilitarianism' 115. See also Hare's review of Rawls' book in the *Philosophical Quarterly* 23, nos 91 and 92 (April and July 1973), and reprinted in N. Daniels (ed) *Reading Rawls: Critical Studies of A Theory of Justice* (Oxford: Basil Blackwell 1975), and his newest book, *Moral Thinking: Its Levels, Method, and Point* (Oxford: Oxford University Press 1981), particularly chapter 9.

77 Hare 'Ethical Theory and Utilitarianism' 115

78 Ibid 119

79 Ibid 116

80 Ibid

81 Ibid 117

82 R.M. Hare 'Justice and Equality' in J. Arthur and W. Shaw (eds) *Justice and Economic Distribution* (Englewood Cliffs: Prentice-Hall 1978) 117

83 R.M. Hare 'Ethical Theory and Utilitarianism' 123–4: 'The commonest trick of the opponents of utilitarianism is to take examples of such thinking, usually addressed to fantastic cases, and confront them with what the ordinary man would think. It makes the utilitarian look like a moral monster. The anti-utilitarians have usually confined their own thought about moral reasoning (with fairly infrequent lapses which often go unnoticed) to what I am calling level 1, the level of everyday moral thinking on ordinary, often stressful, occasions in which the information is sparse. So they find it natural to take the side of the ordinary man in a supposed fight with the utilitarian whose views lead him to say, if put at the disconcertingly unfamiliar standpoint of the archangel Gabriel, such extraordinary things about these carefully contrived examples.'

84 Ibid 124

85 Ibid

86 Ibid 125

87 David Lyons 'Mill's Theory of Morality' *Noûs* 10 (1976) 105

88 Ibid 119

89 Ibid. Recently H.L.A. Hart, in an essay in which he criticizes utilitarianism vigorously, goes on to conclude that 'in the rough seas which the Philosophy of Political Morality is presently crossing between the old faith in utilitarianism and the new faith in rights, perhaps [Nozick and Dworkin's] chief and very considerable service is to have shown, by running up against them, some of the rocks and shoals to be avoided, but not where the safe channels lie for a prosperous voyage. That still awaits discovery' (from H.L.A. Hart 'Between Utility and Rights' in Alan Ryan (ed) *The Idea of Freedom: Essays in Honour of Isaiah Berlin* (Oxford: Oxford University Press 1979) 97).

It seems to me that the most one can claim is that there are very serious difficulties with the utilitarian position, and that 'rights' must be given a firm place in ethics. But this is only to say that a 'highest' stage of moral development is still in process and that amongst those qualifying the inadequate ethical theories are formalists and utilitarians. After all, it is the various formalist schools, too, that have come up short and have been found wanting. David Gauthier, in an article boldly entitled 'On the Refutation of Utilitarianism,' allows this point implicitly when he writes, 'The refutation of utilitarianism is but a negative preliminary – an exercise in cleaning our minds in readiness for the conceptual construction ahead' (in Miller and Williams (eds) *Limits of Utilitarianism* 162). Additional evidence of the intensity of the debate between the proponents of utilitarianism and the formalists can be found in the excellent essays in Sen and Williams (eds) *Utilitarianism and Beyond*, in which it again seems that a way between the two traditions, combining the best insights of both, is being sought.

90 Lawrence Kohlberg 'Notes Toward Stage 7 – Ethics and Ultimate Faith' manuscript (second section entitled 'Notes Toward Stage 7 – Rational Science, Rational Ethics and Ultimate Faith' dated 1.2.75) 3.

91 Kohlberg 'Claim to Moral Adequacy' (1977) 17; Kohlberg *Philosophy of Moral Development* 200. See note 72 above.

92 Kohlberg *Philosophy of Moral Development* 205–7.

93 Peters *Reason and Compassion*, passim

94 Kohlberg 'Claim to Moral Adequacy' (1977) 46; Kohlberg *Philosophy of Moral Development* 222

95 Baier *Moral Point of View* 181; Kohlberg *Philosophy of Moral Development* 159

96 Lawrence Kohlberg 'Stages of Moral Development as a Basis for Moral Education' in C.M. Beck, B.S. Crittenden, and E.V. Sullivan (eds) *Moral Education: Interdisciplinary Approaches* (Toronto: University of Toronto Press 1971) 72

97 Gow *Yes, Virginia* 56

98 Kohlberg and Turiel 'Moral Development and Moral Education' 412

99 Ibid

100 Gow *Yes, Virginia* 93

101 The Education Act, Statutes of Ontario 1974, c 109, s 229 1(c), and Province of Ontario, *Revised Statutes of Ontario* (Toronto: The Queen's Printer 1980) 985, also quoted in Gow *Yes, Virginia* 142

102 John Anderson *Education and Inquiry* ed D.Z. Phillips (Oxford: Basil Blackwell 1980) 122

103 Ibid 70

104 Ibid 191

105 Ibid 209

106 Peters *Reason and Compassion* 34

107 Ibid

108 Kohlberg *Philosophy of Moral Development* 192: 'Stage 6, attained by less than 5 percent of adult Americans.' See also Kohlberg 'Psychology and the Process' 14: 'Only about half of the adult American population fully reaches Piaget's stage of formal, operational reasoning ... demonstrates that such development is not inevitable.' Thus, only half of the population has the mental developmental requirements even to be eligible for Stage Five deliberation.

109 Kohlberg and Turiel 'Moral Development and Moral Education' 412

110 Lawrence Kohlberg 'A Cognitive-Developmental Approach to Moral Education' *The Humanist* 32, no 6 (November/December 1972) 14

111 Peters *Reason and Compassion* 58
112 Richard S. Peters 'Why Doesn't Lawrence Kohlberg Do His Homework?' in Purpel and Ryan *Moral Education* 289
113 Warnock *Education: A Way Ahead* 83
114 Ibid 90
115 Ibid 83
116 Ibid 81–2
117 Peters *Reason and Compassion* 26
118 Ibid
119 Richard S. Peters 'Virtues and Habits in Moral Education' in D.B. Cochrane, C.M. Hamm, and A.C. Kazepides (eds) *The Domain of Moral Education* (New York: Paulist Press 1979) 284
120 Peters *Reason and Compassion* 32
121 Ibid. A somewhat different but important account of two tendencies in mortality is offered by Carol Gilligan in her *In a Different Voice* (Cambridge: Harvard University Press 1982). Gilligan contrasts the more legalistic or justice orientation with another which emphasizes the importance of intimacy and caring relationships. The former, Gilligan contends, is more often present in men, the latter in women.
122 Peters 'Virtues and Habits' 284
123 Ibid 285
124 John Stuart Mill *Autobiography* reprint (London: Oxford University Press 1958) 113
125 Ibid 116
126 Ibid 117–18
127 Ibid 122
128 Aristotle *Nichomachean Ethics* 1103a–b
129 Ibid 1095b
130 Mary Frances Callan 'Feeling, Reasoning, and Acting: An Integrated Approach to Moral Education' in Peter Scharf (ed) *Readings in Moral Education* (Minneapolis: Winston Press 1978) 199, quoting Elizabeth L. Simpson 'A Holistic Approach to Moral Development and Behavior' in T. Lickona (ed) *Moral Development and Behavior: Theory, Research and Social Issues* (New York: Holt, Rinehart & Winston 1976) 168
131 Lawrence Kohlberg 'Moral and Religious Education and the Public Schools: A Developmental View' in T. Sizer (ed) *Religion and Public Education* (Boston: Houghton-Mifflin 1967) 180; Kohlberg *Philosophy of Moral Development* 311–72
132 Plato *Euthyphro* 9e–12a
133 Kohlberg *Philosophy of Moral Development* 319
134 Ibid 98

135 Note the tongue-in-cheek subtitle of his essay, 'From Is to Ought: How to Commit the Naturalistic Fallacy and Get Away with It in the Study of Moral Development' in T. Mischel (ed) *Cognitive Development and Epistemology* (New York: Academic Press 1971). In *Philosophy of Moral Development* Kohlberg does repeat that he is guilty of committing the naturalistic fallacy by urging that the descriptive is-statements of empirical psychologists and the ought-statements of philosophers be based on mutual awareness (page 105). This, of course, is not an instance of the fallacy, for mutual awareness is far softer than logical derivation. Perhaps Kohlberg has come to soften his position so that he no longer alleges that he commits the fallacy but merely 'encroaches upon its territory' without actually trespassing.

136 Kohlberg *Philosophy of Moral Development* 319

137 Ibid 320

138 Hare *Language of Morals* 69: 'Thus, if pressed to justify a decision completely, we have to give a complete specification of the way of life of which it is a part ... If the inquirer still goes on asking "But why *should* I live like that?" then there is no further answer to give him, because we have already, *ex hypothesi*, said everything that could be included in this further answer.'

139 Kohlberg *Philosophy of Moral Development* 337

140 Ibid 336

141 Ibid 345

142 Ibid 368

143 Ibid

144 Ibid 345

145 Ibid 371

146 Ibid 369

147 Ibid

148 Ibid 337

149 Kohlberg *Philosophy of Moral Development* 351–4

150 Ibid 352

151 See note 89 above.

152 Hastings Rashdall *The Theory of Good and Evil: A Treatise on Moral Philosophy* (London: Oxford University Press 1924) II 137

153 Ibid

154 Ibid

155 Kohlberg *Philosophy of Moral Development* 337

156 Rashdall *Good and Evil* 137

157 Ibid

CHAPTER 3

1 Lawrence Kohlberg *Philosophy of Moral Development* vol 1 of *Essays on Moral Development* (San Francisco: Harper & Row 1981) 411. This 'transitional level' Kohlberg labels 'post-conventional but not yet principled.' It represents a growth beyond and a rejection of the previous stages of conventional morality, but is as yet incomplete in its ascent to principles, ie, the morality of Stages Five and Six.

2 Kierkegaard's ample discussion of the absurd is found in *Fear and Trembling* tr Walter Lowrie (Garden City, NY: Doubleday & Co, Anchor Books 1954) 38–64 ('Problemata: Preliminary Expectoration').

3 Friederich Nietzsche *Joyful Wisdom* tr Thomas Common (New York: Frederick Ungar Publishing Co 1973) pages 167–9, no 125

4 William Barrett *Irrational Man* (Garden City, NY: Doubleday & Co, Anchor Books 1962) 5–6

5 Sören Kierkegaard *The Journals of Kierkegaard* tr Alexander Dru (New York: Harper & Row, Harper Torchbook 1959), from 'The "Final Postscript"' 7 February 1846 entry, 98

6 If one abandons the requirement of absolute answers, then search becomes never-ending, and 'truth' a temporary achievement ... If open-minded search is never-ending, then 'truth' becomes a temporary achievement rather than a fixed and final goal, and knowledge becomes an approximation based on the quantity and quality of evidential support. Final justification and verification are possible, but only within the confines of a proposed system of inquiry, or in accordance with proffered axioms, which adopt the convention that axioms are starting points or 'best-up-to-now' indicators of the basic facts of the situation, while facts are doubtable axiomatic beginnings, and conclusions following from those beginnings. The universe appears inexhaustible to us in the practice of learning, teaching, and researching, and the variety of perspectives which may be taken of events appears infinite in valuation, poetry, fantasy and imagination, and the arts in general. Given this state of affairs, it is difficult to teach what we know except against the backdrop of the inexhaustible unknown. Moreover, against this backdrop it is difficult – even impossible – to teach the 'known' as anything more than an interpretation based on a selective perception and/or conception. The result is a disciplinary myth, a great achievement for man but a constricted fixation which ignores the inexhaustible in order to render the exhaustible neat and tidy.

7 Ortega y Gasset says this very powerfully when he writes: 'And this is what

makes man common and woman mediocre, that is to say, what puts them in with the vast majority of human beings. For them to live is to surrender to the unanimous, to let customs, prejudices, habits, topics, be installed within them, give them life, and take on the task of making them live. They are weak animals which, on sensing the weight of their own lives at a moment either dolorous or delightful, feel themselves apprehensive, and then eager to free their shoulders from the very weight which is their being and throw it on the collective group: that is to say, they are preoccupied with becoming unpreoccupied. Under their apparent indifference throbs a secret fear of having to solve for themselves the problems posed by their acts and emotions – a humble desire to be like everybody else, to renounce the responsibility of their own destiny, and dissolve it amid the multitude. This is the eternal ideal of the weak, whose preoccupation it is to do what everyone else is doing' (José Ortega y Gasset *What is Philosophy?* [New York: W.W. Norton & Co 1960] 252–3).

8 Ibid 220
9 José Ortega y Gasset *The Dehumanization of Art* (Garden City, NY: Doubleday & Co, Anchor Books 1956) 14
10 Ibid
11 Plato *Euthyphro* 9e–10a
12 Kai Nielsen *Ethics Without God* (Buffalo: Prometheus Books 1973) 3–5; A.C. Ewing 'The Autonomy of Ethics' in Ian Ramsey (ed) *Prospect for Metaphysics* (London: George Allen & Unwin 1961) 39–41
13 Nielsen *Ethics Without God* 7
14 Ibid 7–8
15 Ibid 9
16 Ibid 10
17 Ibid 11
18 Albert Camus's most accessible work is *The Myth of Sisyphus and Other Essays* (New York: Vintage Books 1955; see especially 88–91), although *The Stranger* (or *The Outsider*, depending on the translation selected) is his best known work. *The Rebel: An Essay on Man in Revolt* (New York: Vintage Books 1956) is his most difficult and systematic work.
19 Albert Camus contends that values are discovered and established in revolt against those who push beyond the limits that one has explicitly or tacitly erected. These limits are not only individual affirmations of what values are basic and not negotiable for the individual, but must be collectively affirmed as well. On this point, Thomas Hanna writes, 'Revolt affirms the complicity of all men around a common value and against a common oppression. It affirms a value which all men possess, even the oppressor himself. It carries

man toward all men, showing that the solidarity of men is metaphysical, or, as Camus puts it, that this value is "horizontally transcendent" of the individual' (Thomas Hanna *The Thought and Art of Albert Camus* [Chicago: Gateway Edition 1958] 98).

20 What Camus actually writes is, 'I rebel – therefore we exist' (*Rebel* 22), but the 'we' is operative and resultant only because life is worthwhile in general and rebellion carries with it the fact of solidarity. To rebel is to be concerned with the horizontally transcendent values. Such values are social in nature – 'we' values.

21 Aristotle *Posterior Analytics* 2.19

22 Martin Heidegger is perhaps the most glaring exception to this charge of existentialist blindness to order in the natural world. In his *Discourse on Thinking* (New York: Harper Torchbook 1966) and elsewhere he pleads with us to be open to the world, to be open to the givenness of the world which, though infinite in characteristics which themselves may be grasped from an infinity of perspectives, nevertheless leads us beyond our present understanding to a freshness of perspective, granting a new awareness of reality. Heidegger terms such openness 'meditative thinking,' which is a 'releasement' to things and which unveils the ultimate, at least in part, and beyond a purely subjective human perspective (cf John M. Anderson's introduction to *Discourse on Thinking* 38). Even here, however, Heidegger is 'existentialist' in affirming that the 'ultimate' or 'reality' is infinitely revealing, the given never complete, and one's perspectives of it infinite in number. To be open to the absolute is not to be in possession of something fixed and final, but rather to view something which glitters from a distance in manifold display dependent on conditions of perspective and the self.

23 Camus's early piece *Noces* (1938) is a sensitive and sensual depiction of the Mediterranean and the warmth of Algiers, with which he then so totally identified and from which he derived considerable meaning. In his 1958 preface to the reissue of a volume containing *Noces* and other early works (*Lyrical and Critical Essays* ed Philip Thody, tr Ellen Conrov Kennedy [New York: Random House, Vintage Books 1968]), he writes of the world as 'divine' and of the great worth of the sun and the sea (page 7). He reflects back to the 'source' of his life's work, and might have been thinking of a passage as simple and salient as this one from *Noces*: 'To feel one's ties to a land, one's love for certain men, to know there is always a place where the heart may find rest – these are already many certainties for one man's life' (page 90).

24 Clarence Irving Lewis *An Analysis of Knowledge and Valuation* reprint (La Salle, Illinois: Open Court Publishing Co 1962) 423–4

CHAPTER 4

1 Walter Goodnow Everett *Moral Values: A Study of the Principles of Conduct* (New York: Henry Holt & Co 1918) 7
2 Clarence I. Lewis *An Analysis of Knowledge and Valuation* (LaSalle, Illinois: Open Court Publishing Co 1946) 383 (hereafter AKV)
3 AKV 391
4 Ibid
5 Charles A. Baylis *Ethics: The Principles of Wise Choice* (New York: Henry Holt & Co 1958) 179
6 AKV 487
7 Ibid
8 Ibid 488
9 Ibid 392
10 Plato *Meno* 99d–100a. Plato's *Ion* is a more detailed analysis of 'inspiration' and not without copious amounts of irony and humour as well. I have written about this theme in 'Plato and Inspiration' *Journal of the History of Philosophy* 5, no 2 (April 1967) 111–21 and 'Plato and Mysticism' *Idealistic Studies* 5, no 3 (September 1975) 255–68.
11 Stephen C. Pepper *The Sources of Value* (Berkeley & Los Angeles: University of California Press 1959) 7
12 Ibid 8
13 Clarence I. Lewis *Our Social Inheritance* (Bloomington: Indiana University Press 1957) 79–80
14 AKV 400
15 G.E. Moore *Principia Ethica* reprint (Cambridge: Cambridge University Press 1959) 2
16 Ibid 3
17 Ibid 6
18 AKV 401
19 Ibid 405
20 Moore *Principia* 6
21 Ibid 6–10
22 Ibid 15
23 For two recent excellent discussions of relativism in ethics, see Bernard Williams *Morality: An Introduction to Ethics* (Cambridge: Cambridge University Press 1972) 34–9 and G.J. Warnock *The Object of Morality* (London: Methuen & Co 1973) 1–11.
24 C.K. Ogden and I.S. Richards *The Meaning of Meaning* (London: Routledge & Kegan Paul, 2nd ed 1923) 125

25 Alfred Jules Ayer *Language, Truth and Logic* (New York: Dover Publications n d) 106
26 J.O. Urmson *The Emotive Theory of Ethics* (London: Hutchison & Co 1968) 19
27 Ibid
28 Comment made by Stephen C. Pepper and quoted by John Dewey in 'The Field of "Value"' in Ray Lepley (ed) *Value: A Cooperative Inquiry* (New York: Columbia University Press 1949) 64. Dewey notes that Pepper's comment was 'contained in the questions and comments preliminary to the present cooperative inquiry.'
29 Ibid 67
30 John Dewey *Theory of Valuation* II, no 4, *International Encyclopedia of Unified Science* (Chicago: University of Chicago Press 1939) 28
31 Ibid
32 G.E. Moore *Ethics* (Oxford: Oxford University Press 1958) 37–8
33 G.E. Moore 'The Nature of Moral Philosophy' in *Philosophical Studies* (London: Routledge & Kegan Paul 1960) 327–8
34 See pages 148–9.
35 John Laird *The Idea of Value* (Cambridge: Cambridge University Press 1929) 44
36 Ibid 44–5
37 Dewey *Theory of Valuation* 30–1
38 Moore *Principia* viii
39 Ibid 146
40 Ibid
41 Paul Taylor *Normative Discourse* (Englewood Cliffs, NJ: Prentice-Hall 1961) 26
42 Ibid 32
43 Monroe C. Beardsley 'Intrinsic Value' *Journal of Philosophy and Phenomenological Research* 26 (1965) 12
44 Cf Moore *Principia* 32–6.
45 AKV 397. For a fuller discussion of the immediacy of intrinsic value in Lewis, see my article 'C.I. Lewis and the Immediacy of Intrinsic Value' *The Journal of Value Inquiry* 9, no 3 (Summer 1975) 204–9.
46 AKV 183
47 Ibid 171–2
48 Ibid 397
49 Moore *Principia* 142
50 Robert S. Hartman *The Structure of Value* (Carbondale: Southern Illinois University Press 1967) 8
51 Ibid 103–6

52 Robert S. Hartman 'The Logic of Value' manuscript, 32. This unpublished manuscript was abbreviated for the article of the same title appearing in *The Review of Metaphysics* 14, no 3 (March 1961).
53 R.S. Peters (ed) *The Philosophy of Education* (Oxford: Oxford University Press 1973) 242
54 R.S. Peters *Education as Initiation* (London: Published for the University of London Institute of Education, by George B. Harrap & Co 1964) 18
55 Ibid 15
56 Ibid 12

CHAPTER 5

1 Robert E. Ornstein *The Psychology of Consciousness* (New York: Viking Press 1972) 10
2 Plato *Apology* 38a
3 Plato *Republic* 439d–e
4 G.M.A. Grube *Plato's Thought* (Boston: Beacon Press 1964) 135
5 Ibid 120–49, and particularly 132–5
6 John Macmurray *Reason and Emotion* (London: Faber & Faber 1935) 37
7 Ibid 38
8 Ibid
9 Ibid 39
10 Ibid 40
11 Ibid 41
12 Ibid 42
13 Ibid 43–4
14 Toshihiko Izutsu *Toward a Philosophy of Zen Buddhism* (Tehran: Imperial Iranian Academy of Philosophy 1977) 80
15 The term is a complex and technical one in Zen Buddhist scholarship, but it means roughly seeing beyond the habitual and ordinary ways of seeing things and oneself, and grasping directly, without thought or ordinary self-consciousness, whatever is before one. See D.T. Suzuki *The Zen Doctrine of No Mind* ed Christmas Humphreys (London: Rider & Co 1969) 28–30.
16 Ernst Cassirer *Language and Myth* tr Suzanne K. Langer (New York: Dover Publications 1953) 32–3
17 Ibid 98–9
18 A fine and brief discussion of the cosmic compassion as central to Buddhist thought is to be found in Hajime Nakamura 'Interrelational Existence' *Philosophy East and West* (In Honor of Charles A. Moore) 17, nos 1–4 (1967) 107–12: 'According to the doctrine of "dependent origination" in Mahāyāna, all

existences and phenomena are interrelated. Even a flower is closely connected with the entire universe; a flower itself has no separate existence in the metaphysical sense. It cannot sever itself from the past. This is true of everything in the universe. The tiny violet droops its head just so much, and no more, because it is balanced by the universe. It is a violet, not an oak, because it is the outcome of the interrelational existence of certain members of a beginningless series' (page 107). The interrelatedness, even Oneness, of all things serves as the basic principle of altruistic deeds and human compassion for all things.

The actual phrase the 'Crimson Heart of Cosmic Compassion' is found in Dōgen *Shōbōgenzō* ('The Highest Truth of Buddhist Enlightenment') ed Eto Sokuo [Tokyo: Iwanami Shoten 1939], book 71, III 11.

19 The major account of Hartman's theory of value is to be found in his work *The Structure of Value* (Carbondale: Southern Illinois University Press, rev ed 1969).
20 Ibid 103
21 Ibid
22 Ibid 112–14
23 Robert S. Hartman 'The Nature of Valuation' unpublished manuscript, 9; Spanish version published in *Anvario Humanitas* (Centro de Estudios Humanisticos, Universidad de Nuevo Leon, Monterrey, Mexico) 1968
24 Hartman *Structure* 112
25 Ibid
26 Ibid
27 Hartman 'The Nature of Valuation' MS 23
28 Ernst Cassirer *An Essay on Man* (New York: Bantam Books, Bantam Matrix ed 1970) 160
29 Charles A. Moore 'Editor's Supplement: The Enigmatic Japanese Mind' in Charles A. Moore (ed) *The Japanese Mind* (Honolulu: East-West Center Press, University of Hawaii Press 1967) 296
30 Ibid 296–7
31 Cassirer *An Essay on Man* 160
32 Ibid
33 Ibid 160–1
34 Hartman *Structure* 113
35 Robert S. Hartman 'The Logic of Value' *Review of Metaphysics* 14, no 3 (March 1961) 408; *Structure* 252
36 Hartman 'The Logic of Value' MS 32
37 Ibid
38 Hartman 'The Logic of Value' 408

39 Ibid
40 Hartman *Structure* 266–7; 'The Logic of Value' 412–13
41 Hartman 'The Logic of Value' 412
42 Robert Francis *The Orb Weaver* (Middleton, Conn: Wesleyan University Press 1900) 58
43 Hartman *Structure* 113–14
44 Robert S. Hartman 'Value Theory as a Formal System' *Kant-Studien* 50, no 3 (1958–9) 301
45 Which, for Hartman, is a state of being which is not only intrinsically good but *morally* good as well. Cf *Structure* 306, 308.
46 Milton Mayeroff *On Caring* (New York: Harper & Row, Perennial Library 1971) 6
47 Antoine de Saint-Exupéry *The Little Prince* tr Katherine Woods (New York: Harcourt Brace & World 1943), 62–71. Seeing five thousand wild roses, the little prince remarks that his lone rose on his mini-planet 'had told him that she was the only one of her kind in all the universe' (62). His friend the fox urges him to look beneath the obvious, for 'You will understand now that yours is unique in all the world' (69–70). The insight comes to him when he realizes that 'It is the time you have wasted for your rose that makes your rose so important' (71).
48 D.T. Suzuki, Erich Fromm, and Richard de Martino *Zen Buddhism & Psychoanalysis* (New York: Harper & Brothers 1960) 1–5
49 Hartman, 'The Nature of Valuation' MS 13
50 George Bosworth Burch 'Respect for Things' *Aryan Path* 31, no 11 (November 1960) 484
51 Robert S. Hartman and Robert E. Carter 'The Transparent Self' unpublished manuscript 82
52 See pages 118–19 above.
53 José Ortega y Gasset *The Dehumanization of Art* (Garden City, NY: Doubleday & Co, Anchor Books 1956) 14
54 Ibid
55 Hartman 'The Nature of Valuation' MS 20
56 Hartman 'Logic of Value' 422. See also *Structure* 224. Discussed in Robert E. Carter, 'Intrinsic Value and the Intrinsic Valuer' *Philosophy and Phenomenological Research* 34, no 4 (June 1974) 504–14.
57 Hartman and Carter 'Transparent' 62
58 Ibid
59 Ibid 66–7
60 Ibid 67
61 Ibid 69: 'Transparency is the pure awareness that you are. This happens, for

example, just the split second you wake up. You just wake up and before you even know where you are, you have the awareness *that* you are.'

62 Ibid 68
63 Ibid 70
64 Ibid 73
65 Ibid
66 Ibid 78
67 Ibid 79
68 Ibid 81
69 Ibid 88
70 Hartman 'The Logic of Value' 426–7
71 Ibid 430
72 Hartman 'The Nature of Valuation' MS 24
73 Ibid 26
74 Ibid
75 Ibid
76 Ibid 25
77 Ibid
78 Ibid 13
79 Ibid
80 Ibid
81 Ibid 15
82 Ibid

Index of names

Index of subjects